COGNITION AND REPRESENTATION IN LINGUISTIC THEORY

AMSTERDAM STUDIES IN THE THEORY AND HISTORY OF LINGUISTIC SCIENCE

Series IV - CURRENT ISSUES IN LINGUISTIC THEORY

Volume 112

Antoine Culioli

Cognition and Representation in Linguistic Theory

ANTOINE CULIOLI

COGNITION AND REPRESENTATION IN LINGUISTIC THEORY

Texts selected, edited
and introduced by

MICHEL LIDDLE
University of Ottawa

Translated with the assistance of

JOHN T. STONHAM

JOHN BENJAMINS PUBLISHING COMPANY
AMSTERDAM/PHILADELPHIA

∞ TM The paper used in this publication meets the minimum requirements of American National Standard for Information Sciences — Permanence of Paper for Printed Library Materials, ANSI Z39.48-1984.

Library of Congress Cataloging-in-Publication Data

Culioli, Antoine.

Cognition and representation in linguistic theory / Antoine Culioli : texts selected, edited, and introduced by Michel Liddle : translated with the assistance of John T. Stonham.

p. cm. -- (Amsterdam studies in the theory and history of linguistic science. Series IV, Current issues in linguistic theory, ISSN 0304-0763 ; v. 112)

Translation of a transcript of the author's D.E.A. seminar in linguistics given 1983-1984.

Includes bibliographical references (p.) and index.

1. Psycholinguistics. 2. Knowledge representation (Information theory) 3. Cognitive grammar. I. Liddle, Michel. II. Stonham, John T. III. Title. IV. Series.

P37.C85 1995

415--dc20 95-2051

ISBN 90 272 3615 1 (Eur.) / 1-55619-566-4 (US) (alk. paper) CIP

John Benjamins Publishing Co. • P.O.Box 75577 • 1070 AN Amsterdam • The Netherlands

John Benjamins North America • P.O.Box 27519 • Philadelphia PA 19118-0519 • USA

FOREWORD & ACKNOWLEDGEMENTS

French-speaking and English-speaking linguistic cultures have seemed destined to pursue separate paths. British and North American practitioners tend to ignore the heirs, gainsayers and transcenders of the framework set out by Ferdinand de Saussure. Although even the most open-minded among them still do not cite French linguistic texts, today I can more easily be assured of at least polite interest for a French linguist's major contributions to cognitive and formal linguistics, than someone attempting to present a posthumous synthesis of Émile Benveniste's research some twenty years ago. My apparent optimism is grounded in the on-going rejection — or, more conservatively, relativization — in the English-speaking world, of so-called 'autonomous' syntax-based linguistics, in favour of more holistic, discourse-oriented approaches. As the stultifying reductions, the artificial-language-based models, the truth-table logic, gradually recede into the collective past, and make way for a return to the formation of hypotheses based on the study of natural languages, real speakers and real addressees, three-quarters of a century of French publications, and continuing explorations in a wide-range of directions, proposing sometimes contradictory solutions, await discovery in the Anglo-Saxon world.

The present volume is an attempt to lift the veil of at least one framework that has been in use in France for decades. In preparing it, my first thanks go to Professor Antoine Culioli for allowing me to translate the transcription of his Seminar, and to the General Editor of the CILT series, Professor Konrad Koerner, for his continued support for this project and enlightened correction of the manuscript — beyond the call of duty. I also extend my warmest appreciation to Professor Pierre Lardet of the University of Paris 7 (Jussieu) for his help in procuring a copy of unpublished documents by Antoine Culioli and to Professor Sylvain Auroux for biographical information. Many thanks to Dr. John T. Stonham for his intelligent and systematic re-reading and correction of my English translation, and for his enlightened comments, to a first re-reader, Paul Peranteau of John Benjamins. My thanks and best wishes must also go to Professor Janine Bouscaren and to her collection of Culioli-related material *L'Homme dans la langue*, a most important enterprise.

CONTENTS

EDITOR'S INTRODUCTION

The objective in publishing this book is to better acquaint English-speaking linguists with a corpus of texts hitherto untranslated, containing the cognitive-based research in formal linguistics of one of the most important contemporary theoreticians in the field: Antoine Culioli (b.1924). In the years following his studies at Paris's prestigious École Normale Supérieure (1944 - 1948), he read Germanic philology at the Sorbonne (1948-1952) where he defended his doctoral thesis on the subjunctive in medieval English (1960), then taught English philology (1961-1969). In 1969, he co-founded the University of Paris 7 (Jussieu) and founded its *Institut d'Anglais Charles V* (English linguistics and civilization), followed by the establishment of the *Département de recherches en linguistique* (D.R.L.) in 1972, and its (C.N.R.S.) *Laboratoire de Linguistique formelle* (U.R.A. 1028) in 1976 —which he headed until his retirement in 1991. Culioli also trained a significant number of researchers and teachers through his Seminars on formal linguistics in his former school of the *rue d Ulm*. Both facets of this remarkable linguist — the indefatigable and exacting researcher, and the pedagogue — will be evident to the reader of the central work translated here.

Enunciation

Culioli's viewpoint is grounded in Émile Benveniste's (1902-1976) revolutionary, though more or less consistent (Normand 1986), answer to Saussure's opposition between languages (*langue*) and individual performance (*parole*). A synthesis of years of analyses performed on a multiplicity of language families, this construct evolved between the 1950s and 1970 into what he termed ***énonciation***.

As Benveniste noted, in a frequently cited article "L'appareil formel de l'énonciation", published in March 1970 in *Langages* No.17 and reprinted in *Problèmes de linguistique générale II* (Benveniste 1974), by enunciation he means 'activating a language by an individual usage act. [...] it is the very act of producing an utterance and not the text of the utterance [...]. This is the act of a speaker who mobilizes a language for his own use' [1] (p.80).

[1] Single quotes will be used for citations given in English translation.

> The individual act of appropriating a language inserts the speaker into his speech act. The speaker's presence in his enunciation makes each instance of discourse an internal centre of reference. This situation is evidenced by specific forms whose function is to place the speaker in a constant and necessary relationship with his enunciation. (p.82)

The point of reference, the origin in all analyses, is the speaker, *I*, when he speaks, *now*, where he speaks, *here* (p.84). This construct enables the linguist to understand certain constants: the difference in value between, on the one hand, the personal pronouns (*I, we, you*) and the demonstratives -- components referring solely to individuals since they exist only in an individual speaking/hearing event (p.83); and on the other, the 'non-personal' 3rd person, dependent upon the speaker and hearer for its discourse value (Benveniste 1966:265). Furthermore, it affirms the centrality of the link between *I* and the present tense, and not only of present time (Benveniste 1966:262-263 and *passim*).

Simone Delesalle (1986:19), at the conclusion of a historical and epistemological study of the term *énonciation* and its Latin and Greek sources, indicates that Henri Weil's *De l'ordre des mots dans les langues anciennes comparées aux langues modernes*[2] contains the first passage where énonciation expresses its present day meaning: 'pulled out of [the grammatical framework of] the sentence, towards interlocution, towards the subjectivity of language and taking the speaker into account when analysing an utterance' (p.20).

As has been clearly demonstrated (Joly & Rouland 1980), Gustave Guillaume (1875-1960) proposes a subject-based analysis of language phenomena as early as 1917 (p.110), thus preceding the publication of Benveniste's conclusions by some fifty years. The foundation, the role of the individual in language as expressed by Guillaume, is, however, more an extension of traditional French psychological (mentalist) linguistics. As Sylvain Auroux

---

[2] whose publication in 1844 went largely unnoticed, but was re-published in 1869 at the suggestion of Michel Bréal (1818-1909) and translated into English by Charles W. Super in 1887; see Aldo Scaglione's re-edition The Order of Words in the Ancient Languages compared with that of the Modern Languages, with other material (=Amsterdam Studies in the Theory and History of Linguistic Science, I, Vol. 14) Amsterdam: John Benjamins, 1978.

(1992:42) has forcefully pointed out, this is in sharp contrast with the position held by Antoine Culioli who clearly distinguishes between the psychologist's domain and that of the the linguist.

The same analysis applies to Charles Bally's (1865-1946) vision of enunciation in both the 1932 and 1944 editions of his Linguistique générale et linguistique française (see Chiss 1986). A cogent illustration of this distinction is the nature of the 'revelation' of enunciation and its formal manifestations experienced by Culioli.

This revelation occurred, according to Jean-Claude Milner (1992:22), when Culioli suddenly realized--as he repeatedly emphasized during the first lectures of his seminar on formal linguistics--that 'a dog is barking' [*un chien aboie*] is ill-formed. The sentence is well-formed, but the utterance should be something of the type 'There's a dog barking' [*Il y a un chien qui aboie*]. No intervention of "the mind" here. Psychology, however, as well as mathematics, logic, anthropology and ethnology are always present, on the periphery, to assist in more fully understanding language phenomena — not only in the framework of the round-table discussions with François Bresson and Jean-Blaise Grizé, but even during his lectures (see Fuchs 1992:222).

In short, theories of enunciation are of varied types. Culioli classifies (Culioli 1980:37-38) them into three groups — the third being his own theory of enunciative and predicative operations. The first includes theories of enunciation based on the rhetoric–pragmatics approach to speech events seen as realizations of internal/prior propositions into utterances, i.e. of *sentence types* into *sentence-tokens* (cf. Oswald Ducrot and his associates). This group underlines referential problems ('truth conditions, intentionality, philosophy of language, language acts' - Culioli 1980:38). The second group includes those theories which equate enunciators and to 'the distance between enunciator and utterance'. They 'can [...] lead us toward sociolinguistic variation, stylistics' (*ibid.*) and probably toward studies of the enunciator in relation to discursive events, historical discourse analysis (see Guilhaumou & Maldidier 1986). Culioli immediately adds that a considerable amount of confusion results in (apparent) commonality between the two groups, and that the various theoreticians, by emphasizing one or another enunciative or discursive component, create what are in fact, undistinguished ad hoc sub-groups.

Culioli 's Enunciative Model in Brief

In describing enunciation, Benveniste insists upon three 'major aspects' or fields open to study: first, the phonetics of individual realizations; second, 'how meaning takes the form of words, in what measure one can distinguish between the two notions and what terms describe their interaction' — the same aspect includes 'the processes through which the enunciation's linguistic forms diversify and are generated'; third (the path chosen by Benveniste), 'within a language, the formal traits of enunciation based on the individual manifestation that it realizes' (Benveniste 1974:80-81).

Culioli constructs his own synthesis of the three, in a theory, not of enunciation, but of enunciative and predicative operations. Culioli insists on form and formal representation in his research. This formalizing approach to enunciation constitutes a break with Benveniste, as he notes in his Doctoral (D.E.A.) Seminar of 1975-1976 (Culioli 1976b:117):

> In this sense, this [type of] processing enables us to carry on Benveniste's work. He went as far as possible in the field of discursive formulation; here the approach becomes formal, inasmuch as once it is elaborated, it functions automatically. Thus, if we produce ill-formed formulæ [elsewhere: 'schemata'], there is an error somewhere, and we must start over.

He also indicates that although Benveniste set down the relationship between *langue*, the underlying system shared by all speakers of a given language, and *langage*, (speech activity as well as an evolving mass of individual speech events), he never constructed a theoretical model of it (Culioli 1985:1). Throughout his own writings, Culioli affirms that a mind-set fashioned by formalization and theorization must prevail to assure a pertinent, consistent approach to the processing of texts, both oral and written. (See below, Chapters 1 and 2.)

His objective is to construct a coherent, unambiguous, complex representation of the means whereby the enunciator's notions become well-formed, meaningful utterances. As we shall see, Culioli imposes a major caveat on the construction of such a model: it must be usage-based — dealing inseparably with meaning and syntax, and actual texts in a variety of languages. Any 'deep' construct on these 'surface' texts must be validated by text usage: by projecting the resulting utterance into the intersubjective space — a simulation of the meaningful situation where it is used — and judging its acceptability. Another form of validation can be cross-disciplinary in character: if the resulting constructs are borne out by research in contiguous fields, especially (cognitive) psychology, including studies on language acquisition (see below, Chapters 1 and 2).

As Culioli declared in his first article on the subject, and as he will maintain throughout the texts cited here: 'There can be no theory of language that denies the grounding of languages in situations' (Culioli 1968a:328). What he calls 'neomechanism', exemplified by generative and transformational grammars, 'skirts round the relationship between utterance and enunciation [and proposes] a language (activities, texts) without enunciators, without situations in which the act of enunciation can take place [...]' (Culioli 1973: 85).

Thus, in a hypothetical top–down reading of the basic model, the first components are physical–cultural properties of a cognitive nature, constructs that constitute notions, and their combination is constrained by their specific values, i.e. meaning in situation. Certain representations of universals, representational constructs as well, combine with the notions to produce the predicative relation or *lexis*; these include, the basic operation of *locating*, schemata for notional relationships and ordering (according to the utterance's configuration). Instantiating the schemata with terms constructed, results in the construction of this basic processible unit, e.g., ⟨linguist - liking - cat ⟩. Thanks to an operation of *quantifiabilization* on the notion, a topological representation of the notional domain, prototypically centred, completes the higher order, fundamental schemata (*schematic forms*) outlined above. Abstract (notional) or linguistic occurrences can be rather typical, not really typical, or not typical at all, and be represented on a gradient as *within the notional domain*, *on its boundary*, or *outside* (see below, Chapters 3 and 4).

Along with *quantifiabilization*, other universal relationships, operations come into play, primarily: *identification*, *differentiation*, and *null relationship*. By locating the predicative relation with respect to the situation of enunciation (I, here, now), the enunciator identifies with the subject, differentiates, or posits that no relation whatsoever exists between them; and situates the moment (time and space) of the predicative relation with respect to now and here. Depending on the language, this will translate as various types of tense and place or tense-place forms. This location of the predicative relation also distinguishes a part of the resultant construct (i.e., an assertive form) representing the situation of enunciation, as the initial point with respect to which other constituent parts are located (Chapter 4).

The enunciator performs operations of quantification, qualification, modality, aspect and diathesis — not mutually exclusive — on the assertive form (Chapters 5, 6 and 7). The results of these operations, specific to the language, are then uttered in response to a situational relationship with the co-enunciator, usually, though not always, the interlocutor — a relationship that has exercised a determining force throughout the enunciation process.

This inevitably grossly simplified summary of the constructed cognitive/linguistic model lacks both the complexity and the subtlety that the reader will find in Culioli's work, and in particular, in the principal text presented here: the 1983-1984 D.E.A. Seminar.

The 1983–1984 DEA (Doctoral) Seminar in Perspective

This work is the best synthesis of Culioli's thoughts on the linguistics of enunciative and predicative operations. Its other great advantage is that the seminar matches an outstanding pedagogue with a class not all of whose members are familiar with the genesis of the theory being taught. The lectures are therefore simply structured, all terminology and procedures benefiting from explanations replete with images and graphic examples.

However, the lectures do have a past and a future — a context which helps put them in perspective within the framework of Culioli's research. Each analysis, each term or metalinguistic representation must be coordinated with passages from other texts in order to make manifest the evolution of his linguistic thought over a span of some twenty years (1968 to 1990). Nothing could be less in keeping with Antoine Culioli's view of linguistics than to present a static panorama of his research at one point in time, like 1983–1984 or even 1994! Although, as we shall see, certain constants in his C.N.R.S. team's research on over forty languages have crystalized into concepts, and a basic pattern of interaction between the empirical, theoretical and formal data has solidified by the time of the Seminar, a great deal is still the subject of experimentation and reflection. However, many of his basic definitions of linguistics and the linguist's specific tasks, for example, have remained constant. Rather than single out variants (often the result of a passing *Zeitgeist*: in the late 1960s and early 1970s, the obligatory references to, Marxism, Chomskyism, and Freudian psychoanalysis, for example), and to avoid repetition, I have summarized most of the relevant passages. Where differences are significant, the adjustments brought by quotations from works written from 1985 to 1990 are deemed an integral part of this process, and thus are of the utmost importance. Given these circumstances, the past and the future could not be relegated to ancillary notes. Each chapter opens with a synthesis of relevant pre-Seminar texts and ends with a summary of those in his later writings.

The composition of a text to which Culioli often refers his reader (before 1980), *Considérations théoriques à propos du traitement formel des langues* (Culioli, Fuchs & Pêcheux 1970) requires special treatment. It contains two parts: the first is a reprint of a previously published article (Culioli 1968b); the second comprises two chapters, the first consisting of notes by Antoine Culioli, Catherine Fuchs and Michel Pêcheux (roman numerals I to XI) on the first part. These notes provide the first published explication of the bases of

Culioli's model. The second chapter is a paper by Fuchs and Pêcheux applying these bases to the problem of determinants.

An English-speaking Presence

In the present volume, footnotes will be reserved for showing equivalences (similarities and differences) with the texts of a somewhat like-minded English-speaking cognitive linguist: Ronald W. Langacker. Since the goal here is not to provide a systematic comparison of their works, references to Langacker will intervene when links between certain passages of Culioli to recognizable North American linguistic terminology or modes of explication are deemed desirable as explanations or complements. It is perhaps important to note that the bibliographies (and, more or less, required reading lists) for the D.E.A. Seminars include references to publications by George Lakoff, John Lyons, and Ronald Langacker (& Pamela Munro), among others. On the other hand, in the works of Langacker, whose research criteria, problems and approaches pit him directly against 'mainstream' (Langacker 1987:2) linguistics, there is only one reference to the French-speaking linguistic culture: Saussure. This can be misleading, however, since he constructs a theory whose basic subject matter is, in fact, that of enunciation from Culioli's perspective:

> We must examine this interface between convention and usage in some detail, for it is the source of language change and the crucible of linguistic structure.
> Let us consider abstractly the various factors involved in a particular instance of language use. It is prompted when a speaker, assessing the total context, perceives the need to find linguistic expression for a conceptualization. The need for such expression constitutes a problem to be solved, and the over-all situation places a variety of constraints on what counts as an acceptable solution. [...1
> The target is therefore a usage event, i.e., a symbolic expression assembled by a speaker in a particular set of circumstances for a particular purpose: this symbolic relationship holds between a detailed, context-dependent conceptualization and some type of phonological structure [...] (Langacker 1987: 65-66)

Moreover, a recent paper on Antoine Culioli's theory, written by one of his closest collaborators, Jean-Pierre Desclés (1992:208), notes some fundamental similarities between this theory and Ronald Langacker's Cognitive Grammar. One can only deplore the lack of intercultural communication that might have enabled Langacker, and other English-speaking researchers as well, to profit from paths already beaten and gain further insight on promising perspectives.

Methodology of the Translation

The original transcription

The original French text of the 1983-1984 D.E.A. Seminar is a transcription set down by Jean-Claude Souesme and edited by Jean Chuquet and Jean-Louis Duchet. It remains very much an oral manuscript. Comprehension after the event could suffer somewhat from the plethora of 'be' and 'have' and personal/impersonal 'you' forms. Another typical transcription phenomenon, i.e. rambling, incoherent sentences, seems to be the result of punctuation difficulties encountered by the transcriber, who may not have heard adequate intonation marks. Any accidental, yet obvious, incoherence has been rectified in the English version presented here.

An explanatory translation

To assure the reader as obstacle-free a path as one can clear to a theory that requires, and indeed commands, a very close, attentive reading, I have decided to specify the meaning of many of the above mentioned 'be' and 'have' verbs. However, since no choice of verbs to describe cognitive and linguistic operations is innocent, and as the more active verbs might well give the text the appearance of one or another school or current, care has been taken to use, wherever possible, only those verbs sanctioned by Culioli himself in his two English-language papers on the subject (Culioli 1983a, 1989a). As for the punctuation, change, when necessary, concurs with the general goal of the translation: clarity through explanation. Thus, when an anglicized literal translation would not convey the meaning made evident both by the Lectures and the twenty-two-year context, an explanatory one was preferred. If clarification required additional words, they are most often enclosed in brackets; all omissions thusly motivated are similarly enclosed. The use of English in the original French text is also noted between brackets, unless it is otherwise specified in the context.

In Chapter 1, in order to extract Culioli's solutions to specific, yet far-reaching, fundamental problems dealing with circumscribing linguistics (the main contribution of the first lectures) — propositions echoed throughout this twenty-two-year period of his linguistic thinking, passages have been selected and ordered accordingly.

The chapter titles do not correspond to similar headings in the original transcription, most sub-headings, however, are simply translations. Graphics in this book are copies of those appearing in the transcription, i.e., the students' reproductions of Culioli's own blackboard sketches.

A Note on Terminology

Although most of the terms used in the construction of the model and its applications are explicitly defined in the passages chosen for translation, some choices require prior explanation. As *enunciative* (*énonciatif*) in Culioli always corresponds to Benveniste's term as explicated above, and is used as such in one of his English-language papers (Culioli 1983a); there is never any ambiguity with its homonym referring to the production of phonetic entities, hence no reason to find another English equivalent. As for the initiator of the act leading to an utterance, in the same paper Culioli uses the term *enunciator*. The act itself *énonciation* / *énoncer* — rendered by 'utterance' as well (1983a:80) — will be translated by *uttering*, a more active and less ambiguous term

Hull (Quebec), May 1995 M. L.

CHAPTER 1

DEFINING THE TERRITORY

EDITOR'S INTRODUCTION

From his first publication on his research in formal linguistics (Culioli 1968a) through the end of the period studied here (1990), Culioli's basic definitions of the linguist's field have remained constant. In brief, the linguist's domain contains the following: homogeneously representable phenomena derived from the relationship between language and the diversity of languages. In this respect, Culioli's works may be characterized by the following traits:

1) this ***language–languages interface****, must override all theoretical and practical considerations concerning the object of a linguist's analyses and constructs;*

2) the phenomena resulting from this relationship — in practice, morphological, lexical and syntactic components of various natural languages examined from the perspective of their appearance in real (or imaginary) contextualized situations of meaningful discourse (texts) or acquisition processes[1] *— must lend themselves to representation;*

3) a particularly productive activity consists of minimally manipulating texts to produce impossible utterances, comparing them to the possible ones and analyzing the source of their incongruity, thus revealing the underlying invariance which constitutes the paraphrastic family.

4) for representations to be homogeneous, the linguist processing these phenomena must respect certain rules of observation, analysis, theorization and formalization, and not ignore the cleavages between phenomena in re-

---

[1] The closest Langacker gets to setting boundaries to what is proper to linguistics, is his definition of a prototypical linguistic unit (Langacker 1987:61): "Prototypical linguistic symbols have for their realization a segmentally organized sound sequence produced by the human vocal apparatus, whereas other kinds of symbols and symbolic systems that we would hesitate to call nonlinguistic depart from this prototype in various ways".

lated disciplines — whose main object is not the language–languages interface — and linguistics;

5) relating such fields to linguistics can, if they are studied thoroughly and their heterogeneity recognized, help to increase the linguist's knowledge about language, the interface, and in particular about relations between cognition and representation.

In his 1968 article on gender in English, Culioli (1968a) proposes a definition of the adjective ***linguistique*** *(as opposed, in particular, to* ***langagier****), first by stating that it will apply only to what pertains to the rules of a language "appropriated and mastered by all speakers" (note 6, p.40). Further on in the same note (p.41), he specifies that it refers to three types of phenomena: "notional partitioning [...] (organizing perceptions, classifying objects, etc.)"; "formal rules that function autonomously with respect to extralinguistic reality"; "between the two [...] complex networks specific to each natural language".*

In his first major theoretical publication (reprinted and annotated in Culioli, Fuchs, Pêcheux 1970), he presents the following list of problems facing the contemporary linguist:

1) Fascination with cut and dry formalization and mathematical solutions to linguistic problems which allow the use of raw empirical data — haphazard, untheorized formalization, possibly the result of cross-disciplinary models or poorly integrated knowledge of mathematics — obviates theorizing as well as any reflection on what is central to linguistics: "language apprehended through natural languages"(p.1), thus "prevents one from giving its full importance to the dialectic relationship between language and languages" (p.2).

2) Formal systems must take into account the dual function of natural languages : communicative and metalinguistic — or ***epilinguistic*** *when this activity is unconscious (p.3) — and, therefore, must not separate syntax from meaning;*[2] *nor lexicon from real and imagined contexts, both immediate and broader-ranging. There can be no unequivocal context-free coding since it would eliminate misunderstanding as well as most metaphors, and relegate rhetoric and style to the rank of mere ornaments (p.3).*[3] *Neither can one*

---

[2] For Langacker as well, meaning is at the heart of the territory (1987:12): "From the symbolic nature of language follows the centrality of meaning to virtually all linguistic concerns. Meaning is what language is all about; the analyst who ignores it to concentrate solely on matters of form severely impoverishes the natural and necessary subject matter of the discipline and ultimately distorts the character of the phenomena described".

[3] Culioli and Langacker agree on the foundational structural import of including nonliteral expressions within the purview of the theory each is constructing, hence within the

"reduce problems of categories to simple generalizations based on frequency" (p.4).

3) In order to avoid these traps the linguist must construct theories of observation, representation and approximation — "to evaluate a model's strength and regionality" (p.5) — as well as a theory of analysis connected to a theory of language, "thus through work on languages, constructing a metalanguage with its rules and working back to languages" (p.7).

In a 1971 paper on linguistics and literary criticism, after emphasizing the importance of the languages–language relationship in his definition of linguistics: "the science whose object is language apprehended through [the diversity of] natural languages [...] I said 'apprehended through', which demonstrates that what is important is this relationship" (1971b:63-64), Culioli shows the need to learn (and not merely to dabble in) other disciplines (e.g., mathematics, psychology, etc.) to nurture thought on language (see especially p.78).

The same year, Culioli (1971a:8) proposes three rules for linguists to set the stage for a "fruitful collaboration" (p.7) with mathematicians (p.8):

First, validating theory and metalanguage against phenomena in a growing diversity of studied languages: "in many cases we are dealing with non-unique and non-contradictory solutions; however, if a contradiction is found, the theory or the metalanguage — or both — will have to be changed". Performing this validation requires a method of calculation and "the goal of formal linguistics is to be able to calculate, if not we simply replace one form of chit-chat by another". The procedures must be exhaustive: "to be exhaustive is to remark that in certain families of paraphrases, some utterances are impossible, then to explain why"; moreover, this should be accomplished by "considering translation to be a particular form of paraphrasing and working to account for apparently heterogeneous phenomena within the same theory".

Second, not to limit the field on grounds of expediency, "nor to confuse, without second thoughts, what is linguistic, metalinguistic and what pertains (empirically) to languages". The linguist "will formulate his hypotheses and

---

linguist's domain (Langacker 1987:1): "The vital problems of current linguistic theory are not of a formal nature, but lie instead at the level of conceptual foundations. Let me offer two brief illustrations. One is the problem of figurative language, including idiomaticity, metaphor, and semantic extension. Figurative language is generally ignored in current theories; at best it is handled by special, ad hoc descriptive devices. Yet it would be hard to find anything more pervasive and fundamental in language, even (I maintain) in the domain of grammatical structure. [...] An adequate conceptual framework for linguistic analysis should view figurative language not as a problem, but as part of the solution".

construct his metalanguage" with the psychologist in mind, and validate them and his calculations (at least partially) by reference to psycholinguistic research.[4] *Without validation by experience, the linguist must abandon them.*

Finally, a more explicit description of the relationship between the linguist and the mathematician who may be responsible for formalizing the "pre-formalized theory consisting of primitive [as opposed to constructed] expressions and explicit rules of construction", which the linguist will produce "either by discovering [...] invariants through successive approximations, or by constructing a perfectible but efficient metalanguage based on experiments (theorized observations)."

The mathematician and the logician have already helped by making linguists more conscious of coherence problems and the need for more rigour (p.15).

EXCERPTS FROM THE 1983-1984 D.E.A. SEMINAR

1. Language and Languages

My purpose here is to present a certain point of view in as coherent a manner as possible and to explain the reasons for this approach.

The first point I would like to address concerns the relationship between *language* and *languages*. In fact the evolution of linguistics shows that it is a complex object characterized by this relationship. This problem has been scarcely explicated except by Benveniste, who posited it without having made a theoretical model of it first; and by Haudricourt for whom linguistics is the science of languages.

A certain metalanguage is constructed — a model — and, on the other hand, observations are carried out on empirical findings. Research is then founded on these data or on empirical findings.

The problem of linguistics, however, is the following: is its object languages or language? For me it is *language apprehended through the diversity of natural languages and registers*[5]. All sorts of related disciplines have been created such as sociolinguistics, psycholinguistics, neurolinguistics, applied

---

[4] For Langacker this is a crucial point: linguistic research must not isolate itself from psychological research on cognition (1987: 13): "Instead of grasping at any apparent rationale for asserting the uniqueness and insularity of language, we should try more seriously to integrate the findings of linguistics and cognitive psychology."

[5] In Culioli (1987:14), 'registers' is replaced by : 'the diversity of texts, oral and written'.

linguistics, computational linguistics, which are not of a descriptive linguistic nature. At one time, we asked ourselves questions to arrive at generalizations, to go from a description in one language to a description in another.

In fact, we have to find a certain homogeneity in languages displaying a high degree of heterogeneity.

Language is a faculty of the human species: there is no ethnic group that does not speak: it is a universal trait. Is it a symbolizing faculty restricted to the human species? Does human language have characteristic traits?

For example, what is peculiar to the human being is his capacity to produce sentences he has not heard before. In speaker-hearer situations, discourse transformation will occur, but what characterizes human language above all is its ability to produce paraphrases. For any given statement, we can provide a definition, a commentary, a reformulation; in short, a class of equivalencies.

A child engages in metalinguistic activity very early: he can relate to an utterance he has heard. The essential activity of language is one of *recognition*. This is second level representation. Linked to it is the ability to *predicate on the predicated*. Example:

He's going to give an answer tomorrow, apparently.

I bet! [*Tu parles!*]

or

– *You think so!* [*Tu penses!*] — an ambiguous statement.

A whole network of relationships is constructed. The human being is able to construct substitutes separable from reality. To do this he must conceptualize a relationship outside the assertion that assigns a value to it.

[*Langue / Parole*]

The problem of language is the following: if it were individual and subjective, no communication would be possible. If it were trans-individual, there would be a coding procedure.[6] It is evident at the level of articulation, but code and coding would be used at all levels: we would have a stabilized universe with "input" and "output" [in English in the original]. But that is not how it works: there would be no misunderstanding nor metaphorical activity.

[6] Langacker (1987) deems this relationship to be a central one to linguistics (p.65): "Putting together novel expressions is something that speakers do, not grammars. It is a problem-solving activity that demands a constructive effort and occurs when linguistic convention is put to use in specific circumstances. [...] We must examine this interface between convention and usage in some detail, for it is the source of language change and the crucible of linguistic structures".

If we were "pre-harmonized", there would be no problem; however we must strive to *achieve* clarity, understanding one another, and that is the activity of language.

(Lecture of 18 Oct 1983)

[*The Intention to Signify*]

The point of view I am defending here is that these errors are, in a sense, like those produced by a machine but they are not the result of a break down. There are conditions which have been termed "of felicity" [in English in the original], i.e., of successful communication between speaker and hearer. The hearer decodes the message: he has received the information, the instructions loud and clear and carried them out. Here is a well-known example: *pre-flight inspection* = making sure that everything is running smoothly. What the pragmatists say in such a case is that there must be a consensus on the wish to communicate: the Cooperative Principle. They also assume a necessary intention to signify and, its counterpart, the intention to look for the meaning of what is transmitted. It can be the intention of seeking to find the meaning the transmitter wished to express, or a meaning behind the first one made out. This set of problems revolves around notions like duplicity, missed acts, lies, etc.

Many of the postulates, the conventions of pragmatics, admittedly with a necessary degree of simplification but including sociological assumptions culturally linked to a particular experience of language, laid down the law and reduced language activity to a *transparent* act between persons wishing to cooperate in order to arrive at a result the transmitter wished to have in mind and the receiver sought to find. We can see that a good number of the criticisms levelled at pragmatics are justified, for all of this is very culturally marked, and that a part of our symbolizing activity will extend, even into areas more apt to foster this crystal clear transparency.

The stance taken with the adoption of "felicity" is that a language act succeeds (even if in certain cases it can fail), and that only the successful cases will be considered. The position I take is that if it succeeds, it will do so because this success has been obtained, it will not be given straight off. There will be adjustments, possibly misses and perhaps a fresh start and finally what can be termed a successful communication.

Thus the symbolic has a certain autonomy with respect to the represented events.

Moreover, the speaker–hearer relationship, as it really is, also includes the possibility of refusing to engage in communication, interrupting, distorting, seeking agreement on a point other than the first proposed by the speaker.

This is what characterizes human language and, as far as we know, is not found elsewhere.

(Lecture of 25 Oct 1983)

[*The Language / Languages Relationship: A Problem*]

The last time, I spoke about the languages–language relationship in a rather allusive manner. When I talk about the languages–language relationship this presupposes a considerable broadening of the field, which means there is a problem relating the two. We cannot deem one to be an extension of the other nor can our study be based on a homogeneneous merger of the two. Two obvious conclusions arise: the need to relate languages and language; the more one deals with problems arising from heterogeneous complexes, the more compelling becomes the need for a form of theorization in which the way to relate heterogeneities may be unknown. In other words, it is essential that we give ourselves a theory of observables before constructing a theoretical model of what we have observed.

Obviously in the areas of psychology, sociology and anthropology the languages–language relationship presents a problem: it is organized in such a fashion that there is a problem to be solved. Without a doubt, one of the great changes of the early 60s seems to me to be setting aside the restriction limiting work to *la langue*, in the Saussurean sense, in order to tackle phenomena in all language activities. While working on a certain region and the exchanges taking place among regions, i.e. multicultural exchanges, we shall have to study problems: to see how the relationships are structured, what importance this has for the language forms used, etc. At present a great many teams are studying these problems called "language ecology", which means that communities structure themselves into a sort of ecosystem. Regulating activities, which are in fact inter-language ones, must be examined, and they in turn imply reflection on activities of collective representation: on the relationship between language and culture.

(Lecture of 8 Nov 1983)

Do we have the right to use phenomena found in different languages as elements of a class of phenomena which I call a "problem" or are these phenomena unpredictable? This question does not have any serious practical repercussions, however, because in general, as a first step, observation is followed by a formalizing of what is generalizable; then we return to our observations that become progressively more refined until we are dealing with the specific.

In point of fact, there are two poles to languages:

1. it can be said that they are totally distinct
2. languages are quite simply historically determined and somewhat shabby reifications of operations that are precisely the same everywhere.

This appears contradictory, though very few people take it seriously. Some generative grammarians do: by means of a universal grammar, from propositions concerning the *generalizability* of certain properties, propositions and categories, they deduce the *necessity* of certain operations.

In actual fact, even in languages of the same family, differences remain. If we look once more at the partitive, we notice differences between French, Spanish, Italian ... But each time we deal with the partitive, we see the partition of a class: we see a sub-class of terms sharing a common property opposed to others. We are working with quality and quantity and so we can say: "I would like a certain (necessarily finite) quantity of objects that possess a certain quality".

If we are working on genera or on all the objects before us, then there is no partition: no asymmetry. In the case of a class, each occurrence, each item can be identified with every other.

(Lecture of 15 Nov 1983)

2. *Observations and Theorization*

[*Forms*]

To simplify things, let us say that the idea of form can be considered from two points of view, on two axes. On the one hand we have *morphology* in the traditional sense of the term, i.e., the morpho-syntactic traits or the strictly morphological ones in languages with declensions, etc.; and it is essentially on these considerations of a morphological nature (whenever I say morphological, this is equivalent to morphosyntactic) that a large part of classical distributional analysis is founded. On the other hand, we have a form which I call abstract form: an *abstraction* [...], in fact a construction based on morphological phenomena previously isolated by a traditional distributional procedure.

[*Methodology*]

This means that whether we like it or not, we shall never be able to avoid a first step — collecting data: observation is never purely empirical but is always a procedure presupposing and entailing theoretical considerations that cannot be dismissed, above and beyond the technical constraints of the particular problem we are addressing. There is always a *theory of observables*. One of the difficulties is that it is almost impossible, unless one gives oneself a theory of observables, to say at some point, "I've made good and exhaustive observations". But what is a good observation? What is an exhaustive observation? We can always find an nth example, a speaker who will contradict us, a dialect that will come up against it. There is always the chance that someone will say: "As for me, after a certain number of manipulations of utterances, I don't know what you're talking about; no one would ever say that". It does not satisfy him and we can see that from this point of view, we really are not in the same position as someone who, at some time might say: "I've 'captured it', like a phenomenon can be captured, I've analyzed it, I'm looking at a snapshot and am satisfied with what my observation has given me at a given moment; I consider it stable". This is one of the major difficulties — which does not mean one ignores it.[7]. On the contrary, we must always keep it in mind and always give ourselves a precise framework even if, at times, the utterance is indeed badly formed. But just as remarkable is a sort of compensation: when applied to phenomena we might have thought studied in the fullest detail, we very often realize that a modelizing procedure makes a good many hitherto unobserved phenomena suddenly appear. And what is more, once one has been alerted, one finds some every time one makes an observation, and asks oneself how others could have left aside so many apparently well-grounded phenomena. In any event, whatever the particulars of your research may be, you will have to do what has been done in traditional structural analysis, by distributional analysis and by a form of analysis whose origins were transformational, and which is now the common property of all linguistics.

[*Possible and Impossible Occurrences*]

There have been a number of changes, however, particularly in traditional structural analysis. When substitutions are made or minimal pairs constructed, the work is done on sentences, utterances, strings (Harris), for example , i.e. on attested texts, and in so doing one verifies if substitution really does pro-

---

[7] This same instability of the object and its content is present in Langacker's theory. The subject matter is *usage events* (1987, p.66): "[...] a symbolic expression assembled by a speaker in a particular set of circumstances for a particular purpose: this symbolic relationship holds between a detailed context-dependent conceptualization and some type of phonological structure [...]". The semantic structure also depends on the specific circumstances as Langacker eschews the assumption of universality (1987, p.47): "A closely related issue is whether semantic structure is universal. I admit to assuming so in the distant past, but I had not yet taken into account the pervasive importance of imagery, i.e., our ability to construe a conceived situation in many different ways (seeing it from different perspectives, emphasizing certain facets over others, approaching it at different levels of abstraction, and so on)".

duce a difference. One works on utterances, strings and sentences that are possible, on the very best form of possibility: reality. What has been added is a search during these manipulations for *what is impossible* and afterwards trying to find out what does not work, what keeps the sentence from being acceptable and what supplementary manipulations will make it become acceptable.

We remain on the level of what we have before us, as we shall notice when we have two utterances or build a square of utterances such that three are possible and one impossible. Example:

The dog is a mammal [*Le chien est un mammifère*]
Dogs are mammals [*Les chiens sont des mammifères*]
A dog is a mammal [*Un chien est un mammifère*]
*Some dogs are mammals [*Des chiens sont des mammifères]

[...] And it is this construct which provides us with knowledge of the class of possibles and of impossibles, information which will prove to be essential for the study we shall undertake later. The problem concerns grammaticality, acceptability, possibility; we must know if we are working with stable intonation patterns and/or explicit contexts. We can then perform all possible and imaginable manipulations to ascertain which are impossible. This is how we construct closer and closer-knit data by means of rigorous procedures. Then we have to conceptualize all of this, whence the need to construct a theory of determination. We can start with a grotesque example, grotesque but possible in a situation where a child discovers that a dog suckles her pups: "Mommy, Mommy, the dog is a mammal."

Sometimes a phenomenon is not found in other languages and we then often speak of a "tertium comparationis", i.e., a third term of comparison to account for non-congruent phenomena in two languages.

Now we can see the need for introducing an abstraction procedure to integrate all these phenomena.

(Lecture of 25 Oct 1983)

In my opinion it is almost impossible to say: "I would not be surprised by something about which I am not too sure". The appearance of something completely unforeseen fascinates. Either it confirms our hypothesis, or it will remain thus for some time and nothing will be able to be said about it. The theorization of problems of abstraction must come afterwards. At some time we shall feel the need for somewhat more elaboration.

(Lecture of 8 Nov 83)

[*Heterogeneous Phenomena*]

What interests me are cognitive and representational activities. [However] I apprehend language only through texts.[8] Given these texts in a language, how does one represent phenomena within this framework, or are these phenomena heterogeneous?

Linguistic activity consists of seeking to construct a homogeneous discourse.

We shall distinguish the life sciences, like neurology, and the social sciences and sciences of structure, of matter. That is the problem of formalization: these are phenomena which cannot necessarily be interrelated.[9] At every moment the linguist sets a trap for himself that is opposed to coherence; if at any time a flaw appears, one must say: "That is not sufficient" or "I have to introduce a new rule".

(Lecture of 18 Oct 83)

[*The Problem of Multidisciplinarity and Finality*]

Here again there has been the same sort of evolution in linguistics. I shall distinguish multidisciplinarity and interdisciplinarity. In *multidisciplinarity*, disciplines must collaborate at some given time, and in *interdisciplinarity*, interaction among participating disciplines, leads to the creation of hybrid, transformed disciplines.

For example, the mathematization of linguistic concepts will no doubt produce a new discipline. Another example: in mathematics in the 17th century, symbolization reduced the notation of certain problems dramatically. Thus, problems can become more legible and their treatment better controlled. Similarly a metalinguistic system of representation is partly a form of stenography in certain cases. The symbol encloses the entire history of a concept. When one can construct operations that satisfy a certain idea, this allows one to perform a type of operation one could not have undertaken previously

[8] Culioli's text-based theory receives an echo in Langacker's *usage-based* theory (1987:46): "Cognitive grammar [...] is a **usage-based** theory. The grammar lists the full set of particular statements representing a speaker's grasp of linguistic convention, including those subsumed by general statements. Rather than thinking them an embarrassment, cognitive grammarians regard particular statements as the matrix from which general statements (rules) are extracted".

[9] Similar misgivings concerning non-specific formalization and the disappearance of heterogeneities are apparent in Langacker, for example (1987:46): "The analytical convenience of assuming that everything in language is discrete encourages linguists to develop discrete formalizations, resulting in general neglect for the many aspects of linguistic structure not amenable to such treatment."

without the help of some ideal machine. Changes in the theoretical conditions of the reasoning will alter the results. All of this hinges on the problem of multidisciplinarity.

One cannot tackle some of these problems if competent in only one discipline: sociologists, political scientists, ethnologists, perhaps specialists in religious studies, etc., are needed. This is most certainly a characteristic of the developments which have taken place. This does not imply that the linguist should not set himself a goal, but for some problems, he is led to work on phenomena which can only be treated by persons specializing in these particular areas.

To summarize this view of multidisciplinarity, either we develop a form of "general-purpose" linguistics, far different from what it has been, or we must establish contacts with other disciplines and thereby bring about a reasonable evolution in ours. The problem of finalities does arise in linguistics.

On this subject, what I consider to be a rather useless discussion has been taking place concerning the corpus. What needed stopping was the magical reference to a corpus defined neither as a stop-gap, nor as a statistically satisfactory sampling. Today the corpus question is only interesting in so far as it relates to the objective one sets for oneself. All linguistic research does have a finality of some sort or another. It sets goals for itself. After all, describing a hitherto undescribed language or unstudied phenomena is indeed a certain type of finality.

Moreover, the linguist must necessarily keep up to date. He must have training allowing him to understand the problem definitions of another discipline. This means that the linguist must not simply be a describer but play a part that goes much further in the area of cultural life because there will be a great number of cultural aspects to a possible public awareness of the specificity of their language.

(Lecture of 8 Nov 1983)

3. *Representation*

[*What is represented*]

The second point I would like to address today is the problem of representations. There is what I shall call a first level or level 1 to which we do not have access: these are mental representations. Reality is conceptualized, imagined, reviewed and we do not have access to these mental representations other than through our actions including our speech — our language activity. Since I cannot base my work on types of phenomena which are not within my scope, nor within the scope of my discipline (but within that of neurology, for example) because the criteria and the evaluation procedures are scanty, I shall say that I do not have direct access — this position is universally accepted. No one, not even a neurolinguist, will say that what he is doing is a part of linguistics: it is a study of language phenomena from the point of view of a neurologist.

[*What represents*]

All we have are representations, that is to say, *text*. This is *level 2*. Text obviously has some relationship with level 1, but this does not specify the nature of the relationship. All we know is that there is indeed activity and so we are going to arbitrarily make a decision. We are going to reduce all this activity to a certain number of operations and decide that we can isolate some operations whose specificity is such that they concern only linguists, from the rest (some of which are biochemical), and call them "linguistic". To say that we are dealing with representations of representations is a play on the word "representation", just as when we say that this word "represents" something — like a "representative" of the people — meaning "it stands for" something [in English in the original]. It is not a term-for-term substitution but it is, nevertheless, a representation relationship. It is not a term-for-term relationship in which an operation of determination might produce a unique, unequivocal representative.

Example:

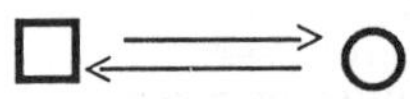

In linguistics one *hardly ever* run across this type of relationship. It would presuppose coding; I would then take my code book and decode the text ... In fact, we posit the relationship between event and utterance from a particular standpoint: the relationship is not an immediate one except in truly ostensive situations, such as: "Look, a mouse!" while pointing at a mouse. Apart from these instances, we shall assume *in principle* that there is no term-for-term relationship between the two levels. Level 1 and level 2 are not homogeneous. We are dealing with phenomena which do not have the same character. We can also say that any text in any given language is much poorer than the result of all the operations which produce the text. This poverty enables the text to produce a great wealth of inter-subjective relations. With some texts, we can always say that words betray us, that they are insufficient to translate our thoughts and, at the same time, be lost in admiration for this lack of equivalence. This is what we find in poetry, for example, and it can produce esthetic effects.

We shall therefore draw the following conclusion: not having access to level 1 and there being no homogeneity, coextensiveness or immediateness between levels 1 and 2 means that I cannot move up to level 1 from level 2. Level 2 does not give me a good, unequivocal representation of what level 1 is. Then we construct *level 3*, a — necessarily metalinguistic — system of representation we can control, since it maintains a certain relationship with level 2. I am constructing a metalinguistic tool to represent textual phenomena and I can reduce it to a system of rules and operations such that they can account for the possibility of having a certain type of utterance and the impossibility of having another, why one needs to use a particular marker to translate into another language and the impossibility of using another.

What we *posit* is the existence of a relationship between levels 2 and 3 on the one hand, and 2 and 1 on the other. It is my hope that by working on the 2-3 relationship, I can eventually construct a simulation of level 1 operations — reproduce the relationship between 1 and 2.

The fundamental constructed hypothesis is that language activity as it appears in this production and recognition process is an activity which produces and recognizes *forms, in the abstract sense of the term* and not in the morphological sense. The real question is: what is this form-producing activity? Why do forms have the characteristics they do to be both produced and recognized? These forms are not the immediate, direct coding of semantic units; the two are not, so to speak, opposed term-for-term. On the other hand, we clearly produce patterns whose level 3 analysis reveals formal properties that make for stability and "plasticity". Adjustment and correction are an integral part of language activity. Missed communications are part and parcel of communicating. They must be integrated into the model.

(Lecture of 25 Oct 1983)

Metalinguistic Systems of Representation

The problem is constructing a metalinguistic system of representation (SRμ) which will enable us to represent the arrangements in a text, the utterances if you will, and the textual strings, as traces of level 1 operations to which we have no direct access. It is a historical fact that there has never been any linguistics where the problem of representation has not arisen. After all, terminology is a much more complex system and in some ways is akin to what one finds in logic since the 19th century, that is to say, on the one hand, what Boole established in *The Laws of Thought* (1846). The title is a program in itself, for Boole proposes by means of a calculus — and a calculus is a form of writing — to try in certain areas, and in particular calculus on classes, to represent what thought operations might be. On the other hand, we have Frege's

Begriffsschrift: concept writing, ideography. It is the work of a specialist in mathematical logic. Indeed Frege was interested in fundamental problems. For the problems which confronted him he created a form of writing, in fact a representational tool. This does not mean that it played a part in the evolution of linguistics. It developed independently, and the ignorance of logic, particularly mathematical logic, shown by most linguists was unspeakable. That was at the end of the 19th century. Then, along with Russell, a great many people recognized their indebtedness to Frege. In the purely linguistic field, practically nothing is available. There is Jespersen, who was quite competent in logic, and his *Analytic Syntax* (1937). He attempted to construct a most ingenious system of representation. Many concepts and ideas have been fruitful and taken up by other linguists who recognized that he had put forward some very good ones. But his system did not prove very productive. With Tesnière and his "stemma" (1959), one is dealing with a sort of term-for-term representation. Then we come to a period of relations between logicians (either in pure logic or in programming, constructing in a formal language for processing by computers) and linguiss with somewhat more rigorous relationships, and the present, where the problem of constructing an SRμ is most definitely an important one.

An SRμ can mean a great many extremely varied things, such as using the *gloss* speakers produce when, given a text, we ask them to make utterances or equivalent commentaries. Roughly speaking, we say: "I don't understand. Could you please reformulate your statement? What do you mean by that?" This happens all the time when one is redundant or when one does not understand what one's interlocutor has said. To push things a bit one could say that using an SRμ is language. Language activity, hence languages, has the potential of being used for metalinguistic purposes. However, one must exit a language before using it metalinguistically.

Secondly we might find a use for symbols — abbreviations of categories that are simply classifications. For example:

The blue hat my grandmother wore on her wedding-day is still in the cupboard.

It's still in the cupboard.

It's still there.

Here we have a fine analysis into immediate components. A hierarchy appears containing nodes, upper and lower levels; and when we wish to study these components we break down the text. If we take a component of the lowest rank and insert it into a unit of the highest rank, we perform a type of analysis often called functional, where the insertion depends on the function. For example:

Paul eats his soup.
N_1 V N_2

We shall draw some conclusions concerning the relation *Paul* and *soup*, and *Paul* and *eat* in regard to *soup*. We shall then have a more sophisticated SR and will be able to continue in the same manner. The problem lies in being able to see that we can cause qualitative transformations, a real leap, in fact a qualitative break when we move from one type of representation to another. But I must insist that *everyday* language can perfectly well be used as an SRμ. For this to be the case, we can see the properties it must possess; foremost, a property by which the terms used have a theoretical status, whether they be primitives or constructs. If they are constructs, the rules of construction must be shown; if they are primitives, roughly speaking, one must present the axiom bringing about their introduction. They must be used explicitly and stably by a community of researchers. The rules governing discourse-links and the development of argumentation from reasoning must be stable and clear.

One might well ask: "Is everything representable?" In my opinion the answer is very clear: no, not everything can be represented. In some cases because the objects cannot yet be represented, in others because they will never be able to be represented, since they possess properties making representation extremely difficult, in particular if we relate two areas like anthropology and linguistics. But knowing from the start that all is not representable does not mean that the undertaking is without interest. On the contrary, it is particularly interesting because we win every time: either we make observations which representations will help us refine, or are dealing with observations such that we can construct a theoretical model upon them and manipulate them thanks to an SRμ, otherwise we do not succeed and we demonstrate that no one can succeed. That is just as good. If we do not succeed others will try and will perhaps resolve what we were unable to. Research then starts to become cumulative. We show that no one will be able to solve the problem by means either of our own Rμ model or of any SRμ. In which case it becomes a great challenge for others who will try to solve the problem and will necessarily make some interesting discoveries. It must be understood that constructing a theoretical framework, giving oneself a type of approach with criteria which are those of scientific investigation is profitable. It seems to me that what I have just told you implies varying degrees of criteria, according to the objectives you set for yourselves, but that it is an approach we find all the time.

Question: "Is it a universal tool?"

We must end up with a number of primitive terms, basic operations, and concatenations, ordered in such a way as to enable us to construct other categories, other operations and be able to control everything. In that sense, this approach has properties of theorization which, if you wish, are universal. However, as it is a very lean system which we can progressively flesh out, it is obviously not universal in the sense of having an answer for every case that could arise. My second answer is that thanks to a system of representations, local theories can be constructed and thus a number of more or less disjointed local theories produced; in pursuing our research we try to establish a relationship between one local theory and another.

Concerning certain phenomena that we shall be able to structure into problems or classes of problems, we shall doubtless be able to formulate them and develop a "problem identification" [in English in the original]. If at all possible, the problem will be of an inter-lingual nature. It can, however, pertain to a given language. What is most important for your SRμ is to always have the same stable system with the same operations, the same sequences, etc. We shall then unify the resulting local theories, then by means of a procedure of even greater abstraction we shall try to unify those areas which have already been somewhat formalized.

An SR must be constructed in such a way as to be both solid and adaptable at little cost.

If one changes points of view every six months or even every two years without bothering with coherence, saying each time: "After all, I see the problems in a different light", one had better have a captive audience.

To return to the languages–language relationship, to the problem of an Rμ, here again I could rather easily show you that it has changed the study of meaning, the semantics–pragmatics problem and the relationship with syntax, for example. Because of the very constraints imposed upon discourse, we obviously have been forced to treat the problem of meaning in a completely different manner: by introducing research on symbolizing, belonging to the domain of language, and not simply by using linguistic representations, belonging to the domain of languages, without bothering to look for operations whose traces are representations. When we are dealing with an SRμ, there comes a time when we must work without being able to nudge ourselves forward: we end up with problems that cannot be treated in the very narrow framework imposed by staying on the level of syntax.

Distinctions made between the different domains like phonetics, semantics and pragmatics still have some use, of course, but a good deal of interpenetration among these domains is quite noticeable. And so I have only one rule of thumb: what is representable? What is not? If it is representable, treatable, I say it belongs to the area of linguistics. This does not mean that what cannot be processed does not belong to linguistics, but that it cannot be processed following the same approach.

(Lecture of 8 Nov 83)

Formalization has two advantages: it is a very powerful aid towards constructing an explicit and stable SRμ, the other is that it enables us to attain certain objectives.

However we cannot assume that we are dealing with a stable pre-defined universe, linked to exterior events by means which are themselves stable. Our intention is to represent everything we can until we can no longer use a homogeneous method of representation.

(Lecture of 15 Nov 83)

As we have already stated, we cannot countenance considering languages to be codes of a stable, universal reality. A text is not a permanent representation of a pre-defined reality, immutable for all speakers. With an utterance or a text string we are dealing with an *ordering* of markers. The idea of an ordering is connected to that of a schema, and thus to *good* canonical forms, regularities ("patterns" [in English in the original]). *Markers* are representations of representations. On level 1, we are dealing with representations; on level 2, representations, separable substitutes, markers, i.e. traces of operations. Hence we are presented with a complex situation: some operations will lead us from 1 to 2 and they are more numerous than one might think because there is also an anterior level, outside linguistics, which is the area of cognitive activity in the broadest sense of the term: the construction of our perceptions, our tastes, our dislikes, our collective representations, objects with cultural properties, physically and subjectively determined.

I remind you that level 3 concerns metalinguistic operations.

When I use the term *marker*, I do so for both positive and negative reasons:

– negative, to avoid the ambiguity produced by the term "mark", all the more important because confusing "marked" and "containing a marker" is a very frequent error;

– positive, because on the one hand it is easily translated into English; it allows us not to speak about the *signifiant*, and it refers to any material trace (this is elementary Saussurean structuralism but it cannot be avoided) which allows us to *classify*, *manipulate* and *process*.

We must be able to isolate (i.e., sort), then we can classify, afterwards we manipulate and finally we process. Markers could be a change in the prosody, an intonational change, a particle, a morpheme or a group of morphemes.

The other approach consists of working in terms of operations and saying: "These markers, these arrangements, these morphemes and these complex markers (for example: when an utterance does not work with a certain supplementary marker or, on the contrary, a certain marker makes the utterance acceptable) are representations of operations" and we must represent the operations of which the markers are representations. One can say: the operations of which these markers are representations must be meta-represented thanks to meta-operations. This will allow me to cross from 2 to 1.

Question: Does every operation have a representation?

The real problem is the one between the SRμ and text strings. In a way it is a simulation, but with languages subjective evaluation always plays a part. Linguistics works on regularities, studying problems that are not only syntactic, but also dealing with partly fleeting phenomena — either because they are subjective or for reasons of dialect, etc. In point of fact, we work on phenommena which cannot be stabilized for everyone.

When we have constructed your SRμ, we are going to come up with chains of operations and we shall hypothesize that whatever the language, we shall find some of these chains. Among the *possible* pathways some are *necessary*. Some operations are necessary, the chains revealing possible pathways and, depending on the language, such and such a path will be activated. This cannot mean that the markers for these operations will always be in the same order. In some cases we shall find a trace of the operations in a different location from where it was found in another language, and in other cases we shall find no markers for an operation. We will be forced to construct a sort of maximum solution which will furnish us with possibles, and we shal say that a certain language prefers a certain sequence, and some operations will be markerless, but sometimes we shall find the problem elsewhere.

(Lecture of 15 Nov 1983)

Formalization

The problem of *form* is one that cannot be avoided. Linguistics has grappled with problems of formalization for quite some time. The first to deal with the problem was Jespersen in his *Analytic Grammar* where he made an effort, albeit a clumsy one, to produce a system of representation. (The book has been translated into French by A. M. Léonard and I wrote the Preface.) A great void followed. Then came Tesnière with his representation by stemma and Chomsky with his use of tree diagrams. The problem of formalization was raised in the 60s and 70s when Harris published his *Papers on Formal Linguistics*. Its formulation then was how to construct a system of representation able to represent text strings and the operations that will give us regulated sequences.

Then came computerization and the development of artificial intelligence which made the construction of a metalinguistic system of representation the specific concern of the linguist. The computer scientist who works on language manipulation introduces simple codes. The linguist will engage in both a technical and a theoretical activity worthy of the name and in so doing will not be overwhelmed.

The development of a theoretical approach is linked to the development of a representational one.

(Lecture of 25 Oct 1983)

4. ***Validation.***

[*Goal and Methods*]

Let us remember that our ultimate goal is to construct an SR which will provide us with a *calculus*, even in a rudimentary form. By a calculus I mean that given a number of terms, I shall establish relations between terms, thus deriving a product which I may say is validated or not validated. Naturally, a proposition can be well-formed, in formal terms, but cannot be validated. There is also another case: at some point I may find myself with terms to which I shall give a certain status (i.e., primitive or construct). By constructing relations I shall end up with certain types of operations and see if these operations are self-contradictory or whether they produce contradictory results. In this case the validation is *not empirical* as if I had asked someone: "Do I obtain a formula interpretable in a given language?" This is a problem of *formal coherence*.

One can imagine in other cases another type of validation having another status, and when working in the *multidisciplinary area* we realize the necessity of having thought about these problems beforehand and of keeping them in mind. For example, when one is working in a related field, with observations concerning, let us say, cognitive activity, and one uses observations from this related field to validate a proposition in the metalanguage, i.e. in the SRμ.

We have just seen the only three types of validation one can find:

– based on the speaker's reaction: strictly empirical in nature;

– through validation procedures based on internal coherence;

– through corroboration from another discipline.

I am leaving aside problems of a statistical nature which really do not belong here. Statistical validation cannot take place in the formal domain. The use of statistics in linguistics will only be valid in certain sectors, and even there we must exercise a great deal of caution.

[*Extension*]

Problem: does our explanation support extension? If we can account for a certain problem and if afterwards we expand the problem by introducing either more empirical data or data from a related area, will construct procedures to account for extension? We can only speak of explanatory capabilities if we possess the criteria to explain these capabilities, if not it is meaningless. We need a system which will enable us to say, for example, that we are dealing with two systems of representation or two solutions in two equivalent systems of representation.

[*Proof in Linguistics*]

The problem is to know when to stop, but there comes a point when one can say: prove it. *There is*, however, *no status of proof in linguistics.* There are rigorous coherent arguments, almost demonstrations in certain cases, but that is all.

ON DEFINING THE TERRITORY FOLLOWING THE D.E.A. SEMINAR

A few years after the D.E.A. Seminar, Culioli, addressing a group of C.N.R.S. researchers from many disciplines, proposed an updated definition of the linguist's territory within the institutional framework of the "language sciences" (1987a: 11-13). He once again emphasized the importance of not succumbing to the lure of "practical" solutions which tend to bypass questions of theory when trying to relate heterogeneous areas, and in particular the central question: how are languages and language related?

Theoretically inarticulated heterogeneity and the lure of disciplines with other objectives, thus different ways of constructing, evaluating and representing observables (the example analyzed is logic), have placed linguistics in the midst of an amorphous mass "in which programs [...] stretch into many areas whose only common denominator is language. Thus the meaning of the term 'linguistics' is diluted, and the crucial importance given the relationship between language and languages is reduced"(p.13). The examples cited are: sociolinguistics, philosophy of language, pragmatics, discourse analysis.

Among the most recent snares, he mentions artificial intelligence and the cognitive sciences applied to texts. Computers

> *impose constraints on us that, for a long time, blocked the theoretical horizon, and what is more, impeded theoretical research. Instead of a subtle form of data processing interacting with linguistics, too often we looked towards simple classification procedures or reductive ad hoc programs to avoid the complexity of linguistic data. In the name of short-term and short-sighted efficiency we too often believed — and too often still do — that one can make do without close analysis and theoretical work. This is what we can notice today in areas like automatic translation and artificial intelligence. Similarly a term like "cognition" shows itself to be dangerously ambiguous, for it is used to refer to mental activity, to simulation, to a whole series of unverified simplifications: of representational activity to neuronal activity, to give but one example. (Culioli 1987a:12-13)*

CHAPTER 2
REPRESENTING NOTIONS

EDITOR'S INTRODUCTION

In this second chapter on the linguist's work, what it comprises and what it excludes, we shall concentrate on specifying the character of relationships of notional representation by means of a preliminary general analysis of notions. Throughout the literature in our corpus, Culioli recognizes and retains the inherent complexity of this representational relationship: neither the representation nor the individual notion is a given. As we have already seen, there can be no unequivocal representation by a primitive, U-language component but properly introduced into the system — out of U-language — it can be used in the SRμ.

Constructing a metalinguistic system of representation remains the goal. Three avenues opened by the study of notions underline its necessity:

1) words in languages do not represent notions;

2) the existence of different levels of notions makes it necessary to elaborate a coherent metalinguistic apparatus for their representation, as do

3) the relationships between occurrences and types of notions.

The presentation of notions, and therefore their representation, evolved slowly between 1968 and 1976. In Culioli, Fuchs, Pêcheux 1970, one senses a hesitation as to the status of notions (p.10):

"[...] for example, tout, quiconque, in English any; an operator that makes one view the class as referring to a 'notion': the noise of a machine, the fragrance of a rose [...]."

The note in Part 2 to which the reader is referred (note XI, p.26) receives its explication in the subsequent chapter ("Lexis et meta-lexis — Applications au problème de déterminants", by Catherine Fuchs and Michel Pêcheux) that distinguishes two types of notions (p.27). The first is "represented by lexical units"; the second is a derived construct (e.g., a nominalization). It adds that any notion (p.28)

> *must be treated like a morpheme or a syntagm functioning with respect to other notions (thus defined); its functioning is determined by the conditions of the production of the discourse wherein these notions act.*

In Culioli (1974), the notion appears in a context where representations already exist and its properties simply determine which operations can be directly performed (p.7). Elsewhere (p.12) Culioli specifies that:

> *a notion has neither quantity nor quality, is neither positive nor negative (to limit our description to quantification and modality) but is compatible with all the values that operations of enunciative and predicative determination entail.*

For example (p.13):

> *we can show that a question like*
> *est-ce que quelqu'un a ouvert la fenêtre?*
> *[did someone open the window?]*
> *consists of scanning the possible values of the predicate (positive, negative), i.e., did open/did not open, without being able to assign either a positive or a negative value to the utterance. In short, in this type of interrogative, one uses the notion of the predicate (which is neither positive nor negative but is compatible with either).*

In the 1974–1975 Seminar (Culioli 1976), he underlines how difficult it is to define 'notion'

> *It is not a concept, much too precise a term, nor is it, strictly speaking, a representation, though one can say that it is a system of representation or representations organized in a certain way.*
>
> *If, for example, we use 'violin', this is a term which refers to a number of physico-cultural properties [...]. These properties are not necessarily universal, they vary from culture to culture, from material to material. This is particularly evident in the domain of grammatical categories like gender, number ... where certain operations are found in all languages either because they are extra-linguistic or linked to language. (Lecture 4, 36-37)*

In one of his 1978 articles (Culioli 1978a:304) we find a first expression of the tripartite classification of notions on which he will further elaborate in the 1983-1984 Seminar :

type α — physico-cultural properties "defined in terms of extension and of a predicative character";
type β — grammatical notions "such as aspect, modality";
type γ — "relations between type α notions"

The genesis of the term 'notion' is more thoroughly explained in Culioli (1981). Notion as a problem arises from confronting the assumption that "the predicate" is the basic organizing and generating construct[1] *within the diversity of languages. The result of this confrontation is the need to introduce "the notion of predicate" or 'notion' (p.49) to serve in this capacity. Culioli identifies a second origin: dissatisfaction with lexicology and lexicography, which reject any adjustment or metaphor, any sense of heterogeneity in the constitution and meaning of words (p.50). Notions are the answer to both difficulties since they are*

> *complex representational systems of physico-cultural properties,*[2] *that is to say, properties of objects resulting from manipulations necessarily a part of cultures, and from this point of view, examining notions inevitably implies speaking of problems of the province of disciplines that cannot be reduced solely to linguistics (p.50).*

A notion is (53-54):

> *a set one can express, such as: 'to read, reading, book, reader, library, etc.' Which means we cannot reduce it to a lexical unit. The latter can serve as a hanger, an entry-point, but that is all.*

EXCERPTS FROM THE 1983-1984 D.E.A. SEMINAR

[*Three Types of Notions*]

Now we are going to look at notions and notional domains. In the representational domain we have essentially three sectors

α — roughly speaking, the lexical domain

---

[1] For Langacker (1987) the basic cognitive unit in languages is the predicate defined as "the semantic pole of a morpheme" (p.97)

[2] Although Langacker (1988:4) defends an organic model language, his heuristic instruments are grounded in cybernetic and procedural models of cognition applied to neurological activity "A complex predicate like [CAT] or [BANANA] is more accurately viewed as a *set* of routines, which are interrelated in various ways facilitating their coactivation (e.g. by inclusion or by the sharing of subroutines) but nevertheless retain enough autonomy that the execution of one does not entail the activation of all the rest" (p.162). In representing the predicate components, Langacker explicitly constructs (an implicitly omnipresent) synthesis, rooting the traditional network model ("In terms of the network model, each of the specifications in a complex matrix is a relation, and the entity designated by the predicate is a node shared by all of these relations" p.163) in an AI-like environment: "We can now identify every entity or relation in a knowledge system with a cognitive routine, typically decomposable into subroutines or even hierarchies of subroutines."(*ibid.*)

β — grammatical categories

γ — what has been called "thought content" (by Benveniste, as well as by Freudians), "propositional content" in logic, or "dictum" (in the Middle Ages and by Charles Bally), or "lekton" (by the Stoics).

[...]

In the *lexical domain*: one must think in terms of a semantic field around a root, a set of representations varying according to the language. In a language such as English, they can be phonesthemes (cf. Firth) such as *glow, gleam, glimmer, glisten; swing, sway* ... . But whatever the culture, we always have a mode, a system of representation based on bundles of physico-cultural properties. When they are physical, they are usually filtered by the cultures, and when they are cultural, there is always a correspondent in the domain of reality apprehension.

If we examine a term, there is a set of associations that will allow *certain* constructions. This term will not have full freedom of movement; its degrees of constraint and freedom are what allows the very construction of utterances. At the same time, connected with all of this, one will have a whole set of relationships, in particular, the primitive relationship *normally entails*. For example: when I hear or read "wet", I associate it with cultural presuppositions, chains of causality, as well as valuing: indifferent, good, bad, therefore beneficial or detrimental, and add to this a subjective point of view: pleasing or disgusting, or indifferent. We have here a real *system* of representation that structures itself according to very stable criteria. This then is what I refer to as the *lexical* level. Words are a kind of *summary* of these notional systems of representation. They are collectors: with a word one can refer to a notion. It evokes all the notion, but the relationship is not symmetrical: a notion will only be partially contained in a word. So, once again, there is no term-for-term relationship; there are always both loopholes and a surplus. In fact it is always possible to have a system based on the word that the word will not be able to hold.

The term *grammatical categories* is meant in the traditional European sense, i.e., the categories of time, modality, aspect, number, determination, etc. They are themselves a kind of representation.

As for the *third sector*, it is a constructed representation which will afterwards yield an utterance. For example:

Paul – lentils – eating

I establish a relationship and a specification. In so doing I construct a representation but it is not lexicalized. It can be: *it is true*, *it is probable*, *he frequently does*, *it's disgusting*, *it will do him some good* ... . We have the possibility of constructing an object detached from reality, for example: *the fact that, the idea that, the hope that ... Paul eats some lentils ...* . If I do not continue, we cannot know whether the process has been instantiated or not.

We are dealing with "thought content". One can then speak of a notion; I shall explain why I use this term and we shall see which properties are common to the notion and to all notional domains constructed on notions thus defined.

(Lecture of 15 Nov 1983)

As I have already indicated, we give ourselves rules for the constitution of objects. (I shall use as equivalents "construct" and "constitute".) And so we are not processing constituted data.

On Level α

With lexical notions, two dangers are to be avoided. One consists in working with a form of general semantics, already constituted since it is said to be common to all representations of the human species. This is why I introduced the restriction of a complex system of representation based on physical and cultural properties. One could no doubt imagine — since we have a good many praxic activities, and that no matter what the culture, we use almost identical sequences of gestures — that we could have a kind of gigantic universal robotics. Where this becomes more complicated is when we pass to the level of representations: *are there universal metaphors*? At the present time it is impossible to solve this problem. We would have to study a whole set of questions belonging to semiology per se, and this presupposes coordinated research. In the area of artificial intelligence it is possible; to a great extent the activity of scientific discourse consists in stabilizing the discourse. Between geometry in one culture and geometry in another, it might be hoped that there can be transfer without a remainder. This is false, however, because mathematical discourse itself carries metaphors and these metaphors can be translated more or less felicitously. To take but one example: *point d'accumulation* in French, is *Höherung* in German, i.e., stacking.

If we look at the other activity's structuring of *praxes* (stabilized behaviour, having a certain regularity — such as a sequence of gestures to produce a transformation), the same holds.

So the first danger, as we have seen, is general semantics and all it entails.

The second aspect is dealing with entirely constituted units. I shall examine two of their characteristics: first, they are already syntactically categorized (noun, verb, adverb ...). You run the risk of carrying with you a categorization which is historically clear but does not necessarily have anything to do with the reality of the observed phenomena. It is not because a distribution, a certain classification procedure has been bequeathed to us by a 2000-year-old tradition that it will necessarily be fruitful.

The second characteristic is that words are a kind of captor as far as meaning is concerned: they are linked to the history and culture of a community speaking a given language, and it is only through forceful imposition that words can be written in capitals that then refer one to general semantics. They are simply material supports for notions.

For example: *eating* refers to a certain way of eating as opposed to *devouring*, *wolfing down*. There is also an opposition between *eating* for animals and for humans. We realize that for a number of reasons words cannot be used as pre-constituted units with ready-made properties — not in the approach I have adopted, i.e., that of generalizable properties concerning language's cognitive symbolic activity as apprehended through the diversity of texts one finds in natural languages.

We therefore have problems with type x notions: I have been somewhat at a loss when faced with ready-made concepts, a conception belonging to general semantics, and an apprehension through words categorized into nouns, verbs, etc.

Level β

We also risk positing as a universal what is in fact the transposition of categories peculiar to one language onto another. We must set out the problem in two terms: on one hand *grammatical notions*, and on the other, *grammatical categories*. We shall then see the relationship between the two and why I have been led to present the problem as I have.

Traditionally, "category" is the attribution of some predicative property which gives us the classificatory principle. One can speak of categorization into noun and verb because they are parts of speech. In English terminology, "category" is used for what was called a part of of speech and is now called a "syntactic class". In the European tradition, the term "categories" in "grammatical categories" is used to refer to major categories of language activity: aspect, modality, number, determination, etc.

These grammatical categories are represented by *markers*. We thus have interplay among markers: cf. the *one* in relation to the *many* – or what would be neither unique nor many for an undetermined, non-negligible quantity. Examples:

'*Il y a de la voiture*.' [There are a good many cars here.
An equivalent utterance in English might be:
There's quite a bit of + *MASS NOUN*+ *here/there*.]

If any person ..., they must ... [in English in the original]

There is a whole set of phenomena related to these markers and this will characterize a grammatical category in a given language. The danger lies in speaking of grammatical categories in terms of markers.

Notions themselves are representations. What they apply to will depend on what the notion is.

If we choose *aspect*, for example, we realize that, on the one hand there is the notion as such, with its aspectual properties: punctual, semelfactive (one time), iterative, continuous ... On the other hand, when we have a conjugated form, certain values are marked by specific forms (accomplished – unaccomplished); it is therefore outside the domain of notions.

On the notional level, a very clumsy terminology is used:

it leads to an endpoint
it is starting
it repeats itself
it only happens once

We have here a certain type of representation such that we are dealing with events we perceive either as resulting in a transformation, or as having a certain stability so that one does not end up with a transformation: stative; whether it be original stative or a transformation has previously occurred. Examples:

In Autumn the leaves are red ≠ copper is red, brass is yellow

Similarly:

The letter is written: stabilized

The process is irreversible; with a reversible one we can return to the starting point. Example: open, closed. With *it is starting*, we put the emphasis on inchoation. With *it leads to an endpoint*, we emphasize the attained or contemplated end. If it is reached, a transformation occurs somewhere.

All this can be reduced to operations with which we are already familiar.

On the other hand, aspect problems are also linked to problems of quantification and qualification: the problem of iteration. It is also the problem of *conation* (from the latin *conare* meaning "to strive"). One very often has a conative value either linked to the notion itself or that can be assigned to a notion (*to strive to, to seek to* ...) For example:

I am seeking to attain

or

I am selling my house: I am seeking to sell it (which we find in Latin and in Russian also).

We introduce considerations in relation to an objective to be attained.

We shall meet these aspect problems again when we define the relationship between modality and aspect.

The classic example in Russian is: *Have you read War and Peace?* The *imperfective* is in the interrogative itself. Why in Arabic are the hypotheses unaccomplished (as in *if he comes tomorrow*) or perfective (as in *if he comes tomorrow = let him come tomorrow* [*qu'il vienne demain*]'), i.e., introducing an event, even a fictitious one.

One will also encounter what is traditionally called the *gnomic aorist*: when one is dealing with general truths, in a great many languages a form other than the present is called for. This is because these utterances can be apprehended as a text string not related to any particular event but as though one had "smoothed" different events.[3] Example: *The early bird catches the worm* [in English in the original]. The starting point is an experience: *the world belongs to whosoever rises early* is the result of a smoothing process — with different occurrences, one proceeds in such a way that they do not appear in their individuality in relation to one another, and one can have a present. One can meet a particular form, aoristic, but can also encounter what I call "granular scanning" (Culioli 1990:183). The occurrences are preserved: an occurrence is taken in its individuality, even if it is presented as imaginary and one draws a general conclusion, something like: *no one has ever seen ...*, *it has happened that ....*

Let us look at problems of *performativity*. They are aspect problems which produce strictures on aspect. In particular in English, a progressive form cannot be used with a performative, except in the case of re-use:

I refuse to obey such orders.

and

So you're refusing to obey. [both in English in the original].

In conclusion we can state that *notions* are never pure in the sense in which one could speak of aspect without relating these *notions* to other problems. They are always linked to modality, determination ...

And so we can speak in general terms, give ourselves the tools of an Rμ that enable us to speak about these problems without being fettered by the specificities of a given language. At the same time we are going to work on

[3] In Langacker (1987:259) the action of "the imperfectivizing progressive construction" is a similar one: "the component states are viewed at a level of abstraction sufficient to neutralize their differences and are thus construed as a kind of mass".

grammatical categories based on marker interplay and this will be in a non-trivial relationship of correspondence (i.e., not term-for-term) with notions which are representations of the order of body activity. The study the linguist undertakes bears precisely on the relationships between notions and grammatical categories. The linguist must step back from language, become interested in areas which are not necessarily classified as being a part of linguistic activity.

Level γ

At some point one is obliged to make a number of decisions, thus the third point (γ) which has been called "thought content", "dictum", "lekton" will correspond to something which can become an utterance, for example: <my brother — to come — tomorrow>. A number of terms (α) can be combined to give us complex notions, and (γ) concerns these. With "thought content" one has a set of constituent terms to be processed, or the whole proposition will be processed, by asking a question, by rejecting, or wishing, or by asserting it. And it is this, this relationship which we shall process in this manner, which belongs to level (γ). One simply establishes the relationship between 'brother', 'to come' and 'tomorrow'. Each of these terms is bound to *clusters* of properties, for example: <you — to read — report> these terms can be worked on; valuing, variants of a semantic or a lexical character (to read — to devour) ... can be introduced.We are then working on observable phenomena drawn from a conversation.

Type (α) notions thus belong to the lexical domain. It is a structured set of physico-cultural properties; (β) is a network of grammatical notions, and (γ) is a network of relationships between type (α) notions.

(Lecture of 22 Nov 1983)

[*Notions and Words*]

Notions, in the sense in which I speak of them here, are perceived through words but *they are not equivalent to the lexical set of a given language*. The problem is to look for stable, general properties that are found, in any case, through the study of phenomena observed always in the context of specific languages and so always through lexical sets.

If at some time we are dealing with the structure of the organizing system of physico-cultural properties, it is not generalizable. If the procedure entails showing that behind these representations there are generalizable properties, this is generalizable. For grammar, the same applies: if one studies grammatical notions as founders of categories, this is generalizable data.

Our first point in this lecture will consist of a number of remarks concerning properties and relationships, certain operations we find, which does not mean they will occur in every instance. First, one only encounters *notions* through *occurrences*. We do not study cognitive activity as it appears through non verbal behaviour, but only through verbalized behaviour. I am not filming someone making a map, knitting or making a table; nor are we concerned with seeing how people taught to tie a knot manage to reproduce it, and all this without verbalizing — which is in fact an aid to trial-and-error learning. In our case we use language, and so, necessarily, text, and sometimes words. The problem of *regulation* is always linked to that of *representation*. What does this mean? Let us imagine that one verbalized strictly for oneself: that language activity would not be at all subject to regulation by another. In a foreign language situation this is exactly what occurs when one's interlocutor is polite. By not interrupting, he does not bring into play the activity of regulation that corresponds to the role of parents "correcting" their child's language production.

One can imagine a self-centered activity in like fashion. However, as linguists we study normed activity where designation plays a part, and the problem of equivalence between the meaning of the concept producer and the actual understanding of whoever receives, recognizes, apprehends, interprets the utterance, is an important one.

For example: I could say "this is a satchel" and someone could say to me: "I would call it a briefcase; satchel is more for schoolboys". One can remark that at every moment in discourse expressions arise such as: *I'm looking for words that can express my thought*, *if I can put it that way*, etc. which show a preoccupation with adjustment. This happens through **occurrences of notions**. One only has access to the notion through text and more specifically through words, but on the other hand, there is no one–notion/one–word relationship. There is always a lack of equivalence.

[*The Prototype*]

Therefore there remains the possibility, rather curious in a sense, of constructing the notion through occurrences of the notion; on the other hand, throughout one's cognitive experience, *types* must already have been constructed which will cause these occurrences to be compared to a notional type.

Some occurrences are *empirical* in character: these are *phenomena*. For these I use the term **phenomenal occurrences**. They are always occurrences of something; but to be able to say that we are dealing with occurrences of a notion, that notion must be already partly constituted. Occurrences are compared to a type that is never stabilized and exists in relation to other notions. From there abstract occurrences can be constructed, for one has the capacity by means of one's representational activity to detach oneself from empirical experiential world data and construct new occurrences, which means that the signification of words, for example, can evolve.

In his apprehension of the outside world, even before verbalizing, a child knows how to do a lot of things. He knows how to tear up a sheet of paper even before knowing how to say: "See how well I've torn up the sheet of paper!" All acts can be representative, even if one cannot verbalize them, one can represent it for oneself. A distinction must therefore be made between *knowing how to represent* and *knowing how to designate*.

If I take the example of an animal, at some point one hears people say "a dog". The next time, one sees another animal and calls it a dog. The first time it was a dog, the second a cat. One will be told: "it's not the same thing". *Differentiation* is introduced.

It can be seen from the graphic that I shall be able to isolate properties. One shall sometimes err: for example,

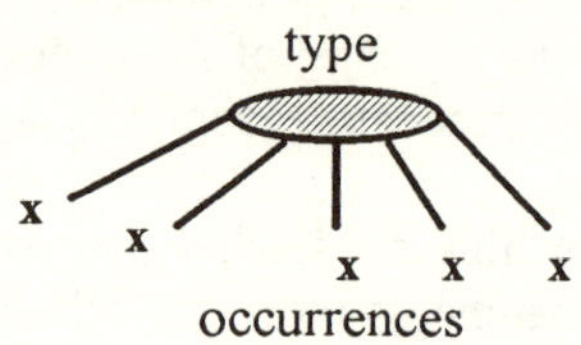

Some trouble could be experienced distinguishing between a wolf and a dog, especially if is a wolf dog, and someone will say: "one lives in the house, the other in the woods" or some opposition of this kind. Little by little a notion is being structured. As one makes mistakes, one see that they invite correction, give rise to admiration, awe, etc., and at some moment one will be able to engage in a discussion and say: "that isn't what I call a ..." or "that isn't really a ...", or again "and I have something like this, that or the other, shall I still be able to say that it is a ...", i.e., what I call **abstract occurrences**. Henri Wallon devoted a great deal of his work to studying these problems in relationship to the psychology of children.

One can notice that the occurrences of a notion are dispersed; they are *representations* and at the same time they represent a dispersion since each occurrence has properties which are its own: one dog's ears are raised, another has pointed ears.

As always some pertinent properties are filtered, i.e., some are dropped and others distinguished if they enable one to posit the identification of the occurrences, i.e., one constructs a **type**. In passing, I would like to make a few remarks on:

- arche-type
- proto-type
- stereo-type
- ∅-type

Within the symbolic activity of the human species the construction of what has been termed "prototype" seems fundamental, *innate*: every human being when viewing events that at first sight appear disparate, sorts them in such a way that he ends up with occurrences identifiable with a type, even if they are extremely diverse colours, actions or phenomena. A large part of our cognitive activity is founded on this capacity to know how to isolate the pertinent properties that enable us to compare apparently unrelated events to types, allowing us to construct abstract representatives detached from reality. In fact there would be no symbolic activity without this ability. In this instance we speak of *prototypes*: "proto" signifying first, primordial, typifying. I more readily use the term "type"; however, when speaking in English, I use the term "prototype". But one finds the notion of "type" in Gonseth, a Swiss mathematician who published *Mathématique et réalités* circa 1925-1930.[4] the notion of type can also be found in Gestalt, in particular in Koffka's book: *Principles of Gestalt Psychology*.[5]

Archetypes are *primitive* types that are in us, in the Platonic sense of the term, or the Jungian sense for those interested in psychoanalysis. They are associated with metaphysical problems.

Stereotypes are types that have been altered by prejudice originating in a culture.

That having been said, one can see that the notion of occurrence is occurrence *of*. It is related to the notion of types. The elaboration of a type is never finished. In fact there is continual *typification*. One acts as though one had stable types when, in reality, they are always subject to a form of *regulation* which is language activity, i.e. regulation from another or from oneself. However, a historically instantiated type, for a given community, at any given moment is not stable.

(Lecture of 29 Nov 1983)

---

[4] Gonseth, F. 1936. *Les Mathématiques et la réalité. Essai sur la méthode axiomatique.*. Paris: A. Blanchard.

[5] Koffka, K. 1935. *Principles of Gestalt Psychology*. London: Routledge and Kegan Paul.

ON NOTIONS AND THEIR REPRESENTATION FOLLOWING THE D.E.A. SEMINAR

Writing in a publication for teachers of English as a Second Language (1986a), Culioli mentions two forms of reference which characterize the notion: ramification as a result of inter-notional relationships created by the user (e.g., sheep and dog as opposed to sheep and lion [p.86]); and abundance as physical, cultural and anthropological properties interrelate in such a way as to refer to a multiplicity of virtualities, "a notional domain" (ibid.).

Later, when addressing an audience composed, at least partially, of linguists familiar with his work (Culioli 1987a), he underlines the importance of economy in the construction of representations (schematic forms or other entities) to assure the coherence of the SRμ, and indicates which are essential (p.116). He also specifies that "every notion supposes a sequence of determinations" (ibid.). To a great extent, the remaining lectures and works on cognition and representation analyze the consequences of this property.

CHAPTER 3

NOTIONAL DOMAINS

EDITOR'S INTRODUCTION

According to the first description of the notional domain: **(p, p′)**, *it can consist of (α) (β) or (γ) type notions (physico-cultural properties; grammatical notions; relations between type (α) notions), each domain having its own topology (Culioli: 1978a: 304). Culioli indicates that by applying operations of determination to the notional category, one transforms the intensional, purely qualitative (α)-type notion, into a "quantifiable and qualifiable linguistic construct". The article proceeds to describe the constituent constructs of a notional domain:*

> *One then constructs the class of occurrences p_i, p_j of the sub-domain* **p**. *Every occurrence p_i of* **p** *has a neighbourhood by construct, thus there exists another occurrence p_j of* **p**. **p** *can therefore be represented by an open.*

A first attempt at a topology of the domain produces a complement of **p**: **Cp** *"closed, by definition (composed, therefore, of the Boundary and the Interior of* **Cp**)*" (304-305). Distinct from the mathematical complement, the "notional" or "linguistic" complement,* **p'**, *can be defined as "the Boundary and the Interior constructed on the mathematical complement* **Cp**" *(p.305). Here,* **(p, $\overline{\text{p}}$')** *is "the topological space derived from notion P" (ibid.).*

A paper presented by Culioli and the resulting discussion involving (primarily) himself, Jean-Blaise Grizé and François Bresson (Culioli 1981), help to refine this first description. Here appear for the first time the relationships between: 1) the domain and a class of occurrences, 2) the attracting centre and the gradient, and, on the other hand, this categorical distinction — a notional domain is not a semantic field (p.54).

> *The class of occurrences is [...] what enables us to grasp a notion [...] to designate it. [...]. (57-58)*
>
> *Thanks to the representations of occurrences abstracted from languages, we can proceed extensionally from a notion constructed as a domain, i.e., that first appears as set of non-quantifiable properties. (p.59)*

Culioli goes on to describe the attractor "a notion defining the Interior of a domain"; it operates by drawing any occurrence back into the Interior "since any occurrence will be identified with it" (p.60). Thus, qualitatively, the attractor contains all the points in the domain by identification (p.61); however, there are quantitative differences in the properties of the occurrences and they enable the construction of a gradient — not a continuous scale — whose anchoring point is the attractor. Differences of degree create a variety of relationships of distance with the attracting centre, and with the Boundary (p.61).

François Bresson's comparison between Culioli's attracting centre and Eleanor Rosch's prototype (p.65) is another major contributing factor to the evolution of the description.

In the 1983 version of a paper on "The Concept of Notional Domain", delivered at a conference on language universals held in 1976 (Culioli 1983a), typification (p.68) and the prototype — equated with the organizing centre (p.69) — are well entrenched in Culioli's model of the notion and notional domains. Further components include the attracting centre, the gradient (p.70) and a potentially open complement: composed of "either Boundary + Exterior, or Exterior only" (p.71), a conceptualization of the Boundary which allows for greater complexity: "the Boundary can be empty [...] belong to the Interior and to the Exterior [...] can stand by itself, or be associated to the Interior or to the Exterior" (ibid.). All of these components will be more fully analysed in the following excerpts from the D.E.A. Lectures.

The reader will note that the Lectures on the notional domain (and the texts from 1984 onward) often combine preassertive and later operations in order to validate metalinguistic constructs by demonstrating their usefulness in explaining the realization of well-formed utterances.

EXCERPTS FROM THE D.E.A. SEMINAR

Notions and Occurrences

I am now going to introduce the term *notional domain*. We are going to posit rational entities: my abstract occurrences (i.e., that I can conceptualize, imagining, roughly speaking, what can be called a transition to the class) of a typed notion are going to constitute the notional domain. If I return to my example, *dog*, I have an idea of what a dog is and I may say to myself: "Now that, that isn't a dog".

There are a certain number of steps. First one touches, then shows, then refers; for example, *where is the dog?*; then one can say: "the dog is a friend" and not "this dog is a friend". One passed from a singular occurrence to the notion *being a dog*. One can invoke the predicate and say: "being a dog is being a friend to ...". One is going to induce *a dog* possessing the first property: every occurrence possible, imaginable is interchangeable, identifiable with every other occurrence — *qualitatively* identifiable. These are abstract occurrences, as in the context where one says: "and if I come across an animal that ..." and describes it and asks: "shall I still call that a dog?". Two distinct properties are therefore necessary. On the one hand, one must be able to individuate, distinguish occurrences, and on the other the occurences must be qualitatively uniform, i.e., they must be interchangeable, identifiable with each other. Naturally this uniformity is always subject to the influence of intersubjective relationships. The occurrences are identified with each other but that does not mean they are identical. This holds true, of course, for the notion — *being red*, for example. Every human being has the ability to classify and to sort. This does not mean that sorting will be performed according to a stable method of designation by all the members of a community, for example. If at a given moment we agree on a certain notion and you analyse distinct occurrences of it, you can state that they are identical. Here we meet the old *langue* / *parole* problem: subjective singularity in relation to trans-individual stability.

One is dealing with a class, however, and these individual occurrences are at the same time considered to be undistinguishable. This term must be used with care. In linguistics, the operation of constructing a class is one of qualifying and quantifying — there is necessarily individuation of occurrences.

A notional domain is therefore the domain of the occurrences of a notion.

(Lecture of 29 Nov 1983)

The Class of Occurrences and Individuation

I would like to insist once again upon our use of the word *class*. It is a hybrid as regards traditional usage. It possesses properties of extensionality that are found, for example, in a logical class, but not all of its other properties. On the other hand it is very close to what one refers to as a classifier in languages with classes, i.e., it is indeed the marker of a quantifying procedure, whatever it may be.

In fact the goal of the operation of constructing a class of occurrences is to make phenomena quantifiable, and thus to be able to process them as though they could be reduced to events, i.e., as if they could be represented by points; and at the same time to perform an operation of clarification or, in other terms, qualifying. Let us examine two examples: a lexical unit and a predicative relation (PR). With the lexical unit *wheat* we can have: *a tuff, an ear, a grain, a bushel of wheat*. I can say: "kinds" or "varieties of wheat". I am able to quantify. If I take a PR: <x – reading a book> I can have: *the fact, the idea, the hope the event, the manner of reading a book*, etc. In this way I specify and at the same time I individuate, an operation that enables me to work on occurrences, events or points. This is germane both to the essential problem: when we, linguists, construct an SRμ, knowing if we can construct manipulable objects. It is also pertinent to how to proceed so that the problem of reference is processed as complex problems of referenciation and not reduced to a simple coding relationship between an external reference and a designation.

The problem must be set out in such a way that we respect the phenomena with which we work. The phenomena are complex, we do not have the right to simplify them if we do not specify that we are doing so and explain why. We do not immediately set out to draw a graphic representation simply because that is how it is done in the sciences. On the other hand, let us not forget that human activity, as it appears to us through languages, has a much greater capacity for abstraction than do linguists when they are working on a language. We must not react by saying something like: "this is abstract, it does not interest me as I am only interested by the concrete content of languages". In this instance, the abstract/concrete opposition makes no sense whatsoever.

I shall now present a set of operations enabling one to construct properties. I shall present them sequentially, whereas they should be presented all at once. In fact braces would be welcome because what I shall state in a) is bound to what I shall state in b) and vice-versa. The operations are not sequenced but much more closely related.

The Organizing Centre

First property: we are going to represent this class of points (I shall say "class of occurrences" so as not to embark upon undesirable elaborations). This class will necessarily contain a centre. When talking about the domain, I shall say that the domain is centred. This means that it necessarily contains an occurrence with a privileged status that serves as its *organizing centre* and — here I anticipate somewhat — *attracting centre*.

Not only is this not removed from reality but, as research progresses, one realizes that it is very fruitful. I insist on the fact that this description has been constructed from observations of phenomena, followed by abstractions, and a return to observation.

An organizing centre means that when one comes across phenomenal occurrences, they are compared to a type that is the predicate par excellence and almost represents the Platonic archetype. At some point, as though it were inherent to our mental activity, we all need to make comparisons to a centre, to a type. As concerns the notional domain, all occurrences are compared to an organizing centre (OC); thus you can state: "they're interchangeable, i.e., qualitatively undistinguishable or "they're qualitatively different" or "they're comparable".

Now, we touch on the problem of constructing the *Boundary*, i.e., what contains properties that belong to two parts ordinarily opposed. In mathematics when one talks about the complement of something, it consists of that which is not something:

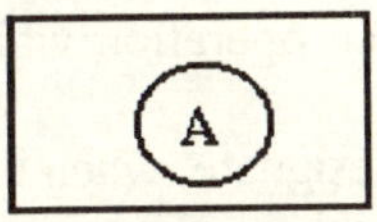

The complement of A is that which is not A. Some linguists have tried to introduce the mathematical notion of *fuzzy sets* [in English in the original]. This notion is apparently useful, for we often feel ill at ease when we have to work with a complement exhibiting the properties of a logical complement. At one time, there were also attempts at working with several negations such that a particular negation could have more or less strength. A negation so strong that it was absolute induced this type of complementarity. A weak negation meant: "it's different but not totally different". But studies based on negations of different strengths never yielded very satisfactory results. When Zadeh invented the idea of fuzzy sets, it was very quickly adopted by a certain number of linguists — the idea was apparently promising. From this [notional] point of view, the topological route seems more interesting and appears to correspond to what is found in linguistic phenomena in a far more productive manner.

To posit the existence of a property and a fringe is not satisfactory. When one is dealing with Boundary phenomena, one must construct the Boundary, explicate how one constructs the concept of an edge. As for the concept of Boundary, I need reasoned-out solutions, constructed arguments.

Identifying and Differentiating

The operation deriving from the first point, i.e., relating back to an OC, is that of identification and differentiation described earlier. It is an operation or a set of primitive operations as well as a sorting activity prior even to classification. Anologies can be adduced: wool which is black to one side and not black on the other, or green lentils, wild lentils and pebbles.

a) Identification

To assert that there is identification, if there exists an occurrence 2 with respect to my organizing centre,

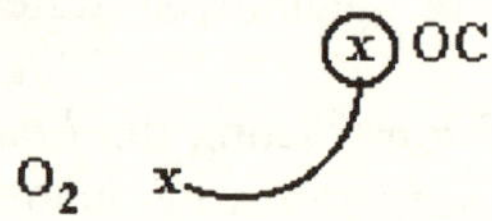

I establish a relationship such that I may affirm that the uncircled occurrence can be accorded fully with the circled occurrence, or that it is different. If it can be accorded, I have represented an operation which can be viewed from two perspectives:

If you ask "is it a ... ?" and you designate, when in the presence of a phenomenal occurrence in effect you are asking "Does the designation for what I am showing you truly correspond to the designatum of this name that has such and such properties?" By means of a phenomenon much more complex than it appears, you have performed an operation of identification. You produce, in certain cases, something that corresponds to *vrai* / *vraiment*, in French, *true or real* or *truly or really*, in English, or some equivalent in another language. In an operation of identification you may say: "now that's a real ... " i.e., there is no property which could mislead you, it displays all the features. When an OC is constructed, it will always have referential properties which are both sociologically stable, and variable from person to person. For example, a book can vary. Some will call "book" all printed matter in book form. Others will reply: "now that isn't a real book, it's a comic book". Others will say: "a book contains at least 200 pages". This is the process of constructing a valuing system, i.e., assigning a value such that it conforms to the OC as I myself construct it or as we try to construct it.

If we take the example of a manufactured product, one can look at its representation in a catalogue; one can also go and see the article in the store. Once more we come across the problems of touching, ostension and progressively increasing abstraction. As for ostension, the catalogue will include an exploded view of an object, or a photograph, or a drawing. Then one will read its specifications outside the drawing. One imagines the object. When neither a list of its specifications, nor a drawing, nor the reference properties is accessible, one imagines the object; and very often imagines the object even when it is present ... . The art of the salesperson consists in selling something by means of verbalization that triggers these types of cognitive processes.

You compare the occurrence of x to the predicate. For example, Y wishes to buy something with which to write. Y is shown various articles, and says "that isn't a pen such as I imagine one", and at some point "now that's a real pen". That is to say that it is a *pen–pen* [...]. The occurrences must conform to the OC, to the idea, the type, what Y imagines to be a real pen, i.e., to the predicate that refers to the notion in its purest form. One assimilates the occurrence to the predicate, which represents the quintessential property.[1] Such is the case in English with *He is no doctor*, for example. He does not have any of the properties of a doctor, he is in no way a doctor.

b) Differentiation

At some point, one asserts that some occurrence is qualitatively "other", i.e. it contains some measure of otherness, minimal or maximal. As we can see, we have the possibility of constructing *zones* inside our domain. If at some moment I have an occurrence (i) and another (j) and I can identify one with the other and with the OC (x), as long as this is the case, I am dealing with a zone which I would qualify as *open*. For it to be closed, there would have to be a break — resulting from the construction of an alternative value, the possibility of having two zones. In that perspective, an intuitive description is relatively simple: for something to be closed, there must be a separation between two zones:

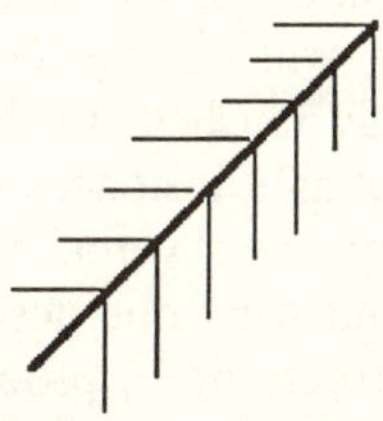

With otherness, there is a double construct: at some point, there is a property that I shall consider to be my OC, and by means of a metalinguistic fiction, I shall lay out an open zone and an *alteration*, i.e., a transformation. Then at some [other] point you will find an occurrence with an alteration,

[1] Langacker (1987:372) also stresses the centrality of the subject's perspective when admitting occurrences into a *category*, often the equivalent of Culioli's notional domain: "Concept X can nevertheless be assimilated to the category provided that the conceptualizer observes a measure of similarity between PT [the prototype] and X and is willing, for the purposes at hand, to overlook discrepancies."

even a minimal one. There is necessarily a break between the occurrence on the Left (x_m) and that on the Right (x_n): there is a space which contains no occurrence. What will be observed is not an infinitesimal transformation (cf. *not in the least*, i.e., I can't even find the slightest trace one can imagine). One will encounter a gap, a break, and this break can contain no value. So an L value, an R value are invariably obtained and one partitions between them. We observe an occurrence to the left and at some point, another with an altered property. It is already something else from there on. Starting at a certain point, something happens: a constructed zone that is *closed on the left*, but the shaded zone is an *open* one, in the sense that it contains no last point, i.e. every occurrence can be identified with the OC.

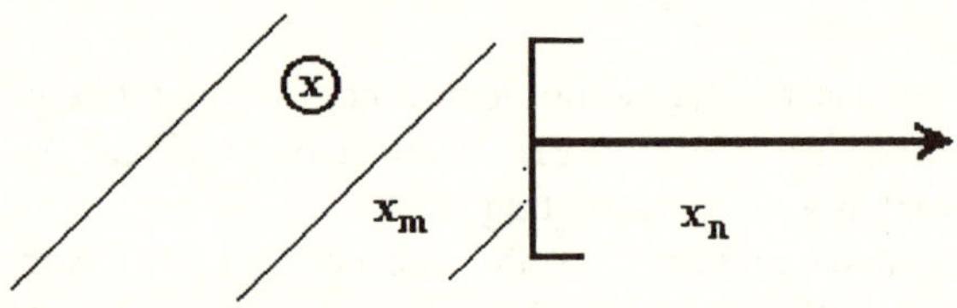

In some instances, however, an end point will have to be reconstructed, for certain specific problems — if, for example, one takes a terminative process, where an end can be foreseen, such as painting a room or writing a letter.

One writes the letter and, at some point says "I'll be finished in two minutes"; 'I shall be finished', but there can be no end point. One cannot say "I finish writing", one is finishing writing: still writing. One must say "I've finished writing", but then one has already finished. In this perspective, one is 'cornered'. Only a few perfectly identifiable instances differ, i.e. in the case where what is done is accompanied by one's verbalization. At the moment one raises one's pen, what one does and what one describes coincide. When one says "that's it", when one reconstructs one's process, one fully realizes that there is a moment when one finished. Depending on whether the construct is viewed retrospectively or anti-retrospectively, one will not observe the same effects.[2] One may well observe a first point without perceiving a last point for the former process or, if one is found, it may be because one is going to reconstitute it.

2 Langacker often insists upon the importance of the perspective of construal, the "vantage point", for valuing notions, a prototypical example being "come vs. go" (e.g., Langacker 1990:62).

[*The gradient*]

Up until now, we have worked with *all or nothing*: either two things identify or not. Nothing prevents us, however, from stating that something is identifiable with something else to a lesser and lesser degree, i.e. it contains less and less of property P, but to a very small degree, it remains P:[3]

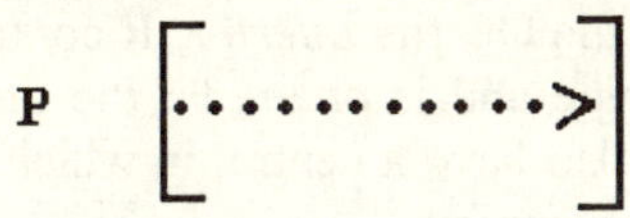

In so doing, I've transformed what I've said and introduced something which resembles a *gradient*.

The term *gradient* is commonly used by physicians and psychologists. I prefer it to the term "scale" for two reasons: first, because strictly speaking, there are no minima and maxima. There is no more a first point than a last point. We can have, however, a purely *imaginary* last point, cf. *He didn't even lift a finger*. This is a *symbolic* representation of *he didn't even make the smallest gesture one can imagine*. Similarly with *not a leaf stirred*, we are employing a metaphor, a symbolic representation, to state that, should one be able to imagine the slightest possible movement, (in any case) even it did not occur.

The second reason for adopting *gradient* is that when one speaks of a scale, one imagines fixed levels such that movement can be made from one level to the next or to the preceding one. In the notional domain, however, what is important are orientations toward the centre, or away from the centre, something which we can represent by an arrow, i.e., movement toward the Interior or the Exterior.

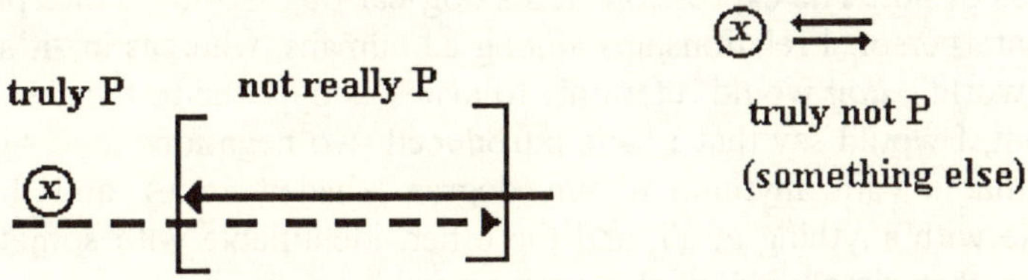

[3] Langacker (1987:371) schematizes the act of comparison with the prototype, here represented by S, in this manner: "S > T = V", where T represents the target, and V the "magnitude of discrepancy between the standard and the target".

The shaded part has properties belonging both to the left and right zones, and depending on whether one starts from the left or the right, one will not obtain the same constructs.

[*Interior, Exterior, Boundary*]

We call the construct around the OC the *Interior*. It contains occurrences identifiable with the OC or the type and is *open*. To the other side, on the right, is the *Exterior*, which may also have a centre, in which instance we are dealing with typed antonyms. For example:

long — short, big — small.

In other instances, the Exterior is constructed on the property which serves as OC by voiding the Interior, and will be characterized by the void, by a null set, e.g., if one says: "*there wasn't even a hint of a human being*". In relation to *containing people*, one can have *to be full of*, *containing people* and *not containing even the slightest hint of a human being*, and construct the fact that there is no one. A scan of the class of occurrences results each time in "voiding", ejection into the Exterior. No term belongs to the Boundary; the Boundary is empty. When one says: "there wasn' even a hint of a living being", one has exhaustea all the possibilities and has, in fact, constructed a null set. [We have seen] an example taken from the aspectual domain: writing a letter. A letter is being written and then there is a point when the letter is written. At that moment, the letter is no longer being written, hence in relation to the process *writing a letter* there is no longer any occurrence belonging to the zone ⟨ writing a letter ⟩. Moreover, when the notional domain is constructed you will evidently construct notions that include the notional domain. For example: *There were no men*, does not say anything about whether there were any women or not. The expression "it's a dog-eat-dog world" is interpreted as defining interpersonal relationships among all humans, whereas in "it's a dog-eat-bitch world", *dog* would refer only to males as opposed to females.

In sum, I would say that I have introduced two negations: one signifying not identifiable with anything to any degree (shaded zone), and thus, not identifiable with anything at all; and the other, identifiable with something to any degree, then simply identifiable with something.

On one hand, we have an OC; then, through differentiation, identification and alteration we construct a network containing *not at all* or *in part*, which enables us to set out on one side **I**, on the other **E**, and to place **B** such that Interior/Boundary/Exterior. And so one finds instances of **IBE**, **IB** in relation to **E**, **I** in relation to **BE**, a null **B** and **IE**. Then there are properties associated with the notions you process. Working on *absent–present* is not the same as working on *raw–cooked*. We know what raw meat is, but we do not know when it is cooked! ...

(Lecture of 6 Dec. 1983)

The operations which I describe here are general ones that I have abstracted from different observations. They present virtualities: everything will not be present in every case. Normally each time a gradient seems possible, there will be a gradient, but there are instances where this will not obtain. In similar fashion, we cannot propose a half-page representation that would set out all possible and imaginable occurrences of β type notions, i.e. grammatical categories. We shall find entities greatly variable in character, like *raw* in relation to *cooked* which are not real antonyms: meat cannot be "uncooked"; whereas *melt* and *freeze* are in a relationship of reversibility.

By means of operations associated with this "template", I construct the model which this representation provides; but it is not as though I had drawn a model on the blackboard. When I create a graphic representation, I do not know where to indicate *cooked* in relation to *raw*, nor *freeze* with respect to *melt* — everything depends upon the predicate. In some instances, the Exterior will be *not doing something*; in others, *no longer doing something*. One can attempt to deal with an amorphous state, or construct by means of operations, a representation which integrates a topology (i.e., properties, an Interior, an Exterior, a Boundary ...). In some instances a given property of gradients may or may not be pertinent.

You must not imagine that this gives you anything more than general tools; constructs will be needed for each specific instance, for each problem, based on these instruments.

A Note on the Centre

Before pursuing my lecture, I would like to return to the question of the *centre*. We know that when we use a term to designate, we always centre it: we relate it to a value considered to be prototypical, to something typified. When we say "did you see the red object there on the table?" this means "the typical object of a typically red hue on the typical table". We would no more say: "it is true that the sun's out", meaning "(the) sun's out", than we say "typical object", etc. It is only during interlocution, when we question statements, that we would say:

"Why do you call that red?"

or

"You call that red? In my opinion it's maroon."

The centre is the minimum to which the interlocutors can agree; and at some point will come a designation, which will have the property of relating back to a centre. Quite obviously, in a good number of instances, it is a product of our interaction with our environment and with others, i.e., roughly speaking, what has been termed pragmatics, which provides us with these typical values. It is clear, however, that these values are typical only for us and that we need criteria of a subjective nature[4] or linked to our social practices.[5] This also concerns fundamental divisions like good and bad. We shall always be influenced by valuation based on a phenomenon of good/bad; attractive/repulsive; beneficial/detrimental. The neutral degree, indifference, can also come into play, it will be level 0.

All we know is that every human being has this tendency to construct centred spaces. Normally we construct a space in such a way that it has a centre, edges and a gradient. Sometimes this model will not be appropriate, but it remains in the background, and can always re-appear as soon as an argument arises or there is a need for precision, etc.

Once again, there is no term-for-term equivalence between the notion and the designation. There is always a little "play", some "slack".

Open / Closed, and Intension / Extension

Now we are going to take a second look at some of the concepts used, in particular *open*. At the the end of the day, it refers to two very simple properties: the first is that there are no first or last points; the second, that there is identification of one point to another.

We could have a first representation such as this:

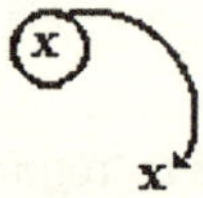

Given a certain occurrence, it is compared to the distinctive occurrence which is the type: the typical or prototypical occurrence. These two occur-

[4] Langacker (1988:63) also stresses the importance of constructing a subjectivist theory of meaning, which he proceeds to do by means of the central role accorded to *imagery*: diverse construals of a property or a situation by real or virtual subjects (Langacker 1987:110; Langacker 1988:63; Langacker 1990:61, and *passim*). As for the subjective — and changing — nature of prototypes, he adduces the following example (Langacker 1987:376): "Elms and maples may not survive as prototypical trees for a speaker who has lived forty years in the desert."

[5] Langacker (1987:403) gives an example of properties whose value cannot be construed outside a socio-political context: 'murdering' vs. 'assassinating'.

rences are qualitatively unaltered one with respect to the other. When the occurrence is related to the predicate as in *a dog is a dog*, one states that it has the properties of *being a dog*. One has posited that there is no otherness. Naturally alternative values can be introduced with *there are dogs and there are dogs*, but in *a dog is a dog* an identification is constructed, one does not establish an identity, since the occurrence is related back to the predicate. In such an instance, there are no first or last points, we simply construct a loop. There is always a starting point and an end point to what we draw on the blackboard, but this is not the mode we are talking about, however, since we are not working extensionally. We are processing intensionally, qualitatively, so to speak, i.e. we are not processing referentially defined occurrences. When I say: "a dog is a dog", this means: when I have some *being dog*, it relates back to *being dog*. You can iterate this operation as often as you wish, it will always be valid.

The second instance that we have seen, is when, on an axis oriented left to right, there are two points such that x_i and x_j are identified

They can be individuated but are not qualitatively distinguishable or discernable. What is confusing is that we seem to be processing extensionally whereas in fact we are working intensionally.

The intensionality is constructed from empirical fragments, since we fragment, we designate. However, this partitioning occurs because we have a tendency to *type* and that most likely we have prototypes. This tendancy is a human property — there is also some element that belongs to the domain of acquired knowledge, but fundamentally I have to posit that it is *primitive*.

To be able to speak of identification, I must extract one point and compare it to the others. It is therefore easier to say i, j, k, even if these points are not *qualitatively* distinguishable.

The third configuration is the following: let us imagine that at a certain moment a certain process has taken place and resulted in a certain state. The process having taken place can be represented in this instance by a *closed* interval, for example: *writing a letter*.

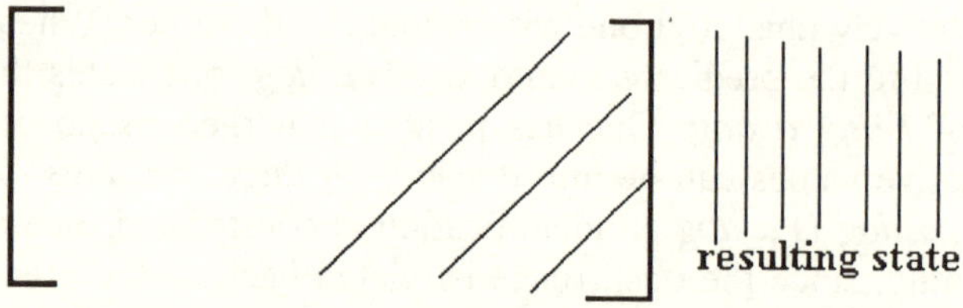

The resulting state is the complement of the closed interval: from now on one is no longer writing, and from now on every point can be identified with any other, and there is a product, a result: the letter that has been written. In certain instances, it's more complicated as in *eating*: *The cake is eaten*. We have a problem inasmuch as we no longer have a product that can be validated referentially or presented empirically. Does a state result from the verb to eat? Yes, since no food eaten is left. Two questions arise that may be complementary: we may be dealing with a resulting state that cannot necessarily be assimilated to an empirically validatable product. This takes place by means of negation.

The state is an open one whose principal trait is being non-closed.

The High Degree

We can now attack the problem of the *high degree* closely associated with that of the centre. On the one hand we have the *organizing centre* (i.e., type) and on the other, the *attracting centre*. There is interaction, of course. By means of a rather arbitrary procedure, I shall separate them and then establish their interaction.

[*Any and "Any old"*]

There may be a property, a trait such as <being red> [/big/] /red/. The backslashes indicate the notion and < > indicates the predicate. If I say "it's red", this means typical red, defined as red in some measure: in the final analysis, one defines negatively. Everything that is more or less red is related back to this organizing centre. Any red will be designated as being red. The fact that it is *any* means that there are no discriminating properties inside my red. When I say *any* [*quelconque* in the original], I am not referring to the word (there is no unique equivalent in English, but many) but to the operation, i.e., if I select several points, they are not in any particular order, they are all on the same level, none stands out or is more important than the rest.

In other circumstances in French, *any* [*quelconque*] will signify a pejorative evaluation: *any old*. If I introduce a negation (from the point of view of the gradient, as we shall see, a negation acts as an inversor), and if *any* means "without importance", "devalued"; *not any* will signify "not any old thing" and will designate something that will be valued.

Any old and *any old thing* are associated with *not much*, *not a big deal*. It happens that in French *a big deal* [*grand chose* in the original] is primarily used in a negative way. However, when you remove *not*, you are left with *a big deal* which signifies *something of importance*. During the manipulation that we have just performed, when you construct in such a way that the operation appears to be exclusively an identification of any term with any other, it can activate what I have just described or a gradient resulting in a devaluation. When you invert by adding the negation to *any old thing* or by eliminating the negation from *not a big deal*, you increase the value. Hence there are two movements in relation to my attracting centre

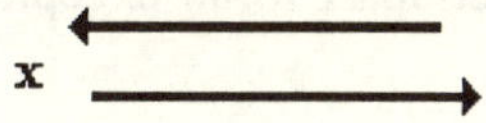

Some

Let us examine another problem: *someone / somebody* [*quelqu'un* in the original]. This means "an occurrence of a human being". *One* refers in this instance to *non-negative, non-null* no matter what the qualitative variations may be.

Differing from *any*, which necessarily indicates that there are a number of occurrences and that the occurrence being examined cannot be distinguished from the rest, *someone / somebody* has been individuated. The occurrence is related back to my *attractor*. What is interesting is that *somebody* means *someone important*, that is to say, not anyone. If I say "if you meet someone", it signifies "whomsoever". If it is in an affirmative assertion, it will refer to a particular event: *I met someone*; but if you are dealing with an identification: *he's somebody*, you will note that this is appreciative; it means *this is not anyone*. It provides you with a distinguished term, separated from the rest by a particular property which, in this instance, is associated with good / bad.

Now take the construction referring to inanimates: *something* [*quelque chose* in the original]. Let us examine the expression *that's something* signifying "that is not nothing".

Nothing provides the Exterior, which is empty. Add the negation, it triggers a movement across the Boundary and *not nothing* can be used in an appreciative sense.

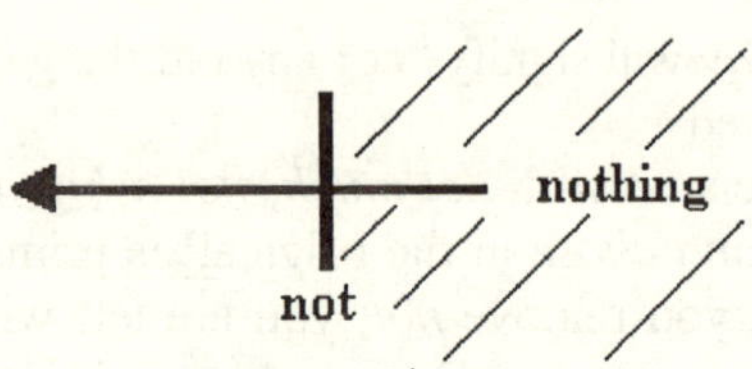

Let us take the canonical English example *some*. In *some car* [in English in the original], it can mean "that car is quite something" [*pas rien*, not nothing] or on the other hand, "that's some car", i.e., "that isn't much of a car". To say "that is not nothing" can mean: "that is not nothing and that's good" or "that is not nothing and that's bad". It is not nothing either among entities to be rejected or among those to be valued: it is set apart to an exceptional degree, to the high degree.

[*Orientation of the Gradient*]

This means that when we construct our gradient, one direction is headed toward a less and less strong (or a weaker and weaker) degree, up to a posited last, imaginary, point: *not in the least* or again *not at all* where all refers to the Interior and to the Boundary, i.e., "there is not the slightest trace, whether I view the property as defined typically or in altered forms".

This provides an orientation and, I repeat, there is no final point: it is imaginary. I construct the minimum when I need to construct a point which signifies "here is the last point before the Boundary". And on the other hand, when I go in the other direction, there will be a stronger and stronger degree; degree here signifies the quantity of a quality. Thus, if I say "something is hotter than something else", insofar as the quality *being hot* is concerned, there is a greater quantity of it. Hence, once again, we are dealing with problems of valuing and qualitative transformation: from *hot* the movement is toward *boiling*, an increase, but once more no last point, only a superlative. If there is no final point, you have the high degree, or an intensive. The opposite of an intensive is a down-toner [in English in the original]. In some instances down-toning continues until extenuation. Its counterpart is simply an intensive and that is all.

[*Coincidence of the Organizing Centre and the Attracting Centre*]

Here is a problem I have not studied: why do the attracting centre and the organizing centre seem to coincide in some instances? For example: ***a book is a book*** means "it's important, one doesn't throw it away", but also: ***it isn't very important, it can be replaced***. We see that this operation which consists of referring to an attracting centre is compatible with both. On the other hand, what if I posit a first term and then the occurrence, for example: *tall, he's tall alright*. I posit a first term, then I place it in an enunciative space: let us speak of *being tall* in relation to him — I say "he's tall". This effectively induces the high degree, meaning that it is undisputable; such a degree is not situated in the Boundary zone, but in the high part of the gradient. We can see that it passes through *really / truly*. What one can notice in the high degree is that each time a predicate has properties that can be *gradated*, the operation of relating back to the predicate will activate this high degree. When the predicate has no degrees, like *occurring*, there will be no high degree.

(Lecture of 13 Dec 1983)

Constructing the Notional Domain

[*Designation and Representation*]

Analysing relationships between designation and representation (in the sense of notional representation, i.e., the construction of a centred notional domain), leads to distinguishing two possibilities. One can be exemplified by *president* in *as for being president, he only has the title, the appearance, the name*; the other by: *now he's what I call a president* — "he's all president, has all the attributes, the look ...".

In the first instance, *being president* is culturally linked to institutional questions. By saying "he only has the title, the appearance", one introduces a distinction between the designation (being designated as president) and carrying out presidential functions. From this opposition we can derive *he's not a **real** president*; we construct a representation of the notion *being president*, then we choose an occurrence empirically situated in relation to given subjects in a given spatio-temporally specified situation, and note that there is no equivalence between my idea or the general idea [of *being president*] and the person's behaviour such as I construe it.

Now he's what one calls a president provides us with the opposite: the designation here evinces the essential value, the centred quality. By designating, then, I predicate a centred notion

In general we end up with *what one calls a president*, i.e., the consensual ***one***, what everyone agrees to consider to be ... . But we do not state what it is; in a sense, to be a real president is to be like him.

Here we find, in another form, the old problem of the arbitrariness of the linguistic sign: designating does not necessarily imply an essential equivalence — all that is required is the agreement to designate by a certain name. On the other hand, there is the notion that the designation is equivalent to what it designates — this movement from one to the other is perpetual and unescapable.

[*"No more, no less"*]

Now, if I say "he's president, I have nothing to add" or "he's president, nothing more", this will activate additional pathways. In theory we can distinguish the first operation which consists of isolating a marker to which I assign a metalinguistic function; and as soon as I activate it, other markers bond with it: *he's president, no more, no less*, etc.

In *he's president, no more, no less*, the *no more, no less*, can apply to the relationship between *he* and *being president*, but also to ***what I say***. Let us consider these two one at a time. We shall provide a rough gloss:

1) *he's president, neither more president, nor less president, nothing else*.

2) *he's president, I state no more, I state no less*.

Here again it can go either way.

Let us look at the first instance. What is called *president* refers to the representation of *being president* normally shared by all reasonable persons. Every occurrence will be identified with every other occurrence: I end up with **a centred domain**. The entire domain can be reduced to this centre or this point expanded such that every occurrence having been identified to every other, every occurrence is in the proximity of the typical value. We then have neither *more* nor *less*.

Imagine constructing a gradient on it:

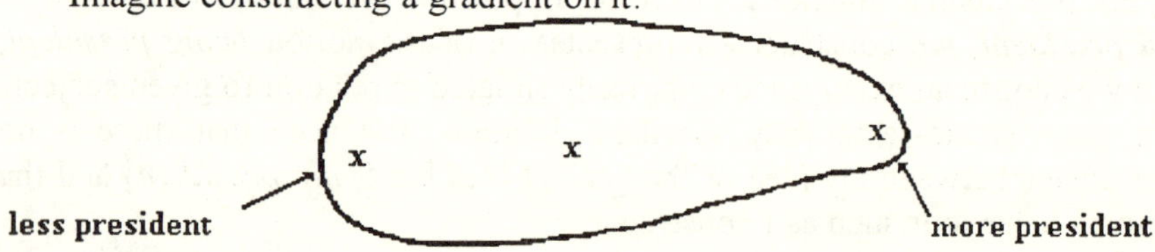

If I say that I cannot perform this operation, this means in fact that I am dealing with an *open*, i.e., with everything that is the typical property without any alteration and, in this instance, the entire domain is equivalent to *being president*, nothing more.

What could alternative values include? We have a property P /being president/

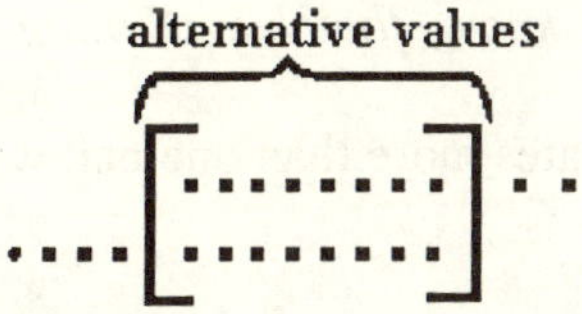

then, in some measure, even minimally *being president*.

On the other side: *not president*.

It is the interplay between the interlocutors which will displace the Boundary.

[*Distinguishable occurrences*]

Let us examine the second instance. There is a point where it differs somewhat from the first. (We can reduce a good number of the problems involved in constructing a class of occurrences in a domain, to quantification and modalisation.) I am presented with the following possibilities:

1) I distinguish one occurrence with a certain value and there can be another, different from it.

2) there will be not only one, but another.

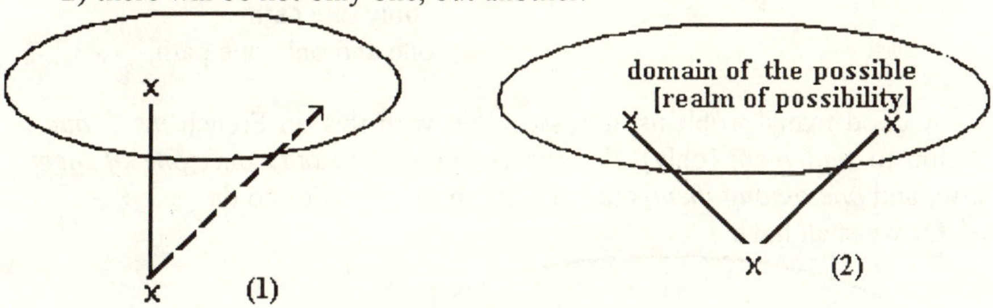

I constructed two each time; this signifies more than one, a minimum of two. The dotted line indicates that this relationship may be realized but is not necessarily present — it corresponds to *in any case, at least*: (1).

If we process distinguishable occurrences of the same property, we shall find markers such as: *among others, for example*, *notably*, etc.: (2).

Other is ambiguous. *Another beer* is usually interpreted as meaning "a second beer", but one could interpret it as meaning "a different beer", which does not mean that it will be qualitatively different.

Other used metalinguistically could prove ambiguous.

And so you see that we have three possibilities and can set aside the first, i.e., when no relationship is created, nothing constructed about nothing: *I have nothing to say, I don't know, that has nothing to do with it, you're barking up the wrong tree*.

The second instance activates more than one pathway.

One, and only one

In the third instance, there is *one*; however, we shall see it is the realization of two possibilities. There are in fact two ways to construct one path: we have one path from the outset, or more than one and we remove as many as necessary to leave but one.

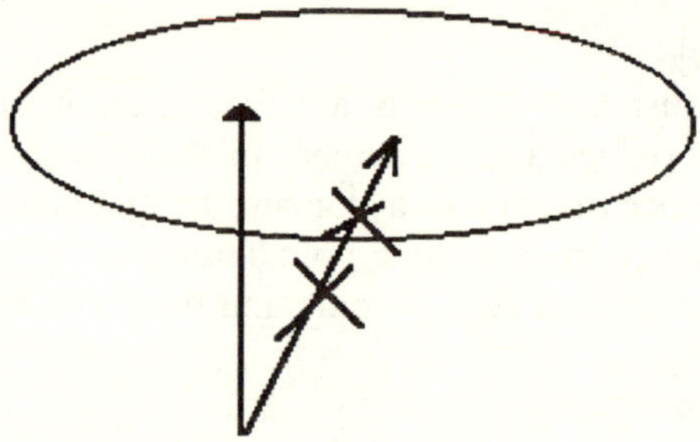

only one path
one and only one path

A good many problems are associated with this: in French *ne ... que* in relation to *seulement* [only]; *the one* as opposed to *only one*, *one of them / those*, and *one among them*, etc.; in English, *a* in relation to *one*.

Or we shall have:

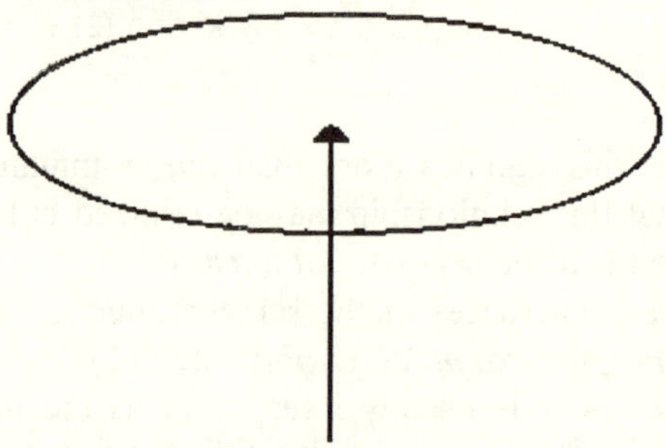

one, no more
I state no more

This corresponds to a predication of existence by which one posits a term without stating that there is one — and possibly more; without stating that there are more than one or that there is no more than one. One can, in a sense, define negatively.

When you say "nothing more, nothing less", etc., you are constructing a great number of additional values. This is without a doubt one of the greatest sources of ambiguity.

If we tackle the problem of modality, we shall find one and only one pathway, and this then is the *necessary* path.

The other instance will be centring on *possibility*, in one way or another. This status is more complex. It corresponds to what I have called "weakly unique" as opposed to "strongly unique" (i.e., one and only one path). In a sense it is a weak necessity.

The Boundary Revisited

I would now like to take up once again the problem of the Boundary. First point: the Boundary is a construct. It is one of the necessary conditions for conceiving an interval. There can be two zones such that on one side a certain state exists, another state on the other.

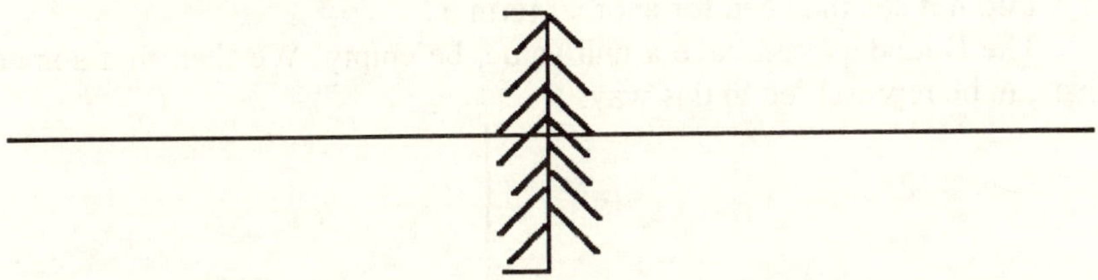

You can consider that you are dealing with instances as small as you wish; in any case, you can always insert a partition between the two, i.e., something which belongs neither to the left domain, nor to the right.

Another way of conceptualizing this is to imagine an overlap. We then separate the two zones but keep them in contact without any overlap.

The Boundary results from the construction of alternative values:

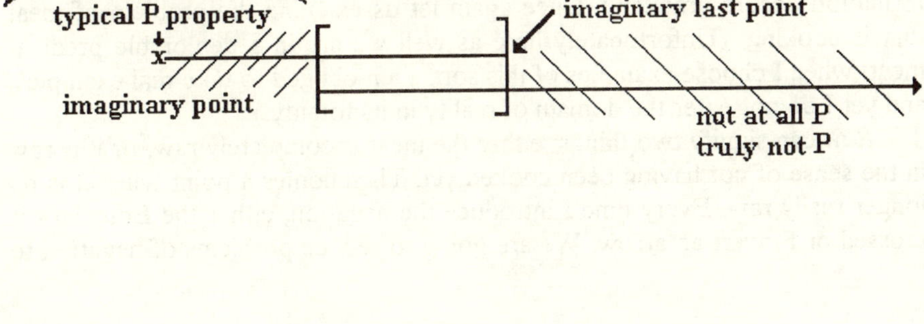

We start from P with its typical value, and on it we construct a gradient, decrease it until we can say "there isn't the least", "the smallest", and at some point, exit. This zone then has an *imaginary* end point. On the other side, there is *not at all P*, really not P, totally other than P. Then we move toward the left and find less and less *not P*, until we reach a point which is not at all *not P*. In so doing we have defined a zone which is open, without alteration (to the left): P, nothing more, nothing less. To the right is the zone comprised of everything that has the property *other than P* without alteration. Between the two, we have this intermediate zone to which we shall return later.

In the case of pronouns, between locutor and interlocutor there is no Boundary, no confusion is possible. When we are dealing with an enunciator and a co-enunciator, the situation is different and more complex since they are not physical persons, emitters–receptors.

In short, we must not confuse partition and Boundary. Instead of saying "Boundary", I could have said "airlock"; why not? In a submarine it is the intermediary zone that allows one to pass from one environment to the other. However, what I have just described corresponds to the *topological Boundary*. I do not see the need for another term.

The Boundary can have a null value, be empty. We then find something that can be represented in this way:

The Boundary then introduces a disjunction between **p** on one side and $\overline{\mathbf{p}}$ on the other: when working in a system with two values, in such an instance we have constructed an empty Boundary.

Let us look at the electric switch, for example: either it is on or it is off; either it is open or it is closed. In this case, there is a leap, a movement from one side to the other. One can, however, imagine a situation where the transformation occurs gradually. Once again let us examine the problem of meat that is cooking. (Unfortunately here as well we are in a deplorable predicament: when I choose examples of this sort, I am obliged to take real examples, and yet I do not enter the domain of reality in its totality.)

Raw can signify two things: either the meat is completely raw, or it is raw in the sense of not having been cooked yet. Then comes a point when it is no longer really raw. Every time I introduce the negation, either the Boundary is crossed or I invert an arrow. We are going to reduce problems of negation to representations we can manipulate. We shall then abstract a simple, applicable rule.

Hence, we shall set out *not really p*, and it will be less and less p, less and less *raw* as it becomes more and more *cooked.* Then will come a point when we shall say "that's it, it is no longer raw". And that point is subjective. Afterwards will come *truly not raw* and *not at all raw*. Let us take them in reverse order: *not at all raw*, then *truly not raw*, then *not really raw* which means: *not really raw, not really cooked.* We can construct in one direction or the other.

Traditionally, we call the left part the *Interior*, the right part, the *Exterior.* The Interior is open. The Exterior is also open. In fact it is the Interior of the complement.

Traditionally we call the complement closed if the Interior is open. In this instance the complement will be: Boundary plus Exterior. If you choose the Exterior, the complement will be the Interior plus the Boundary.

We must rid ourselves of the simplistic idea that the complement is a mathematical or logical complement with two values, one of which is the complement of the other. We do not wish to be caught in the trap of a fully constructed negation which would appear to function like *that which is not*, since *that which is not* is much more complex. To start with I worked on **p** and $\bar{\mathbf{p}}$. Then I realized that this construal avoided the problem. I then interpreted $\bar{\mathbf{p}}$ as being the closed zone, in topology. In fact, it is much more complicated than that. Finally, I call it **p**, **p'**, to remove any ambiguity. This enables us to understand that the complement is not given once and for all. That is the whole notional domain as we can construct it. Afterwards we shall decide what our complement is. It can be the complement of the Interior, i.e., the closed zone plus the Exterior. It can also be the complement of the closed zone (Interior and Boundary): the Exterior.

Let us imagine that we wished to construct the modality of the possible, i.e., *what is* and *what can be*. *What is* will be represented by:

and *what can be* by:

for this can be or not be. We oppose all of this to *that which cannot be*, that is to say, the impossible. In graphic form:

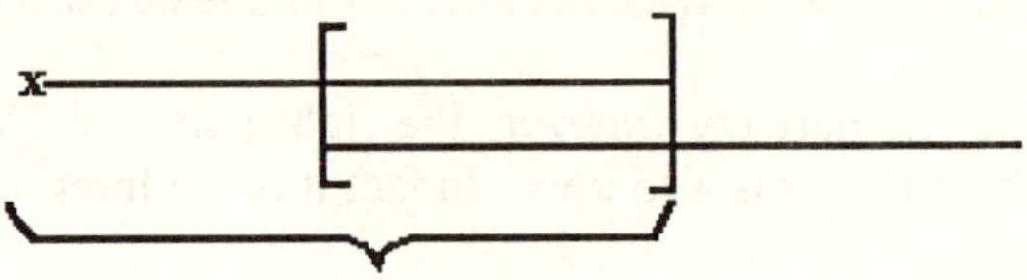

possible

Now, we shall examine the modal and aspectual problem of *wishing to do something*. If one wishes to do something, one has not yet done it. At some point, one is in the zone where one is trying to do it: in the Boundary zone of conative occurrences. When one crosses to the other side, one says that one has "succeeded", in French "*réussi*", whose etymology signifies "to go out once more" — "*uscire*" in Italian. One has crossed once more to the Exterior since, as of now, the deed is done. In a very intuitive way, we realize that there can be representations enabling us to perform trans-categorical operations: not only to construct categories, but also to bring together lexical and grammatical problems, modal and aspectual problems, quantification, modal and aspectual problems.

(Lecture of 20 Dec 1983)

Up until now we have proceeded in a non-specific manner and have enabled ourselves to construct a variable model, a model of variations; you cannot say "the notional domain is this in relation to that". It is a construct comprising an Interior, an Exterior and a Boundary, perhaps an Interior and a Boundary in relation to an Exterior, or an Interior and an Exterior, and a Boundary distinct from both the Interior and the Exterior. We have given ourselves the means to construct the representation which will serve us.

We are going to move on to some additional considerations which derive from this construct. You realize, of course, that together we have raised an extremely complex set of problems that I shall now explicate.

Intension and Extension

The first concerns the relationship between intension and extension. It is sometimes called: realization / unrealization, or realized / virtual.

Example 1: [*The Possibility of a Relationship*]

When I posit a relationship between *John* and *coming*: <John – coming>, the relationship is not validated. I do not say that John will come or that he will not, nor that it is possible that he comes or not; I simply envision the possibility of a relationship being established between the two that could be validated either positively or negatively, or in the form of any other modality which you may find.

In this instance, we are not analysing an event in the sense that *John has come* or *John hasn't come*, or *John is coming* could be called events ... . Nor are we analysing a future event *John will come*. We are processing a domain that we construct: the domain of the values that can realize the relationship <John – coming>. We are analysing events as second degree metalinguistic ones. The relationship mentions the two terms that constitute the event. It does nor refer to an event in the real world. Either we analyse a class on the generic level, or we process it in such a way that after a certain number of operations of quantification you can state "there are some that ... , there are some that ... not; there are some x's that have this property, some x's that don't".

Example 2: [*The Comparative*]

This tool is better suited than the other one.

It could be that *the other one* is not suited at all. If I say "oranges are sweeter than lemons", no one will infer that a lemon is sweet. Anyone can validate it. We cannot avoid an analysis, a semantic one, of our stock of prior knowledge. Having said that, we construct an utterance which clearly signifies that oranges are sweet and lemons are not. This is how one constructs the comparative in a good many languages. There are, essentially, three ways to do so:

– The first is by constructing a notional domain with two zones such that you introduce a difference: oranges are "on the sweet side" with respect to lemons. A relationship is established and, whatever the degree of the term to the right, the term to the left has a higher one.

– The second process is that in numerous languages you have a predicate signifying: to exceed, to surpass.

– The third process is to use a form of negation, as in French: *l'orange est plus sucrée que* ***ne*** *l'est le citron*.

If we take the example of concessives, such as: *As cunning as he may well be, he still was caught*, you will notice that that we were able to construct a relationship pertaining to values that cannot be defined referentially, if by referential we mean extensional, but which can perfectly well be defined referentially if this means "being located inside a network of abstract references that provides us with all we need to perform the operation of referentiation."

The Problem of the Boundary

The other problem that arises is that of the Boundary. We are accustomed to almost always working with two values: true – false, or to working with three or n values but only after giving ourselves intermediate values. However, we are working on constructing entities, metalinguistic objects that will be useful to us, thus the problem is one of constructing the Boundary. This not only concerns problems of properties of notions that could be transformed (cf., raw / cooked), it also involves a whole set of problems associated with modality, for example: what status to give to *seeking to*. In Russian, in many instances, the imperfective has a conative value: *wanting to do something*, in relation to the perfective which can present a value of realization, *stricto sensu*. *Wanting to*, *seeking to*, *striving to* are not in the zone where the event is taking place, nor in the zone where it has taken place, nor in that where there would be no relationship at all.

Similarly, there are all the problems concerning *hardly / barely / scarcely* [*à peine* in the original]. For example:

It is hardly / barely / scarcely sketched out. Is it or is it not?

He is hardly / barely dressed. Is he or is he not?

He had hardly / barely /scarcely entered.

I shall have to place *hardly / barely / scarcely* to the right or to the left of an open zone-marker or a closed one ... . I am going to impose very strict constraints upon my representations. Graphic representation provides us with constraints that keep us from doing just anything.

With *hardly* / *barely* / *scarcely* you will meet with Boundary problems. Similarly with reckoning: *it must be one p. m*. What is this operation which, in French is marked by the verb *devoir*, and in English by *must*? Or what about *that'll be the shutter banging; it'll have come loose*? What is this operation marked by the future? We are in a zone where we have no definite values, outside the universe where we could say "yes" and "no" by means of "yes – yes" and "no – no", i.e., with two perfectly stable values.

Negation

Now we come to the problem of negation. It is everywhere: when we analyse alternative values, the Exterior, absence, the void, we process operations of negation.

Concerning negation we can only have two attitudes: either we seek to eliminate it or we consider it to be primitive. Personally, I do not think it can be constructed as a derivative — we cannot do without the operation of negation. I am forced to posit it as being primitive. This means that when I construct my Exterior, I shall do so based on a notion that I shall first apprehend in its positive form as an Interior.

We come across negative value predicates like *fearing*, *hating*, which do not behave like other predicates containing a negation, such as *not liking*. In the first instance we are talking about a negative value by referring to semantic considerations, and in others it is a problem related to considerations involving segments, syntax to a certain extent.

In some instances negation will be constructed, in others it will be a given based on those negative experiences of which I have just spoken. In French, *ne ... pas* is composed of two parts. *Ne* refers to the primary operation of negation: the term indicates that it is an operation that inverts the orientation, it is an *inversor*. In some instances, the process will be reversed; in others the inversor undoes the previous state; in yet others, it is suspensive: if you say "don't open the window", this means "leave it closed".

Pas is the marker of minimal occurrence; it signifies an abstract occurrence. It is the minimal positive quantity of the occurrence of a given property.

In English *not* comes from *ne* – $\bar{\text{a}}$ – *wiht*, which has given *naught*, *nought*. $\bar{\text{a}}$ is a scanning marker and signifies "ever". You construct a class of occurrences, you choose any one occurrence: *wiht*, which has given *whit*, in *not a whit* is the representative of the abstract occurrence. Hence, any occurrences are not inside:

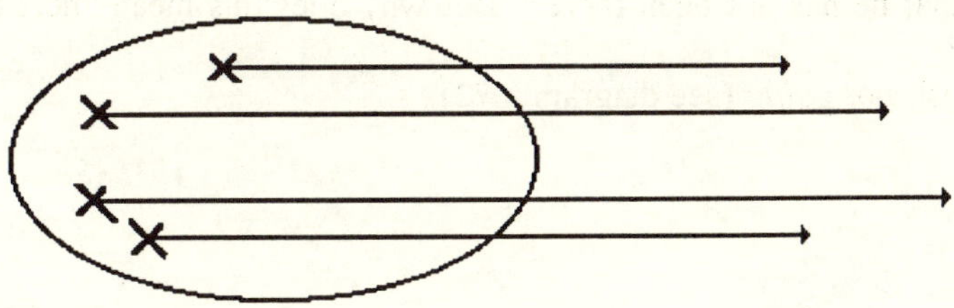

and if no occurrence represents property p, this means that it is *not p*. It has no p in any measure, to any extent [in English in the original]. We have no trace whatsoever of p , it is thus an operation by which, in effect, we construct the exit, that is to say, found the construction of the Exterior. Hence a situation where, as concerns intension and extension, we cannot say "it's primitive and therefore entirely given". It is at the same time primitive and a construct.

Each time we come upon a primitive operation of negation, linked to it are construction operations entailing that, in a given domain which we construct as a positive one, we shall, by performing alteration and emptying operations construct a negative predicate. Thus it is a problem of gigantic complexity.

[*The Negative Interrogative*]

As for the rhetorical question, it is a problem related to the notional domain in a rather complex fashion. Let us take the example:

Where has he not travelled?

or

Has he not travelled?

Whether it be as a mark of surprise, or to call someone to witness to something, we can see what this refers to: I preconstruct somewhere that *I expect that he has travelled.*

[Particularly in French], the interro-negative is not a request for information concerning equiponderant values between which you cannot make up your mind. You can only ask biased questions, weighted on one side or the other. Why is it, as is often said, that the interro-negative sounds like a request for confirmation? We shall add a counterpart to *where has he not travelled?*: *has he even travelled?* We put into question the very fact that he has travelled.

Once again we remark that we are not simply working with *inside / outside, yes / no.* The rhetorical question asks: "Does a place exist about which one can say that he has not been there?" But why does this mean "he's been everywhere"?

Let us posit *not going* (see diagram p.72)

The occurrences re-enter the Interior of the domain:

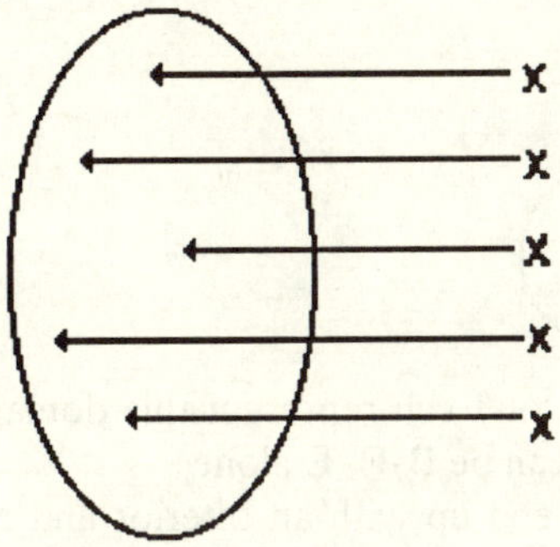

[*Equiponderant Interrogation*]

The real problem with the negative interrogative is knowing what is an interrogation and why, in some instances, it will be compatible with a request for information concerning equiponderant values.

In instances of equiponderant interrogations, a scanning of possible values occurs: positive or negative, for example: *being here* and *not being here*. This means that all values other than the possible ones are impossible values. As in this instance the class of possible values has been exhausted, this means that the class of impossible values will be null. In fact, the problem is much more complicated, since an interlocutor can also reply: "I don't know", "I don't want to answer you".

In equiponderant form, this gives me: yes / no; here / not here; Interior / Exterior.

I shall construct an interrogation if I cannot decide. I am in the **IE** position. I ask some one whether **I** or **E** will be chosen. I have as much of a chance that he will respond with the value **I** as with the value **E**. In certain instances we shall present a value as being improbable: *Is your brother really here?* means "I didn't expect him to be here"; we notice the pre-construct. For there to be a surprise, there must be pre-construction. When analysing the request for confirmation *Isn't your brother here?*, we find the opposite pre-construct.

[***Positive, Negative and the Domain***]

Why is it that in some instances I can bias, weight, introduce the notion of a pre-construct? Here we can use the model of a cam. Why a cam? Because the movement travels from one plane to another, only to return to the initial plane, graphically:

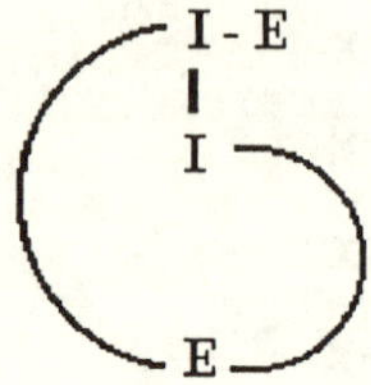

A term represents the entire domain: **I-E**, or I can represent this domain by **(p, p')**; **p'** being the complement of **p** — it can be **B-E**, **E** alone, ...

For example, in this particular instance, I end up with an Interior and an Exterior: *eating* and *something other than eating*, if it is qualitative, or *eating* and *not eating at all*, if it is quantitative. When I designate this, I use a term to refer to this complex notion. It so happens that languages use the *positive* term. When I say *eating*, it refers to <eating – not eating>. We see a sort of lexical designation that, from the point of view of values inside predicative and enunciative operations can refer just as well to a positive value as to a negative one.

In the same way, if one says: "this book is interesting", the statement is invariably interpreted as meaning: interesting in some way, but certainly not a null one, i.e., "it has some interest".

If I say "this book is uninteresting", this means: "without interest". From which I can derive that **the book is only slightly uninteresting* is anomolous, whereas *this book is only slightly interesting* is acceptable. Here we are dealing with an Interior having an attracting centre, so that when we say *interesting*, the occurrence evinces an orientation towards the high degree. *Only slightly* inverts the arrow, points toward the Boundary: it turns you away from the attracting centre.

Uninteresting is formed in such a way that it is in the Exterior: it has been constructed by removing the smallest particle of interest. You cannot construct a gradient; you cannot have *only slightly*. *Only slightly* belongs to the Interior of the domain.

If I examine *the book's interest*, *interest* can signify interest and lack of interest. *Interest* designates the whole domain.

If I say "the coat of paint is thick", this means "very" or "too" thick. By using a predicate of a form that is not comparative, one produces a value which, in a language like Latin, would entail the use of the comparative. When we say "it's thick", this means "on the thick side in relation to what would be needed". However, if we say "thickness", it signifies either "thick" or "thin": a term that designates the domain in all its complexity, including the complement. The complement is always a construct.

Hence **IE** is a privileged relationship: given **IE**, we have a relationship such that **IE** is distinct with respect to any other value. **IE** is on a plane which some call "virtual". It is, in fact, a *representation* with which we can work: we can mention it, use it as an infinitive, a substantive, a nominalized predicate. Hence, we cannot say that it is virtual — it is a virtual value, if you wish (cf. our first example: <John – coming>).

We also have a privileged relationship in the positive value: **I**. When I arrive at the [outside] end of the value **E** — we have seen how to construct **E** — I shall continue my operation and be brought back to the value **IE**. This demonstrates to us that to negate, one must first construct the domain on which the negation will operate. In this sense, as I have already stated, negation is always both primitive and a construct.

(Lecture of 10 January 1984)

There is a problem concerning which — in my opinion — lexicological studies have not been well carried out: constructing antonyms and determining their status. In some instances, an antonym or a negative term is constructed by evacuating the positive occurrences, as in *uninteresting*. In others you construct an antonym because you have a second, associated, domain, the complement of the other, hence Exterior to it. In re-examining the very useful example of *raw* and *cooked*, I find properties of both types which construct their mutual incompatibility.

To speak of *open* or *closed* concerning *raw* or *cooked*, makes no sense, since they are not inherent properties.[6] When I am at the stage of designating, I am dealing with the concept of the notion as an *open* to the extent that, as long as there is designation, I say "this is raw, this is raw ... ". From this point of view, if I do not take degrees of alteration into account, every occurrence is considered to belong to the domain composed of enunciative occurrences of such properties, none of which can be distinguished from the others.

In short, I construct the notional domain that enables me to answer a number of questions. However, when I plunge it into an enunciative space,

[6] This distinction between inherent and non-inherent properties, and the differences in description it entails, resembles Langacker's position concerning cognitive domains and the objective and abstract properties which they include. The properties concerning time, dimensions, and other 'basic domains' are probably inherent (Langacker 1987:148). Yet we may construe events (linguistic and otherwise) structured by these properties — and thereby value them, in very subjective fashion (imagery).

that of assertions, for example, this will activate additional operations. For example, when I am dealing with a positive assertion, it is invariably centred: this will yield one and only one value. I can then plunge my domain into a modal space, this will activate other operations. It is therefore impossible to say "once open, always open". The domain will be able to take in additional properties such that one property will absorb another.

Pouvoir and Constructing the Notional Domain

[This section is based on verifiying the acceptability of juxtaposing *pouvoir* (being able, can) and *bien*, and *pouvoir* and *fort bien* in French. In English, *bien* requires a variety of translations according to the context.]

The following example illustrates the complexity of these problems: *X could have left the window open*, with respect to *X left the window open*. At some point I construct a notional domain that is the relationship between <X> and <leaving the window open>, such that, in this instance, I can assign almost any value — *he left it half-opened*, *he didn't close it well*, *he didn't leave it open*, *he's the one who left it open*, ... The positive assertion *X left the window open*, signifies that the speaker, as enunciator, endorses the idea that it is truly X who really produced the event. There is only one value remaining through elimination of all others possible.

Now *X could have left* ... signifies "it could be X, it could be another", or "since I am speaking about X, perhaps he left the window open". In effect, *could* applies to the relationship. We see that *could* means that it may be the value which validates the relationship you establish with respect to a situation, but it may well not be. I set aside more complex values such as *it's imaginable that he's capable of*. You superpose an epistemic value and a root value, to use a jargon very much in fashion at present.

You can see that I have superposed a set of problems: assertion, then a modalisation of assertion, and now I shall introduce the interrogative: *Who could have left the window open?* This gives me a representation of the class of assignable values which I am scanning. I have constructed a space in which I would say: "It could be so-and-so, it could be so-and-so ... "

If I insert *really* [*bien*]: *X really left the window open*, I notice that it is immediately interpreted as a reiteration, a confirmation, i.e., a back reference to what was stated or noticed earlier. This signifies "it is truly [*bien*] X who ...". *Truly* applies to the relationship between <X> and <leaving the window open>.

Now, *X could well* [*bien*] *have left the window open* is impossible without a polemic value. To really function as such it needs *very well* [*fort bien*], and it then signifies "it is perfectly imaginable that X left the window open".

Thus *well* [*bien*] gives one value in one instance and another, completely different, elsewhere: concessive, polemic (cf. "given his foolishness, he could well ... ", or "I don't care, ... "

Very [*fort*] is therefore necessary to the well-formedness of the utterance. It *centres* anew and will at some point evince the high degree, and so will identify with the attractor. Why this operation is necessary for the well-formedness of the utterance must be explained. We must explain why *can* and *well* constitute a centre-less operation, that a centre is needed and that, therefore, one must centre. If a polemic or concessive value is required, it means opposing two terms, two enunciative components. According to some, one can be posited, however this has no importance in relation to the rest. At this point, there is no longer any incompatibility between *can / being able* and *well*: *He may well [peut bien] have done it, it doesn't matter.*

If we were dealing with an infinitive not in the past tense, this would induce a value of *being well able* [*pouvoir bien*], for example: *You can / may indeed leave the window open. You can / may indeed* enables us to find one of the values of *indeed*: a scan of conative occurrence values, and *indeed* indicates that at some moment we move into the positive domain. *You can / may indeed leave it open* means "you can / may nevertheless, anyway, all things being considered (so you see that there is scanning) do nothing to prevent the window form remaining open". I am obliged to use this circuitous route because *leaving* signifies "not doing anything so that ... is not / does not ... ". This helps me understand the relationship between *laisser* and the causatives, cf. *lassen* in German, *let* in English, and similarly in all the Scandinavian tongues of the Germanic group.

Now I shall examine the interrogation: *Who could have left the window open?* Here the opposite holds true: it is impossible to use *very*:

* *Who could very well have left the window open?*

The interrogation marks a scanning of all possible values:

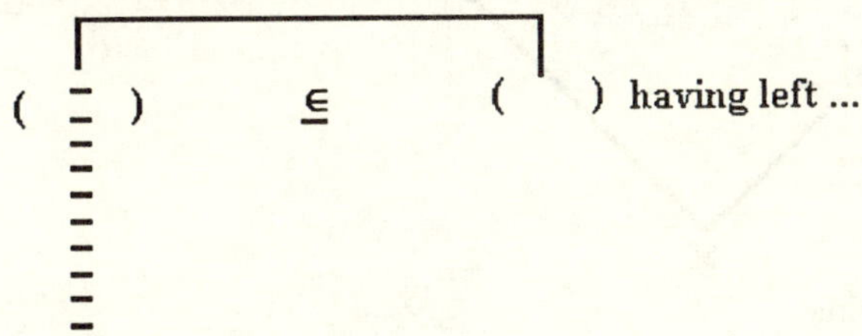

I establish a relationship between a place and *having left* ... and I ask myself what value will acceptably instantiate this place. *Being able* is compatible with this scan, so is [*bien*]. *Very well* [*fort bien*], among other operations, centres and thus, blocks the scanning; it is therefore incompatible with the interrogative.

In *X could have left ...* , we can represent *being able* by a bifurcation activating, in this instance, two values; thus, the Boundary will be considered empty.

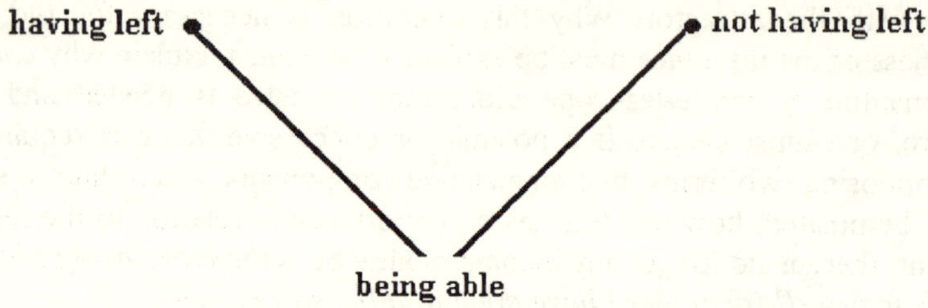

If one says "he could have left ... ", this is the equivalent of *he could have left ... but he could have not left ...* . Once more we find the phenomenon explicated by the cam diagram. If one says "he could have not left ...", this also triggers *he could have left ...* . *Being able* is located at a point from which we can visualize the two values. It must be on an external plane:

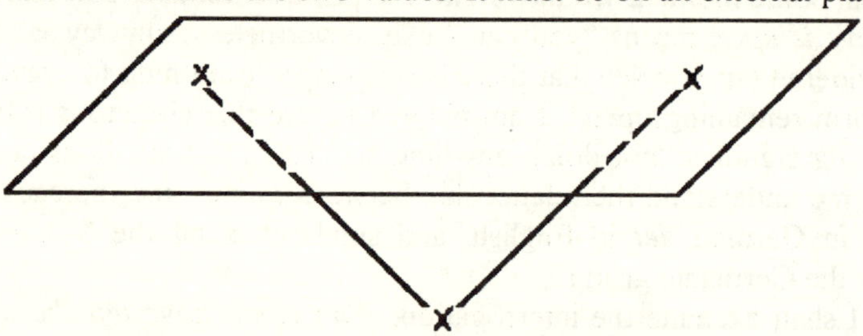

If we analyse *he could not have left the window open*

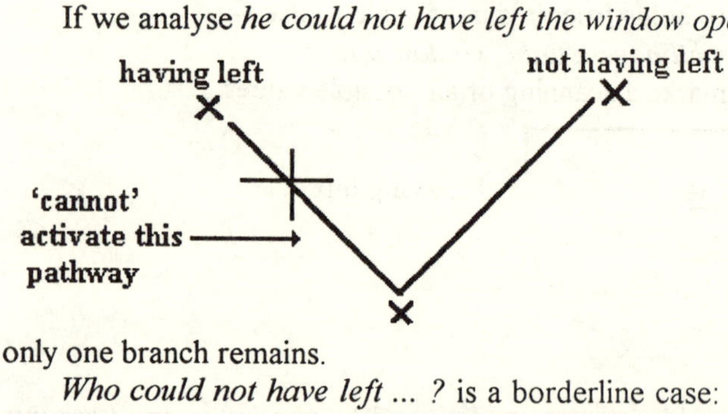

only one branch remains.

Who could not have left ... ? is a borderline case: it can mean "of whom can I say that it is unimaginable that he left the window open?". This is the only possibility. In fact it blocks scanning. Either it is a true predicative relation and the scanning is blocked, becomes impossible; or we construct a type of notional domain: the class of those who could not have left the window open, and scanning becomes possible once more.

The marker *bien*, requires at least two occurrences. Activated operations can include:

identification, for example: *He has really [bien] arrived.*

scanning: *Where in the world [bien] can he be?*

scanning with an exit: *You'll surely [bien] end up by ...*
He'll arrive eventually [bien]

centred scanning, etc., i.e., all the possibilities.

In identification, the second term possesses a recognized existential status; in scanning, a derived existential status. With *he has actually [bien] arrived*, I am processing a certainty, a past event: it is an event that has occurred. If I process the future, it is a form associated with non-certainty. If we add the marker [*bien*], this will immediately come to mind: *he'll end up* [*finira bien*]; however, *ending* is the best example of moving from one zone to another, crossing the Boundary.

(We also come across the double status: *either ... or* [*ou bien ... ou bien*]. That is to say "let's try a value; let's try another value": let us give ourselves such and such a value as our working value.)

X could not have done that, is ambiguous: I can mean "given X, it is unthinkable that X did such a thing", or "given an event that has occurred, it is unthinkable that X did it". In such an instance, one cannot affirm who is responsible for the event in question, all one knows is that X belongs to the class of "impossible values".

If we proceed without a negation, we find a "sporadic possible", for example: *Alsatians can be obese* (cf. G. Kleiber, "L'emploi 'sporadique' du verbe pouvoir", Colloque de Metz, 1981).[7]

The relationship <Alsatian – being obese> is not impossible. Once again we find the logical construct of possibility, the equivalent of *there are instances where ...* . It does not suffice, however, because we can come across values like *there are quite a few* and even an interpretation with the high degree seems possible. In such an instance, I have to work up from the impossible. If the relationship it not validatable, this is the 0 degree: if there is no relationship between *Alsatian* and *being obese*, this means that, no Alsatian being obese, I can say of every Alsatian that he has 0 degree of obesity.

---

7 "L'Emploi 'sporadique' du verbe *pouvoir* en français". *La Notion sémantico-logique de modalité*. Acts of the Colloquium of Metz. Edited by Jean David & Georges Kleiber (= *Recherches Linguistiques*, 8). Paris: Klincksieck, 1983. 183-203

If I start from the impossible, and then enter the notional domain of positive values, I can process this movement in two ways: either through an analysis of a quantitative type — *there are some*, or of a qualitative one — *rather obese*. Once again we encounter the problem of the attractor.

In this instance we have processed the impossible as if it were an empty class; thus we work on the possible as referring to a class of non-null values. The complement will be Ø:

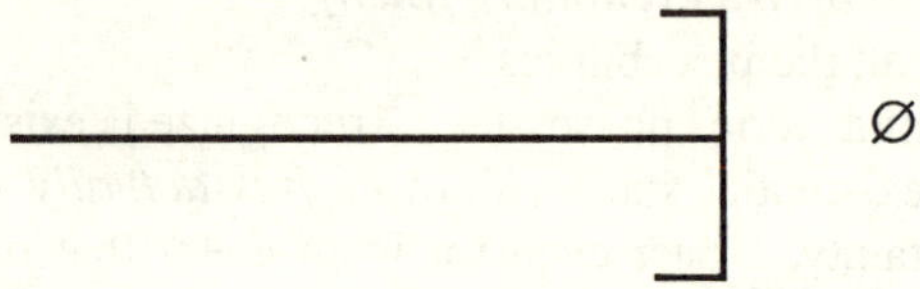

then moving back to the left, I enter the domain of positive values.

As for interrogatives, in some instances they do not aim at obtaining information: some rhetorical questions are practically interjections. For example: *Who's the idiot who left the window open?* We must always take this into account. The complexity of what I am trying to elucidate by means of the notional domain allows for this plasticity, this characteristic *deformability* by each enunciator.

(Lecture of 17 January 1984)

[***Trans-categorical Analyses and the Turn-back Point***]

Once we have constructed categories, our work consists of performing trans-category analyses: we must not set aspect on one side, modality on another, and quantification on yet another, completely compartmentalizing the operations. We must demonstrate the existence of transverse operations creating trans-categorical relationships. Behind all of this, lies the problem of constructing the reference: either designations are bi-univocal, or we are dealing with much more complex operations of referencing. Concerning the notional domain, I draw your attention to the following point: imagine that we construct a plane on which I choose a point from which I organize all my locating network (see diagram p.80):

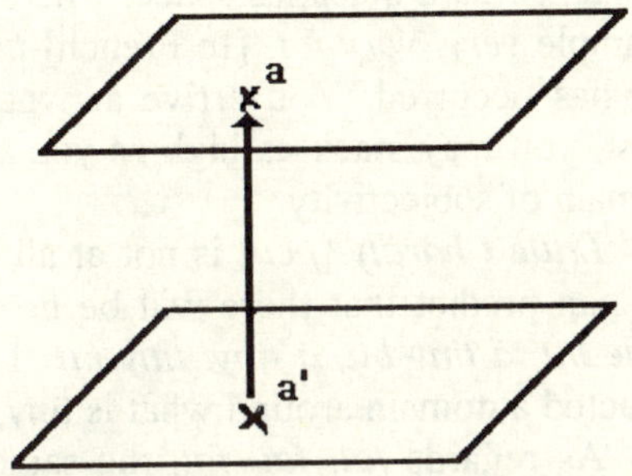

Then I construct another point:

by separating this plane from the former. This point will be considered, in a very loose sense, to be a projection of the first point. The move from **a** to **a'** can be accomplished in such a way that leaving **a'**, results in a return to **a**. However, since they are separated, I can imagine that the pathway activated might not return to the starting point: it could diverge in one direction and not in the other. **a'** is the point which I have called the **turn-back point**. Heading back, given two values (0 and 1), could activate pathways to value 0 or value 1, or no returning pathway: a stay on the separated plane, and induce neither value 0 nor value 1:

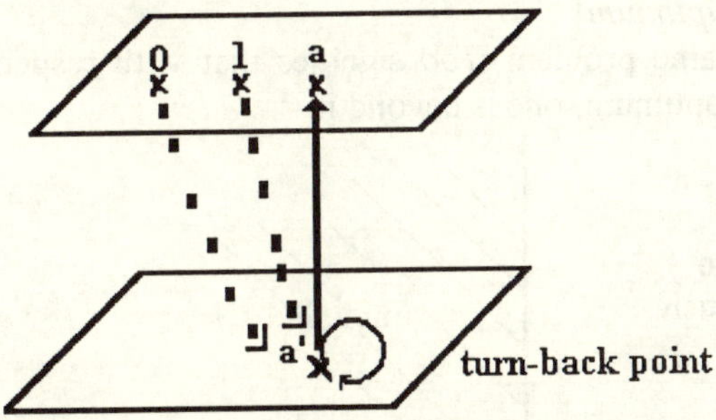

I have constructed a set of possibilities that expands very quickly. This is the problem raised by certain modalities: possibility, necessity, hypotheticals, etc.

Our problem is being able to construct enunciative spaces exhibiting properties of coherence so that we can always assert that in our metalinguistic discourse "the rule just posited, the operation just elucidated is appropriate or not, is validated or not".

A Second Look at the Attracting Centre

Before proceeding, it appears useful to me to take another look at how one must understand what I have called "the attracting centre". It must be visualized as a stacking space. There is no last point. Let us re-examine the example *very, very fat*. [In French] *très* etýmologically indicates that a crossing has occurred. You arrive at what is not an end point and, in theory at least, you may stack as high as you wish: *very, very, very ...* . We are in the domain of subjectivity.

Little / hardly [*peu*] is not at all constructed in the same manner, and so we can predict that there will be no reduplication. We can find, however, *a little bit, a tiny bit, a tiny, tiny bit*. This is acceptable because you have constructed a domain around what is tiny, tiny.

As regards *fat, fat, fat*, the same obtains. *Fat* provides the designation, that is all. In this instance, the problem we have set out is the relationship between designation and predicate. If one says: *he is fat*, this can have a great many significations, for example: *I find him fat*.)One will then be asked: *how fat?*. One might answer: *this fat* or *fat, fat*. One can also reply: *fat, fat, fat*. This means "everything you'd call fat, every property composing the fattest", in English: *fat as fat is*. In some instances it means "too fat with respect to" and one then performs a comparison. There is no longer any relationship between the designation and the predicate, without some form of determination.

[*The Problem of the Optimum*]

Too, too, raises the same problem. *Too* signifies that with respect to a level considered to be the optimum, one is beyond it:

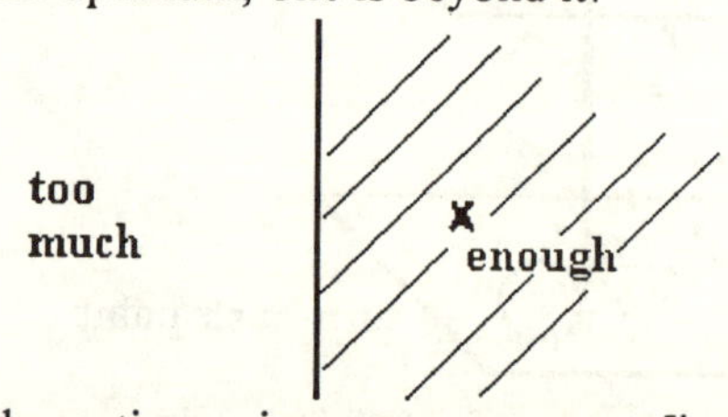

If we do not take the optimum into account, *assez* [in French], *enough* in English, *nug* in Swedish will signify "sufficiently". However, *enough* will serve as an intensive: it will transfer any occurrence that does not possess this optimum level to the side of the attractor. In English this is the case in *fair enough*, or in Italian in *allegro assai*. "*Nug*" in Swedish is used as a sentence intensive. [In French], *assez*, when not inducing the value *sufficiently* is used with predicates that, in themselves, activate the high degree: *rather brilliant* [*assez génial*], *rather extraordinary* [*assez extraordinaire*]. *Assez* is used to signify "rather" ["*pas mal*"]. In French three terms refer back to the negative side: *mal, peine, rigueur*. From the viewpoint of a gradient, they eject the occurrence into the Exterior, while *pas mal*, [*not bad / rather*] returns it to the

Interior and can just as easily mean *rather*, i.e., *not too badly, no more*: *He didn't manage too badly* [*Il ne s'est* ***pas mal*** *tiré d'affaire*], as it can mean *very*: *He's rather mad* [***pas mal*** *cinglé*]. This raises an interesting question concerning the relationship between rhetoric and language activity. Possessing down-toners, understatements, reinforcements, etc., coexists with the property of not having, for example, only one colour to indicate the positive and another for the negative, i.e., something unequivocal.

[*The Absence of Counterparts for Borderline Occurrences*]

The problem is that there is no side-to-side equivalence. *Bien* exists, but is not its strict equivalent. There is no equivalent for *scarcely/barely* [*à peine*]. What is the opposite of *scarcely*? What is the opposite of *effort – suffering* [*peine*]. The same holds for *rigour* [*rigueur*]. There is in fact, *easily* [*facilement*]: *This metal can be shaped if need be* [*à la rigueur*], *can scarcely be shaped* are acceptable, but you will notice that *easily* does not have the same status as *pas mal* in the opposition *mal/pas mal*. It does not configure as positive on one side, negative on the other. For example: *that's great* [*à la bonne heure*] exists, but *that's not great* [*à la male heure*] does not. A type of sorting takes place among possible phenomena.

[*The High Degree*]

As for the high degree, we can ask ourselves whether there is a limit to the degree. To an extent, there is none: one can say "it's big, big, big"; one can also say: "it's as big as" and use an external reference point. Then we find such expressions as *everything you'd think of as big*, where we appear to be working extensionally. *What is referred to as big*, relates back to the predicate *per se*, without any other qualification, at its most absolute. When dealing with predicates, such as *running*, *being big*, etc., it is difficult to define them according to a set of properties, as we can for individuated objects: a book, a duck, etc.

[*Constructing an Unattainable Exterior*]

So, when you have constructed your domain with your centre, etc., you can always exit the domain and construct, from this point of view, an Exterior that will be unattainable. This is what occurs when we say: "He's so stupid, it's unbelievable" or "He's so rich, it's just not possible" As for *more than* and *big* in *he's more than big*, we can always build a sort of hierarchy and say *he's more than intelligent*, which amounts to saying *brilliant*. You can leave the notional domain while maintaining contact; this induces such expressions as *not possible*, which does not mean “impossible” in the strictest sense, signifying elimination.

ON NOTIONAL DOMAINS FOLLOWING THE D.E.A. SEMINAR

To explain the notional domain to non-specialists (Culioli 1986a), he refers to “a set of virtualities” (p.86) centred by the prototype (p.87).

In (Culioli 1987a), he specifies that:

***IE** can also be construed as a site previous to a choice between **I** and **E** and leading to a possible validation either as being identified with the property of the attractor (**I**), or as being radically different from this property (**E**), for example (once again): in an equiponderant interrogative (Culioli 1988b: 98-99).*

*An example of an occurrence on the Boundary is afforded by a particular instance of negation as applied to the opposition ‘I agree to help / I refuse to help’: ‘I don’t refuse to help’. Whereas ‘I refuse to help’ positions the occurrence in **E**, ‘I don’t refuse to help’ enables positioning in **I**, without excluding an occurrence in **E**; “in short, we are on the Boundary, whence the ambivalence” (100).*

Finally, in a paper published in 1989, fully explicates the nature of the attractor and its relation to the gradient:

> *Now the term attractor should not be interpreted as an attainable last point (there are no first or last points on the gradient), but as the representation of the imaginary absolute value of the property (the predicate) which organizes an aggregate of occurrences into a structured notional domain. (Culioli 1989a: 200)*

CHAPTER 4

UTTERING, ASSERTING AND INTERROGATIVES

EDITOR'S INTRODUCTION

The two most important points raised by Culioli with respect to these notions are: the distinction between enunciators and locutors, and the relationships between the situation of uttering, the lexis or predicative relation (PR), and spatial-temporal coordinates that constrain utterances in general, assertions or interrogatives in particular. In the following chapters we shall see how he accounts for diverging types of assertions, but here we shall first examine his constructs on notions to obtain assertions.

Preassertive Constructs

The Schema of Primitive Relationship

The basic construct joining notions is the primitive relationship. Culioli first mentions it in Culioli (1968b), positing on theoretical grounds the existence of a prelexical "grammar of primitive relationships", prior to any distinction between syntax and semantics (7-8). Note VIII (Culioli, Fuchs, Pêcheux 1970:20) indicates that even though one cannot formalize raw surface text, its syntactic diversity derives from networks of semantic effects and that by theorizing about thse networks, Culioli "was led to posit the lexis schema".

The primitive relationship is analysed in greater detail in Culioli 1971 where the operation of orienting is first applied to it. The relationship is tripartite: ***a****, the source;* ***b****, the target;* ***p****, the relator. The primary orientation, from the source toward the target, is dependent on the properties of the three notions (p.9). Orienting the primitive relationship constructs a primary schema containing a starting term and an end term.*

In Lecture 5 of the 1975-1976 D.E.A. Seminar (Culioli 1976:49), he remarks that in a primary schema — now predicative relation — 'eater', as opposed to 'eaten', is normally accepted as a starting term, thereby constructing "a coincidence of

> *the source in the primitive relationship,*
> *the starting term of the predicative relation,*
> *the constituent term of the enunciative relationship, and*
> *the construct representing the agent."*

In analysing the problem of constructing referential values in a variety of languages (Culioli 1976:42), he finds that primitive relationships belong to three major categories:

> *operations: identification and localization [including possession, p.41];*
> *relationships between properties and the organization of space, which produce the structuring of events;*
> *relationships between properties and agentivity from which derive intersubjective relationships, the set of animates ... (ibid.)*

The Lexis Schema

The note (Culioli, Fuchs, Pêcheux 1970, note VIII: 19-24) corresponding to a cursory remark on the creation of a lexis from a lexicalized state of continous semantic–syntactic matter by means of a "filtering process"(p.8), provides a description of the lexis schema and justification for its composition. This schema is more systematically discussed in note IX (24-29): it is composed of three empty places

> *of the form:* $\langle \xi_0, \xi_1, \pi \rangle$ *which reads: first proposition (or starting point of the relationship), second proposition (or finishing point of the relationship), and predicate (or relationship between the two points). (p.24)*

Not having yet integrated the concept of the **notion** *into his model (as we saw in the previous chapter), Culioli here suggests the presence of a "lexical filter" which selects three lexical items (represented by X, Y, R). An "operation of attribution" dependent on the properties of the three items termed "primitive relationships" assigns these terms to the places, thus producing a lexis* $\langle X, Y, R \rangle$ *(24-25).*

Culioli (1976b) also insists on the difference between $\langle \xi_0, \xi_1, \pi \rangle$ *and "arg., arg., pred."*[1] *in generative semantics: 1) the latter simply represents one relationship (that of the predicate) between the first argument and the second; whereas the lexis schema allows for many more intra-lexical relationshps, and the lexis, even more relationships with Sit. 2) "in a lexis [schema], the places are empty, i.e., they are abstract relationships", but the*

---

[1] Langacker (1988: 100-101; 1990: 167) also argues againt this representation: lack of information concerning "the internal structure of any of the three predicates. [...] nothing explicitly shows that [X and Y] have different roles with respect to [R], or what these roles are. [...] how [X and Y] connect to [R], and what permits this combination [...] are left unspecified. [...] there is no direct characterization of the composite semantic structure that results from integrating the three components".

status (filled/empty) of the places in 'arg., arg., pred.' is ambiguous" (p.108).

In order to account for a multiplicity of languages where one does not or cannot express the origin of the process by means of a subject–predicate relationship, the model's representation of a lexis must adopt the form:

$(\ ) \ r \ b \in a$

*"meaning that the place represented by parentheses is not empty, but is in effect instantiated by **a**, and that '(   ) r b' is located with respect to **a**, its locator"*[2] *(p.110). Thus this ordered relationship ("**a** is the source [origin] and **b** is the target and [...] **r**, a predicate supposing an ordered relationship") is oriented "by positing a starting term" (p.113). It is also a representation of a "relationship called that of possession (an object belongs to / a book is on)" (p.120).*[3]

If the textual utterance's diathesis is active, then orienting the lexis implies "selecting the source term in the primitive relationship to instantiate place ξ_0 in the lexis schema" (Culioli 1982:12).

From Lexis to Assertion

When he first defines the lexis, (Culioli, Fuchs, Pêcheux 1970: 8) this "preassertive" component of the model contains "terms compatible with ordering, but not yet ordered". To become an assertion, a lexis must be modalized and stylistically modulated , the latter inducing prosodic traits and / or permutations (ibid.). Together they produce "a pre-terminal string whose elements are partially ordered and weighted" (idem). The note corresponding to the stylistic modulation as opposed to other forms of modulation (note VII: 18-19), specifies that it refers to "the enunciator–subject taking charge of the discourse". The same note (p.18) cites Culioli (1968a: 46):

> *each [lexical] unit refers to classes with their properties [...], but also with 'qualities' that depend on a subjective evaluation (for example: affectively [...] — positive, negative, indifferent; concerning the relationship with the object [...] — individuated or not, this being linked to a specific situation.*

---

[2] When accounting for "static configurations" (Langacker 1990: 224) in his analysis of subject/object asymmetry, Langacker arrives at the conclusion that "the profiled relationship is rendered asymmetrical by the very fact of one participant being elevated to the status of relational figure" (p.223)

[3] Langacker 1990: 338 "What all possessives share, I believe, is that one entity (the "possessor") is used as reference point [...] for purposes of establishing mental contact with another, the target"

Later in the text, Culioli remarks that the lexis and the positive assertion "have the same form (except for order and some other differences) [...]" (p.13); whereas "negation is applied to the lexis, which, in itself, is neither positive nor negative" (ibid.).

Operations of assertion defined as "the enunciator–subject taking charge of the lexis" (note IX, p.25) activate a closed set of "intralexical relationships [...]: either $\xi_0 \in \pi$*, a choice that can be represented by:* $\langle (\ ), Y, R \rangle \in X$*; or* $\xi_1 \in \pi$*, which one can represent as:* $\langle X, (\ ), R \rangle \in Y$*" (ibid.).*[4]

In an article in which Culioli's objective is to specify the distinctive nature of formalization in the processing of natural languages (Culioli 1971a), he describes a primary form: $\langle \xi_0, \xi_1, \pi \rangle \in a$*: the lexis schema is located with respect to the starting term of the primitive relationship primitively oriented by its component properties (p.9). Also written* $a \in a\ R\ b$ *(ibid.), the primary form not only marks the orientation from* **a** *toward* **b***, but also serves as the object of an operation that further "constrains the relationship of the starting term", a "loose relationship": 'it's* **a** *and only* **a** *that* **R***' / 'there's at least* **a** *that* **R***' / '***a R***' represented by: . —* $a\ .\ R\ b$ *" (p.10).*[5] *He then proceeds to examine the obvious connection with transitivity and explicates well-formed derived schemas for the representation of the passive voice. (The relationship between aspect and diathesis on which his demonstration is founded, will be seen in Chapter 7.)*

Uttering

Culioli (1973: 88-91) addresses the specificity of the enunciative domain, "defined with respect to the enunciator $\mathcal{S}_0$ *and the moment of uttering* $\mathcal{T}_0$*" (p.88).* $\mathcal{S}_0$ *grounds the "intersubjective space [between it and* $\mathcal{S}'_0$*, the co-enunciator] of every situation of uttering" (ibid.), while* $\mathcal{S}_1$ *represents "the first occurrence of a subject in the utterance [...] an utterance subject in relation to [located by] an enunciator–subject", as opposed to the traditional syntactic view of the subject (idem).*

If 'I' identifies with (=) $\mathcal{S}_0$*, and 'you' differs from (≠)* $\mathcal{S}_0$*, (p.88) other components of utterances correspond to more complex values. 'Who' in 'Who*

---

4 For the sake of clarification, we can compare these locating relationships to the explication of dependency relationships proposed by Langacker (esp. 1990:169-170) where the potential combinations at the semantic pole of such units as [MAN], [CAT], [FIND], are seen as the result of correspondences (construed as identifications) between the landmark, the trajector, and the landmark–trajector relator components of these units.

5 Langacker (1990:167): "[...] I am not concerned with trying to predict the valence of a morpheme on the basis of its internal semantic structure. In fact, I do not think it is possible to predict valence in absolute terms. [...] Instead of absolute predictability, we must settle for predictability of a weaker sort, one more generally appropriate for language [...]."

opened the window?'represents a class of values other than the scanned possibilities, since no criterion allows the enunciator to choose one possibility in preference to another — a class of imaginary values. Its representative: 'who' in this instance, "is the **image** *of the first enunciator and therefore represents $\mathscr{S}_0$'s assertive act, origin of all uttering" (ibid.). Culioli also calls 'that' an* **image** *(p.89) in 'I say that I'm hot' or in any other declarative utterance. This utterance translates into the following schema:*

$S_1 = \mathscr{S}_0$; Q *[that, que]* $= im\ \mathscr{S}_0$; $S_2 = im\ \mathscr{S}_0$; $\Rightarrow S_2 = \mathscr{S}_0$

and (I say) 'I'm hot', into:

$S_1 \quad S_2 \qquad S_1 = \mathscr{S}_0$; $S_2 = S$; $\Rightarrow S_2 = \mathscr{S}_0$ *(idem).*

In Culioli (1975), the author proposes the following definition of uttering: "Uttering is constructing a space, orienting, determining [quantifying / qualifying — see below, chapters 3-5], establishing a network of referential values, in short, a system of location" (p.10).

The sixth of his 1975–1976 D.E.A. Lectures (Culioli 1976b) emphasizes the importance of maintaining a space between the instantiation of the places in the lexis schema and any utterance. The direct result of instantiation is not an utterance but "a cluster of relationships", operations ["voice, aspect, modality, ..."] performed on the lexis and inducing a variety of utterances "belonging to the same paraphrastic family" (60-61).

As for the starting term, it can be neither **a**, *nor* **b**, *as in: 'He was told the story by Paul', but it will be "the locator for the rest of the utterance, itself located with respect to the situation of uttering" (p.65).*

The predicative relation only becomes such when it is located with respect to the situation of uttering : $\langle \lambda \rangle \in Sit$ *(p.127). In certain instances, in particular that of the present progressive, in order to distinguish the predicative relation from an enunciative operation, Culioli constructs the following schema (p.138):*

$$\overline{(\ )\ r\ b\ \in}\ a\ \in\ a$$

> ***a*** *is a substitute for Sit [...] as in "John is driving the car", where the operator* $\in$ *of the predicative relation (the one derived from "John drives the car") is absorbed [...] and the operator* $\in$ *of the enunciative relationship is then marked specifically either by 'is' or 'was'.*

As in his 'Notes on determination and quantification' (Culioli 1975:10), Culioli also specifies that T, with respect to $\mathcal{T}$, *is not the time of the utterance, but rather "the time of the event to which one refers by means of* *an utterance on which one constructs a referential value enabling refererence to an event." — "time" includes aspectual and modal as well as temporal relationships (p.115). He later describes the difference between processing the domain of "curls",($\mathcal{S}$ and $\mathcal{T}$) and that of "straights" (S and T). In the first instance, one "processes a relationship between the term locating a predicative relation being formed and the situation of uttering" (p.151); in the second instance, one processes*

> *predicative relations that constitute an utterance, and thus construct a referential value establishing a relationship between a language act (i.e., producing and recognizing this utterance) and an event [...] to which one refers." (ibid.)*

Linearizing

There is a difference between **starting term** *and "initial term" as can be seen in the following [oral!] example:*

'There's John, his brother, [well,] motorbikes, he repairs them really well'(p.150)

the starting term is 'he'; 'there's' will occupy the initial "with respect to which other locatings will be organized" (ibid.) It will constitute a trace of locating by the situation of uttering ($\mathcal{S}_0$ $\mathcal{T}_0$), whereas 'his brother' and 'motorbikes' are **constituent locators** *(Culioli 1978a: 303-304, note 4).*

A further specification of the nature of the distinction between first argument, starting term and constituent locator (topic or theme) is afforded by a paper on metalinguistic representations (Culioli 1982). The components designated by these terms do not necessarily coincide (p.16). The constituent locator can contain more than one term, and must be stable: "a proper noun (in the widest sense of the term), a generic (every occurrence in a class can be identified with every other occurrence) or a subset of the class, or a back-reference" (ibid.).

The interrogative

Culioli (1976b) outlines the effect of enunciative operations on the lexis, the predicative relation, in these general terms: "depending on the operations of quantification brought into play, the enunciative operations will impose constraints on the predicative relations" (p.159). The weighted interrogative is the result of two operations (Culioli 1978:315): elaborating a pre-construct, and establishing a new locating relationship based on the co-enunciator. In a note, Culioli specifies that

> *from a strictly formal point of view, questioning consists of (1) constructing a predicative relation located by the enunciator ($\mathcal{S}_0$); (2) constructing a second location [act of locating] starting from $\mathcal{S}_0 \neq \mathcal{S}_0'$" (ibid.).*

EXCERPTS FROM THE D.E.A. SEMINAR

We are going to reduce the interrogative to a relationship between subjects consisting of an exchange of information or passing information from one subject to another, and in a simplistic fashion, we are going to concentrate on this aspect of questions, even though we know that interrogation does not only serve to request information. Now, if I say "What if we went somewhere?", everyone construes this as a suggestion. It is not a direct request for information. If I say "Why do that?", while shrugging my shoulders, it signifies "there's no reason for doing it". It is a rhetorical question. In *Now, why would you want him to buy a car?*, the interrogative removes the first locutors assertion from the field of validatable assertions. There are also hypothetical interrogatives: *Were it to rain, then we would change our programme*.

[*Enunciator / Co-enunciator vs. Locutor / Interlocutor*]

To construct an interrogative we have at our disposal the enunciator and the co-enunciator. In the present instance, however, we can say locutor and interlocutor, since the locutor can be identified with the enunciator, and the interlocutor with the co-enunciator. They are interchangeable. Let us recall some basic notions: there is a locutor S_1 and an interlocutor. We shall represent the subject of the utterance by S_2. If S_2 identifies with S_1, the utterance will show *I*. If the locutor says "I", there is identification with S_1 as locutor, and this is why *I* appears. If you find a difference with respect to S_1 (i.e., where S_2 is identified with S'_1 — the interlocutor), then the utterance evinces *you*.

I may have "disengaged" myself from this relationship, in which instance the third person appears.

An occurrence may produce a loop necessarily resulting in identification. A second occurrence will show differentiation, and a third, neither identification nor differentiation (and so the value of a break ω), and finally a fourth ($*$) will concatenate all three.

The locutors are clearly distinguished, separated from one another. Locution acts can be represented by closed intervals: someone starts speaking, then stops ... . The act always appears as an event of the type *starting to speak ... no longer speaking*.

There is another problem: enunciator – co-enunciator, which I represent by $\mathcal{S}_0$ and $\mathcal{S}_1$. They refer to several important concepts. They are abstract entities that I integrate into my SRμ for specific reasons. The first is that this enables me to study the connection with problems of argumentation, of collective representation, or of constructing the uttering subject, and leave aside the epistemic universal subject, a sort of blind spot. The second reason is that with "locutors" we are dealing with factors linked to individuated, distinct events. Strictly speaking, one cannot be "another", one cannot be the interlocutor. One can be one's own interlocutor, but that is another matter. One cannot say to someone: "you would like to do that". This is the problem of subjective predicates: no one can say: "you are ill", except the doctor who says, in effect, "I pronounce you ill". One cannot say: "you are afraid"; one can say: "you seem ... ".

We are dealing here with predicates referring to prior states, they cannot be used other than in the first person, or in the third person in indirect discourse.

[*Locution / Assertion*]

Enunciators are entities that I shall call *individuatable* but not necessarily individuated. In some instances, they can be reduced to one global entity, and in others, they will be distinct. If I am a locutor making this identification throughout, I shall say "I", especially if I am a locutor–asserter. To be able to assert, to produce an assertion, I must declare it publicly: an interior assertion is not an assertion; but there also needs be the commitment of someone who takes responsibility, who guarantees your statement or who wishes to assert something despite your position.

If it is simply an instance of locution, you do not really have assertion. For there to be responsibility, one must guarantee what one states. In an institutional setting, the guarantor could be sanctioned if what he guarantees does not materialize. If at some time one asserts — in the fullest sense of the verb — that a certain event will have such and such a consequence and it does not follow, if one produces an assertion or a theorem and others realize that it cannot be reproduced experimentally, or if others can demonstrate that one's theorem is erroneous, as one has guaranteed it, this can possibly have repercussions; sanctions may be taken. Now we can see the importance of not having merely a locutor. This is clearly shown by the problem of silent disavowal: one is asked to take an oath; one can do so while silently disavowing it. In such an instance, the locutor has indeed taken an oath, but the enunciator (asserter) did not guarantee it.

In some instances, the enunciator and co-enunciator are distinct; then the locutor is identified with the enunciator and the enunciator is identified with the locutor, as — in fact — the enunciator is constructed on the locutor. In other instances, they can be fused. This is what occurs with the French pronoun *on*, for example, or in rhetorical questions, or in the fictitious questions of an author who, while writing an article, asks himself spurious questions. In this instance, it is somewhat as though he were constructing a fictitious interlocutor because every enunciator is, in fact, constructed with respect to himself as his own co-enunciator.

The Interrogative and the Notional Domain

Let us return to the interrogative: there is a question and an answer. We shall leave aside for the moment questions without answers. A question means that I who ask the question am somewhat uncertain. Not knowing means, to simplify once again, having the choice between several solutions. We could complicate matters if we wished. If one says "is he right?", this could signify: "to what degree is he right?". It all depends on the predicate; if it can assume a gradient, "to what degree?" is a possible signification. If it is a predicate of the type *is he here? / isn't he here?*, possible values are: all or nothing. In any case, at some point I shall be able to represent the initial state by means of the entire domain **(p, p')** where **p'** represents the linguistic complement of **p**. In the most basic instance, this gives me something corresponding to **(p, $\overline{\mathbf{p}}$)**, if I am working with two values ($\overline{\mathbf{p}}$ being the strict complement, in the mathematical sense).

To ask a question amounts to placing before another all the possibilities in such a way that the answer will be , in the simplest instances, **p** or $\overline{\mathbf{p}}$. The two pathways are equally possible. In a biased, non-equiponderant question such as: *Might he perchance have come?* conveying surprise, the two pathways are no longer possible.

There is, however, a request for confirmation when we solicit an affirmative answer, a confirmation of what we wish or expect — something we find in the negative interrogative, as in the use of *n'est-ce pas*, and of tags [in English in the original] in English.

We now have all we need: the enunciator – co-enunciator, and the values **p** and **p'**, and we are going to represent their relationship in a cam diagram.

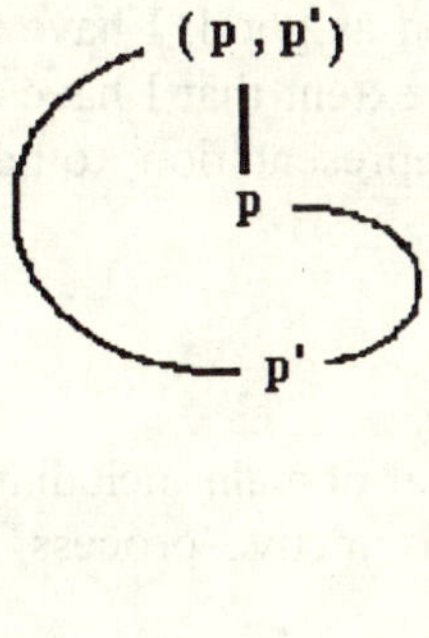

(Lecture of 24 Jan 1984)

A Note on "heuristic approach"

Our approach raises a great number of questions as we go along. It is a truly *heuristic* one in one sense of the term. The most current usage is linked to its etymology: discovery processes, manipulations, techniques that enable us to discover phenomena, that help us to make observations. A second meaning is associated with computer processing. One can say that one is dealing with a heuristic system if, in certain types of problems, it discovers procedures that will lead to a solution. It is therefore a system that has properties of discovery. The third usage is mixed and it is the one I use: a representational system has heuristic properties if it obliges you to ask additional questions and thereby seek additional explanations.

I shall distinguish beween three possible instances:

1. a target and a 0-distance locator

2. a distance with only one path

3. a distance with the possibility of two paths (i.e., more than one)

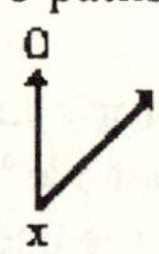

If our target is the circle, we miss the the target if we do not attain the circle. If we construct a boundary that provides the closed interval of all possibles, even missing the target will not be bad.

One will notice that we have reproduced the construction of a notional domain by constructing possibilities, possibilities valued as good. I have here an apparatus that will run almost autonomously to the extent that I have only to ask additional questions concerning my system of representation, to be led to perform new operations.

[***The Interrogative and the Notional Domain (2)***]

We shall now pursue our study of the interrogative.

The notion **P**, **(p, p')** provides us with the notional domain including its complement. Let us take a simple situation with a disjunctive process, i.e., where **p'** corresponds to the logical complement ($\overline{p}$).

To simplify, we can reduce our interrogative here to a yes or no question. In the intersubjective schema of interrogation, we establish a relationship between $\mathscr{S}_0$ and $\mathscr{S}_1$ (where $\mathscr{S}'_0$, the co-enunciator is distinct from $\mathscr{S}_0$), and in an equiponderant interrogative we start from **(p, p')**. Both possibilities **p** and **p'** exist; we cannot choose **p** or **p'** and consider that one becomes the necessary value:

(p p') ($\mathscr{S}_0 ... \mathscr{S}_1$) (relationship between the two)

step 0 : $\mathscr{S}_0$ presents $\mathscr{S}_1$ with the two possibilities that $\mathscr{S}_1$ will scan.

p is in the initial position for reasons linked to the cam: the value of the interior, the positive value, let us say, is representative of the whole domain, including its complement.

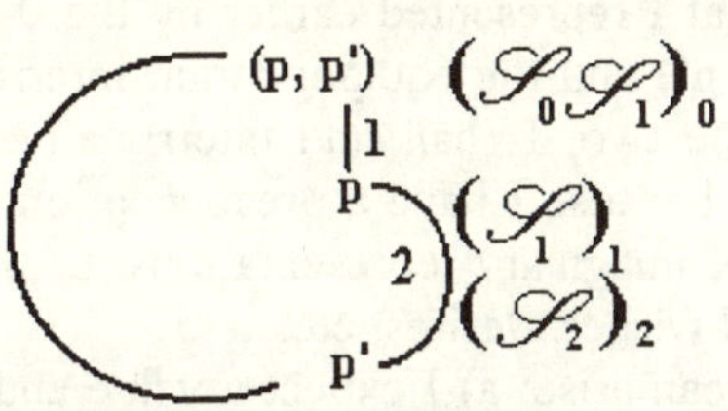

As long as this mechanism is not halted by a decision taken by $\mathscr{S}_1$, it can keep on running: we can ask someone: "did he come or didn't he?". No answer. "Did he come or didn't he? ... " No answer, and so forth ... Either *he came* or *he didn't come* will stop the mechanism. Then we can process the complement: *I'd say that he came and that he didn't* or *he didn't come but it's as if he had*. As can be seen, from a very simple system, we can derive a whole set of modulations. The approach consists of being able to simplify, and at the same time, introducing additional explanations.

The whole game of questioning consists of provoking a response that distinguishes a value: **p** or **p'**. We could have represented it this way:

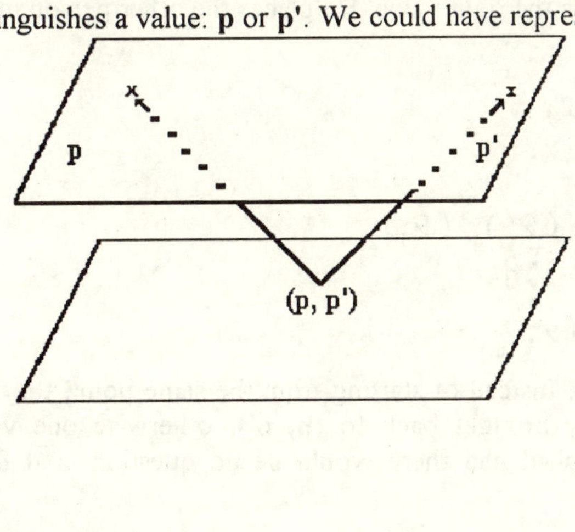

Biased Questions

We shall then be dealing with a pre-construct. "Pre-constructed" means that it can be related back to a form.

I make a distinction between notions, and primitive relationships between notions that are already pre-constructs. For example: between *matches* and *box*, relationships of content to container, of interior to exterior, or contact come to my mind. After having made this remark, we can return to our problem, which consists, in effect, in distinguishing a value, i.e. it is a problem of valuation. We have seen two instances: first, the true value we can distinguish in *he came*. No scanning is necessary since the target has already been reached. This is what I represented earlier by the 0-distance loop; at the opposite extreme, **(p, p')** and the equiponderant interrogative that we have just studied. Between the two, I shall find interrogatives weighted more to one side than the other, because I have a preconception of the expected value — this is the domain of imaginary representations, or those deduced from clues, or fulfilling personal wishes, desires, etc.

Two instances can arise: a) I expect a value and I ask someone if he can confirm it; b) I can expect a value, someone proposes a different value, and I ask him to confirm, not the value I expected, but rather that what he has said is really true.

1st Instance:

Let us take the same schema with **(p, p')** and $\mathscr{S}_0 - \mathscr{S}_1$. **p** is the value distinguished as the starting term. In itself, **p** is neither positive nor negative — it could be: *I expect that he did not come*. For the moment, however, we shall start with a simple instance where **p** is positive and **p'** negative.

Here $\mathscr{S}_0$ expects **p** to be the right value. He places the other person in the complementary position.

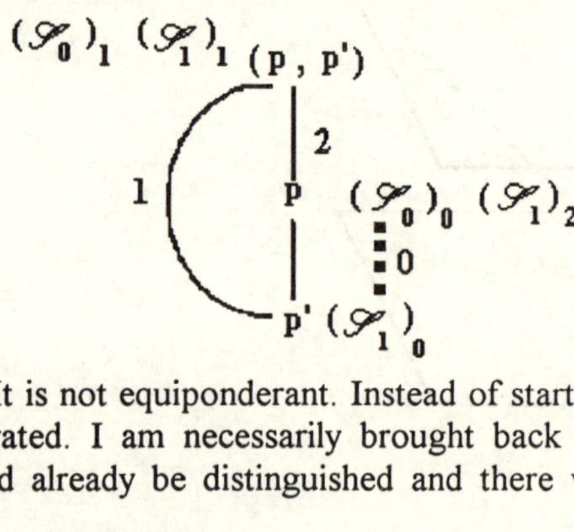

It is not equiponderant. Instead of starting from the same point, they are separated. I am necessarily brought back to **(p, p')**, otherwise one value would already be distinguished and there would be no question; and from there to **p**. I made two moves to find myself back at the point to which I wished to draw the other person, i.e., the value which I want confirmed.

2nd Instance: Weighting by a Pre-construct.

$\mathcal{S}_0$ will privilege $\mathcal{S}_1$'s pre-construct: it may be one he attributes to $\mathcal{S}_1$ because of a preconceived idea, or one he derives from an external clue, or through a verbal preparation, i.e., previous text that clears the way.

This can be represented by the following graphic, $\mathcal{S}_1$ being in **p**, and $\mathcal{S}_0$ in **p'**:

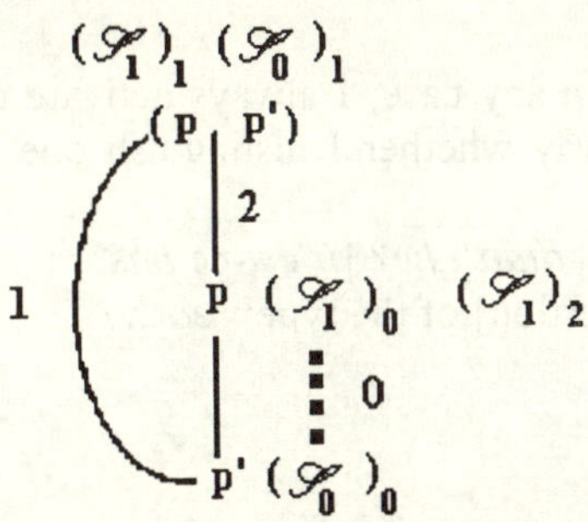

$\mathcal{S}_1$ is questioned so that he will re-assert what $\mathcal{S}_0$ posited as $\mathcal{S}_1$'s pre-construct: $\mathcal{S}_1$ is brought back to his pre-construct — verbalized or not.

This schema is evinced as *you don't say*; *no ... that's incredible*; *don't tell me it's true*; or *go on!*; *you're joking*. Another reaction can be *really?*, a rejection, a questioning of what has been asserted. $\mathcal{S}_0$ asks $\mathcal{S}_1$ to confirm not his own pre-construct, but rather a pre-construct external to $\mathcal{S}_0$. All these expressions indicate surprise, which means that expectations have been deceived. To say that they have been "deceived", signifies that a value differing from the expected one has been obtained.

A great number of languages introduce the interrogative expression by means of a final morpheme corresponding to a disjunctive *or*, for example: *il est venu ou quoi?* in standard French, *il est venu ou bien?* in Swiss French, [*(well?) did he come or what?*].

The instance *isn't it?* [*n'est-ce pas*?] is a complex problem in that it compounds the negative interrogative problem and that of it is [*c'est*]. What is *c'est* in *c'est qu'il est venu* [*the fact / trouble is that he came*]? We must ask ourselves why *it is that* [*c'est que*] does not function as the positive of *is it that ... ?* [*est-ce que ... ?*] from a semantic point of view. We can say:

"He came, *didn't he*?' [*n'est-ce pas*?] as well as "Isn't it a fact that he came?" ["*N'est-ce pas qu'il est venu*?"]; however there is no counterpart:

** He came, is it a fact?* [** Il est venu, est-ce*?], for *Did he come?* [*est-ce qu'il est venu*?].

It is that [*c'est que*] and *is it that* [*est-ce que*] are not directly related other than by morphology. There's a twist somewhere; they no longer correspond exactly, and the linguist's work consists in elucidating why this is.

For the interrogative, we can construct three configurations and induce three values. The three configurations are: *he came?* [*il est venu*?], *did he come (* is it that he came)?* [*est-ce qu'il est venu*?] and *did he come?* [*est-il venu*?]

Let us examine *he came?*

1. it is equiponderant (yes – no). In any case, I always activate one of the forms, but without marking in any way whether I distinguish one or the other (**p** or **p'**).
2. [weighting, seeking confirmation] *didn't he?* [*n'est-ce pas*?]
3. [rejection, questioning of the assertion] of the type: *really?*

For *est-ce qu'il est venu?*:

1. yes – no
2. * *didn't he?* [**n'est-ce pas*?]
3. *really?*

For *did he come?*

1. yes – no
2. * *didn't he?* [**n'est-ce pas*?]
3. surprised, in disbelief

(Lecture of 31 Jan 1984)

The Three Configurations

We are going to attempt to elucidate why we can obtain one, two or three values depending on whether the question is *he came?*, **is it that he came?* [*est-ce qu'il est venu?*] or *did he come?*.

We can perform another test by inserting *only / even* in addition to *isn't it* [*n'est ce pas*?] and other manipulations noted in the previous Lecture. This will give us:

Did he even come? [*Est-il seulement venu*?]

Est-ce qu'il est seulement venu?

but

* *il est seulement venu*? [* *he only came?* is not an intensive]

We can plainly see that *he came?* is an interrogative modulation of an assertive-shaped sequence. On the other hand, *did he come?* quite obviously does not have an assertive shape [...]. *Est-ce qu'il est venu*? comprises two parts, it is a composite: one refers to *he came?* [*il est venu*?], hence of an assertive shape; the other *is it that* [*est-ce que*], draws us toward the interrogative.

Another test: if the verb *croire* [*believing*] is added, the interrogative and the negative forms require the subjunctive [in French]:

– *I believe that he came.*

– *Crois-tu qu'il soit venu*? [*Do you believe that he came?*]

– *Je ne crois pas qu'il soit venu*. [*I don't believe that he came.*]

– * *Tu crois qu'il soit venu*? [*You believe that he came?*]

When processing an assertion, we are dealing with one and only one value. When one asserts, one guarantees, one takes responsibility for one and only one value.

The interrogative imposes the scanning of possible values. One must not fixate on one value. If I find something of the *he came* type, it derives from an assertive operation through which I both posit a predicative relationship, and say that it is located by a network of coordinates: (straight S) $\rightarrow$ Sit_2. This is the locator of the event to which we refer by constructing the utterance on a predicative relationship; Sit_1 is the locution locator, and $\mathscr{S}it_0$, the origin locator.

The text string becomes an assertion if, at some point, something like this occurs: *I who am speaking insist on saying that I believe what I have just said by means of the text to be true*. There must be identification; someone can, in fact, say: "I who am the one who says of me that it is I who speak". There needs be this functor of locution and it must necessarily relate back to an origin. This functor provides a certain consistency throughout the various locution events.

For Sit_1 and $\mathscr{S}_0$, as soon as one pronounces an utterance that does not refer to a single event, but to a class, as soon as one speaks in general terms, there needs be a functor somewhere such that one can relate these unique locution events to it, enabling one to take charge of generality from a cognitive point of view by a process of generalization.

Sit_2 is located with respect to an event. In every instance, an operation will establish relationships between these locators and others. A privileged instance is *I*, since one describes, about oneself who is speaking, something which concerns oneself at the moment one is saying it.

He has come, an assertion, comes down to the construction of a relationship that will become an utterance because it is related to this system of coordinates. Evinced, it becomes a designation, just as an object is designated.

Here is something that I shall represent between angle brackets: ⟨he has come⟩ This is an as yet unasserted predicative relationship, since it has not been located with respect to Sit_2, Sit_1, $\mathscr{S}it_0$. It is what I have called the notional domain of the relationship between *he* and *having come*. Roughly, this corresponds to the construction of the domain with an interior and an exterior, and as we are processing only two values, it yields (*he – having come, he – not having come*).[6]

1. *He came?*

When we posit ⟨he came⟩ ∈ [located with respect to] Sit_2 (S_2 T_2), in Sit_2 we are either dealing with a value that enables me to perform all my calculations with respect to Sit_1 and $\mathscr{S}it_0$ — or there is no assigned value. This is what occurs when I designate the relationship and it is not an assertion. If I say "he came, he came, he did not come ... ", It's almost as though I were producing for myself the objects that these predicative relations are, naturally located with respect to me, the locutor, but not referring to an event in such a way that I could state: it is true, it is false. At this point, it is as though we had empty parentheses ( ) bearing no assigned value, filling Sit_2's place: this place remains open, hence compatible with either a positive or a negative value. External to these two values, it remains an object of contemplation, designation, meditation. Here is one of the sources of the deception, since the produced text is disconnected from reality, while having the appearance of an asserted utterance.

He came? diverges from the text string considered an assertion or the representation of a predicative relation that will provide an assertion. It is the prosodic marker that will reveal the final value. It can function as an assertion *he came* and as ⟨he came⟩ compatible with ⟨he did not come⟩

He came? is therefore compatible with everything:

– with ⟨ ⟩

– with an equiponderant interrogative

– with the schema based on a pre-construct: $\mathscr{S}_0$ constructs *he came* as a representation of what he considers to be expected, normal, desirable, and $\mathscr{S}_0$ asks $\mathscr{S}_1$ for confirmation.

We can represent all of this in graphic form:

[6] Whereas for Langacker (1987:278), the scope of the analysis must be much broader and include an examination of all valence relationships between the two linguistic 'units' (entrenched linguistic expressions): "It is only by virtue of having certain substructures in common that two component expressions can be integrated to form a coherent composite expression. To the extent that we regard the component structures as distinct and separable entities, we can speak of **correspondences** between their shared substructures, i.e., between certain substructures within one and those substructures within the other to which these are construed as being identical".

assertion is:

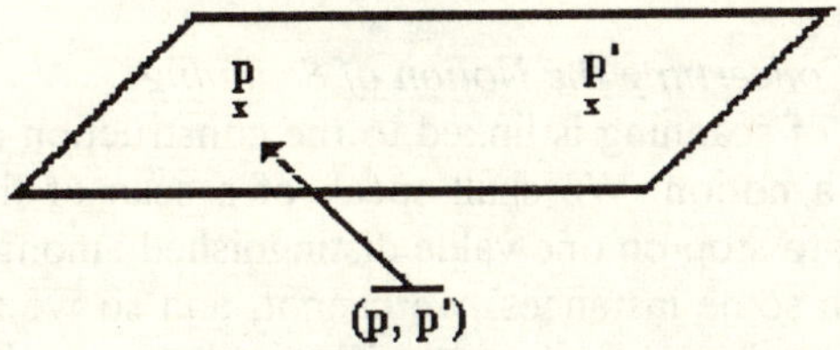

the interrogative is:

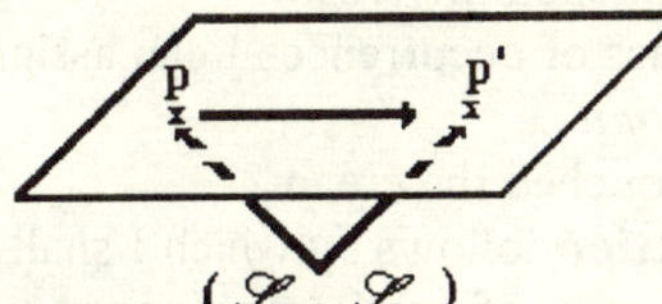

He came?, No answer → *He came?* etc.

One instance is based on a pre-construct and tries to draw S_1 to $\mathscr{S}_0$'s level, i.e., to the desired value

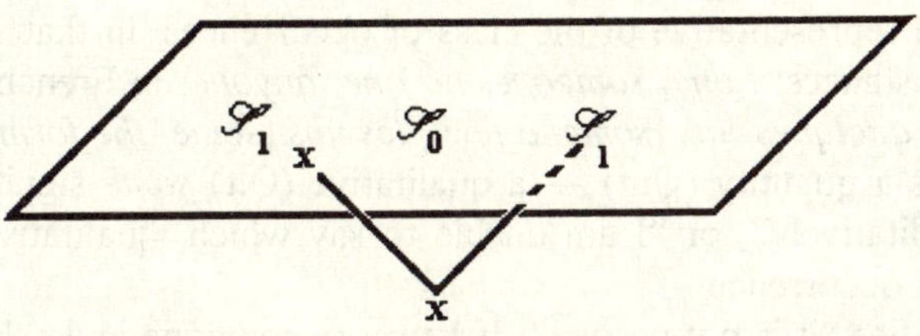

He came?

The other instance is based on a pre-construct of $\mathscr{S}_1$, and $\mathscr{S}_0$ asks $\mathscr{S}_1$ to confirm what he has said, a value which does not correspond to what he expected.

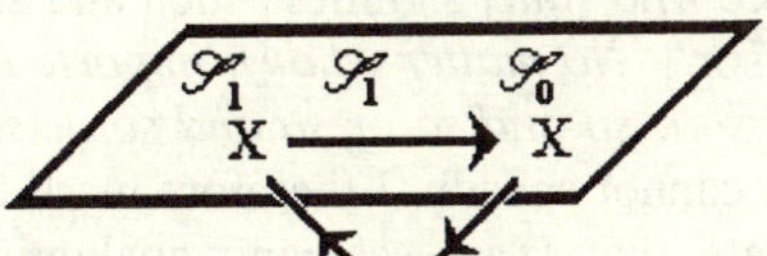

There is *scanning* of the possible values between the three nodes. It might be a good idea to redefine this term.

Reminder Concerning the Notion of Scanning

The notion of scanning is linked to the construction of a class of abstract occurrences of a notion. We shall speak of a scan of the class K. We scan without wishing to stop on one value distinguished among the others, or being able to do so. In some instances, we cannot, and so we may resort to asking someone else; in others, we do not wish to, thus a modalisation will follow, and not turning to someone else.

If I say: "Who has touched the cream?"; this gives me:

( ) has touched the cream?

I shall construct the class of occurrences I can assign to this place: representations, i.e., all the *ones that* ...

$(\ )_k \in (\ )$ has touched the cream

An operation of **extraction** follows by which I shall extract an occurrence that I may designate by the sum of its elements, or some of its existential properties ... , and this yields a particular occurrence taken from the class of occurrences.

$(\ )\ Qt_l \in (\ )_k \in (\ )$ has touched the cream

If asserting takes place, this will induce

Someone ....

one is the vestigial representative of the class of occurrences, in that we only find it in certain instances: *none*, *someone*, *no one*, *anyone*; in French, *un* in: *aucun*, *quelqu'un*, *quelques-uns* [*some*, *a few*], *les uns* [*some*, *the former*].

Qt_l represents a quantity (Qnt) — a qualitative (Qlt) *some* signifies "no matter which, qualitatively", or "I am unable to say which, qualitatively", in any case a non null occurrence.

Someone signifies "it is not no one". If I turn to someone and ask: "*Who* touched the cream?"; I then scan all the Qt_l: so and so or so and so or so and so. *So and so* refers to nothing more than a representation by which I designate a totally abstract value.

I can also say "someone, no matter who". In so doing, I reinforce the qualitative scan, since *who* [*qui*] signifies "such and such or such and such or such and such a person". *No matter who* [*n'importe qui*] is the equivalent of: *no matter which person: so and so or so and so or so and so*. There exists a non null value that I cannot specify. I therefore mark that in my speculations I am forced to indicate that I am scanning qualitative values. By explicitly marking that several values can be considered acceptable, I am obliged to modalize, and will induce:

Anyone [*n'importe qui*] *could have touched the cream.*

* *Anyone has touched the cream.*

To explicate the scanning we must construct a bifurcation for *being able / can* [*pouvoir*]:

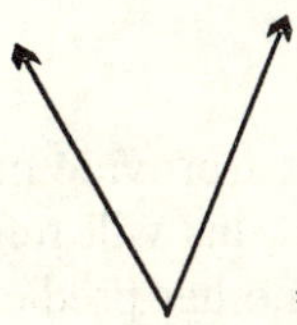

= among others

as opposed to:

= asserting, as the absence of any distance rules out the construction of a boundary.

one path, no more

in any case, anyway.

Similarly: * *No matter who could well* [*bien*] *have touched the cream.*

but *Who could really* [*bien*] *have touched the cream?*

Bien marks identification, but also the result — and in this instance, *bien* marks the scanning of the occurrences of representations of assertion. By saying *who*, one refers to the whole class of assignable values; *being able / can* induces several values, and *bien* is the marker [in French] for the operation by which one scans the class of assignable occurrences. *No matter who* is not acceptable since it contains properties of the type *someone* which stops the scanning at a particular value; furthermore, such an incomplete scan makes it incompatible with *bien*.

Totalization

There is also a scan with totalization. In many languages, an operation of totalization, applies to the predicative relation, whereas in French, one can have the impression that it applies to one of the arguments. We can process [...] assertions like:

dogs are mammals
and *every dog is a mammal*
all dogs are mammals

Every dog ... signifies: "as long as I provide myself with a representation by whose means I signify ⟨being dog⟩, this will refer to a predicate which, in turn, has the property of referring to another predicate: ⟨to be mammal⟩". This instance very often induces a deontic value: *Every dog eats Xg of meat* signifies "every dog *normally* ... " — a necessary relation with one path. I do not posit any deviance. If it concerns human animates, this necessary relation is often tinted with deontic values associated with institutional problems. I move very easily from taking note to a normative discourse with judicial connotations: what is good, what must be done ... .

In any case, there indeed exists a scanning operation, inasmuch as I construct a class of abstract occurrences of ⟨being dog⟩, i.e., of what is a typical dog.

2. *Did he come? (*is it that he came?) [Est-ce qu'il est venu?]*

This comprises *he came* [*il est venu*], *is it* [*est-ce*], and *that* [*que*]. We shall represent *he came* by λ (a predicative relation)

$\langle \lambda \in [\quad] \rangle$

He came will be located (it is as though there were a Sit_2) and I am going to clear this place. In this instance, I shall construct a back-referencing phenomenon of the same type as *the weather is rotten — It's true that the weather is rotten*. This phenomenon is generally associated with a modality, and appears as a completive introduced by *that* [*que*]. The square brackets in the schema indicate that I am processing a symbol, here Sit_2, but one that I have emptied, as opposed to a specified attribution.

If I say: *that he came* [*qu'il soit venu*], *that* is the **image of the enunciator**. The back-referencing is performed by means of a symbol taking various forms depending on the language: a demonstrative, a relative, or a component representing the identification of two terms, such as in Greek, or in Slavic languages — Bulgarian and others — *da*.

I posit *he came* and I perform a back-referencing operation as if I were clearing it of all enunciative components: the back-reference of something that is no longer an assertion, but contains all the properties of an assertion. This is what appears in *that he came*. Then I posit a scan of the possibilities of locating with respect to the entire network of enunciative coordinates: *is locatable*, as opposed to *is identifiable with*. The responses induced by the scanning can be stated as *it is the case* or *it is not the case*.

$\langle \lambda \in [\ \ ] \rangle \in, \notin$ Sit *is* or *is not*

If there is interlocution, one will find:

$\langle \lambda \in [\ \ ]_{\mathscr{S}_1} \rangle$

$\mathscr{S}_1$ subscript indicates that my starting point is this sort of disasserted assertion posited to be another's. It results in: *est-ce qu'il est venu*?, compatible with the other component *is or is not the case*, and then the three nodes.

You're telling me that he came. Is this the case?

Initiated by someone else, the utterance returns to that person.

Furthermore, you cannot ask yourself for confirmation, as in:

$\langle \lambda \in [\ \ ]_{\mathscr{S}_0} \rangle \in, \notin$ Sit

since you assert that $\mathscr{S}_0$ affirmed something and then asks whether his assertion is true or not.

This should enable us to understand why we only find two possibilities / delimited degrees with *est-ce qu'il est venu*? [*did he come? / *is it that he came?*]. The first is the first one presented above. If I now include $\mathscr{S}_1$ and $\mathscr{S}_0$, I shall be able to say to $\mathscr{S}_1$: "you asserted".

3. *Did he come? [Est-il venu?]*

We now move on to *instance 3*: such as *Is it hot out?* [*Fait-il chaud?*]

$\langle \lambda \in (\ \ ) \rangle$

I use ( ) because there is no operation of disassertion. The predicative relation is posited as having no possible bias with respect to anything else: it is truly the construction of the notional domain **(p, p')** without any possible pre-assertion, without the possibility of including $\mathscr{S}_0$, $\mathscr{S}_1$. That leaves only one possibility: the equiponderant question.

(Lecture of 7 Feb 1984)

[*Asserting*]

I would like to re-examine certain notions used last week, and firstly this one:

$\lambda \in [\ \ ]$

The objective is to explicate the problem of assertion, and then that of disassertion, in instances where an assertive form is compatible with an interrogative, either equiponderant or biased. In effect, we must put some trust in markers: every linguistic approach is based on a sort of trust in the relationship between the representations and the phenomena to which we cannot accede directly.

Assertion is a metalinguistic concept, and just as we can construct an assertion, at some point we shall be able to disassert, for example in a back-referencing phenomenon.

We must always process forms, whereas pragmatics processes effects and/or uses, and is little concerned with forms: simply as vectors bearing meanings. What is important to us, is to understand the passage of one form to another, a certain value will be induced by superposing two forms, i.e., a modulation.

For there to be an assertion, there must be a notional domain. This is what $\langle \lambda \rangle$ represents: a notion on which I shall construct a domain. If the notion is predicative: a notion of a predicative relation, it is a **lexis**. $\langle \lambda \rangle$ can be the value **(p, p')**, and can be set out as a positive or as a negative for the sake of simplification. In an assertion, we can see that this notional domain, which represents a great number of possible representations, will be located with respect to Sit (i.e., Sit_2, Sit_1, $\mathscr{S}_0$), with respect to a subjective system (locutor and enunciator) which endorses and guarantees, and with respect to a system of spatio-temporal co-ordinates, as well as S_2, the subject of the utterance. This will enable me to say that such and such a relation is validated for a specific moment, or in the case of the generic, for every occurrence that I can produce.

The very fact of having constructed a location with respect to Sit_2, Sit_1, $\mathscr{S}_0$, will, in the notional domain — and if I am dealing with an assertion, oblige me to choose one and only one value: a filtering operation is performed on $\langle \lambda \rangle$.

An utterance is a theoretical construct: it is produced by locating a predicative relation with respect to Sit.

[*Operations on the Lexis*]

The lexis is both a propositional content and an empty, abstract schema. If I set down: $\lambda \in$ Sit, it processes as though I had written $\lambda \in (\quad)$ Sit. Depending on the instance, it will have a value, or it will process like a variable and refer, somewhat like a schema, to an abstraction, or it will have a value and I shall clear its place, an operation I represent by square brackets: I leave this value in abeyance.

We find this in relatives, for example:

The man who came is called Z.

We can also say:

"A man came. He is called Z."

I am then going to set down: [ ] came; [ ] indicates that a value is assigned to this place, that I clear it and will possibly re-use the same value.

I clear *a man* and set down: [ ] came. As I have constructed a second occurrence, *a man* becomes the first occurrence: this is the operation of **extraction**. $Qt_1 \cdot Qt_2$ is the operation of **pinpointing** coupled with an identification. This gives me:

The man $\in$ *[ ] came is called Z.*

Qt_2 Qt_1

I insert the symbol for location: the back-reference is located by the term from which I constructed the relationship. [...] $\in$ necessarily evinces as what has been termed "qu-" in French, or "wh-" in English.

We find this type of relationship when we construct, then deconstruct a relation so as to reconstruct another. If I put down: *The man who came (for a man did come), this man is called* Z, we can see that our starting point is *a man came*: we construct *the man who came* and also *this man is called Z.* Now, if I construct an interrogative starting from a disassertation, this will give us:

$\langle \lambda \in [\ \ ]\ \text{Sit} \rangle \in, \notin \text{Sit}$

In fact, I should have noted: ( ) Sit.

For a given value of Sit_2, "$\in$, $\notin$" signifies "is or is not located", i.e., "is or is not the case".

Note:

I will recall here the mirror value of $\ni$ dual. This relationship is *not* determinist, in the widest sense of the negation: it can be so, it can be not so.

For the value of $\in$, one can have ω, the value of a break or detached value, and $*$ which is either one or the other, or neither one nor the other.

If I want to construct a substantival clause, I have:

$\langle \lambda \in [\ \ ]\ \text{Sit} \rangle$

then I back-reference from there:

$(\ ) \in \langle \lambda \in [\ \ ]\ \text{Sit} \rangle$

que [in French] or that / ∅ in English

It is very often a component that is either specifically relative, or a type of deictic, for the relationship of identification is precisely term-for-term.

If I say "give me that watch", while pointing to it, and if there is only one, that is the watch; if there are several, it is the one to which I am pointing; however, if I say: "give me the watch" and there are several, the watch to which I refer is no longer evident.

Negative interrogative: Did he not come?

One must keep in mind the problem of the relationship, in the cam, where the positive form refers both to the positive value and to the domain (i.e., positive and negative values):
he came → ⟨he came⟩; *he came* represents the entire domain. *Did he come* [*est-il venu*] can at no time be assertive; it can be found in: *sans doute est-il venu* [*he probably did come*], *peut-être est-il venu* [*perhaps he did come*], where there is modalization. It can have the value of a hypothetical: *est-il venu, je m'en vais* [*if he came / has come, I'm leaving*]. What is very clear, however, is that in French one can say: *alors arrive mon père* [*then / thereupon enters Father*], but * *then arrives he* [* *alors arrive-t-il*] and * *then arrives this / that* [* *alors arrive-ça*] are impossible. From this point of view, *did he come* [*est-il venu?*] is a very peculiar form, constructed in such a way that it is a marker, an indicator that something, a certain type of relation has occurred: from *he came* I abstract a metalinguistic representation ⟨he came⟩, then: *did he come?* I can obtain two answers: *he came* (yes); *he did not come* (no).

As for the negative interrogative, on ⟨he did not come⟩ I construct *did he not come*. Whereas when processing *did he come* on the cam, both **p** and **p'** were available; here, starting with *he did not come*, I am brought back to *did he not come*, and from there to *he came* and only to *he came*.

Since the positive form represents both values, the positive form transposed into an interrogative format activates the two possibilities. When the starting point is the negative form similarly transposed, only one possibility remains, as the negative form does not represent both values (positive and negative).

[*The Negative interrogative and Configuration 2*]

We shall adopt the same approach for: *did he come?* [*est-ce qu'il est venu?*]: is that what really occurred? From *it is*, I can abstract ⟨it is⟩, from which I derive *is it*. *Is it* enables yes – no, and corresponds to a scan of all possible values, hence the impossibility [in French] of * *il est venu, est-ce?* [*he came, did he?*]; whereas *n'est-ce pas* [*isn't it / didn't he?*] weights the question, enabling the answer: yes. The starting point for *est-ce* being *c'est*, representing **(p, p')**, the interrogative form cannot be interpreted as biased, as an assertion. *Est-ce* induces a movement to the higher node:

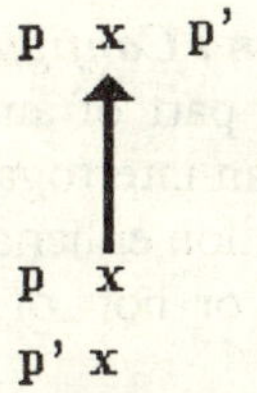

Isn't it [*n'est-ce pas*]'s starting point is *it isn't* [*ce n'est pas*], it is no longer equiponderant, but rather biased towards the positive side. For example:
Isn't it [a fact that it is] raining? [*N'est-ce pas qu'il pleut*?]

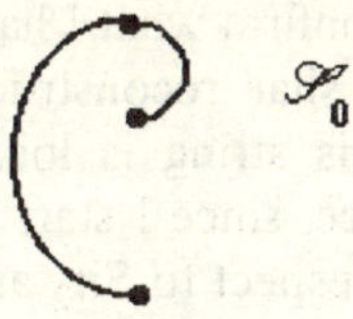

it is not $\mathscr{S}_1$
and it relates back to the holding state.

In the instance where *he came?* expresses surprise, $\mathscr{S}_0$ and $\mathscr{S}_1$ are in **p**:

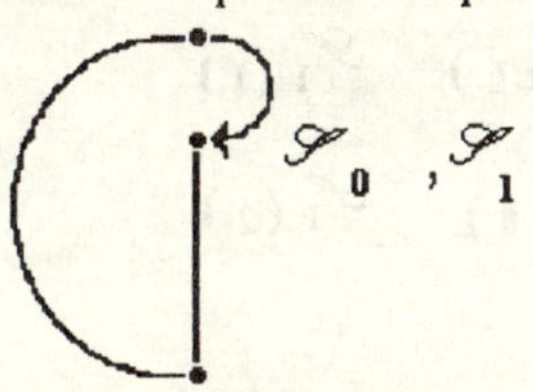

If one assigns a value, one can no longer scan the entire domain.

(Lecture of 14 Feb 1984)

In one instance, we start with something that has the form of an assertion. From there we construct an initial form and an initial value. The initial form is *he came*, and by adding a prosodic marker, I produce a biased interrogative *he came?* [*il est venu?*] if I think he came, and ask for confirmation.

In *did he come? / is it (a fact) that he came?* [*est-ce qu'il est venu?*], *that he came* is neither positive nor negative, it has a positive form; *that he should come astounds me*; *that he should have come is [quite] impossible*, as values, are no more positive than negative. We find here the same problems as with *thickness* as opposed to *thick* referring to *thick* or *thin*.

[*The Negative interrogative and Configuration 3*]

Did he come? cannot be part of an assertion. The problem is knowing from which point to start. In an interrogative, we construct a relationship between $\mathscr{S}_0$ and $\mathscr{S}_1$, and we question either a relationship about which we do not know whether it is validated or not, or what has been said by another. In short:

1. I cannot answer: is it this or is it not this?

2. You say that it is this; can you confirm what you have just said?

and finally

3. I think this; can you confirm what I have just said?

With *didn't he come*?, I shall reconstruct the initial, original form ⇒ *he didn't come*. I posit that this string is located with respect to a locutor–enunciator, and in this instance, since I start from the interrogative, I shall indicate that it is located with respect to Sit$_2$ and $\mathscr{S}_1$ — *he came* is located with respect to $\mathscr{S}_0$. This gives me state 0. From state 0, I move to 1: *didn't he come*, and from 1 to 2: *he came* [...], the value.

This is a way to process relationships of form. It simulates exchanges, it is a representation:

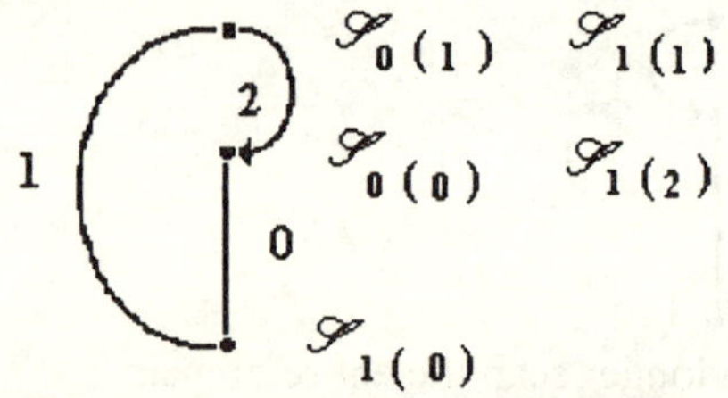

This means that $\mathscr{S}_1$, whatever his position, will eventually be drawn back to point 2, the point with respect to which I have constructed a relationship then a shift, and the end point must be neutral. The value depicted here is the following: *we are entirely in agreement to say that he came*.

In this instance, I have consistently spoken of the locutor–enunciator, as one cannot say: on the one hand there is someone, a physical person, who thinks something, and on the other, another physical person who thinks something else. It is a system which, in order to function stably and enable a multiplicity of values, must be reduced to very basic relationships involving a neutral point and two nodes, two positions. For the purpose of clarification, I used $\mathscr{S}_0$ and $\mathscr{S}_1$, and there really is someone who asks the question, someone who answers and it usually is the person from whom we expect an answer. This signifies that we are dealing with *locution* phenomena and *enunciative* phenomena, in the sense of representing and constructing domains which we process.

[*From Equiponderance to Tags*]

As for the the equiponderant question: *did he come?*, and for reasons linked to the problem of the cam, there is a positive term that functions either as a term having a positive value, or as a representation of the relationship without any specific assigned value, i.e., a representation of the positive-negative value.

Starting from *did he come*, I can derive either: *he came* $\in \mathscr{S}_1$, or ⟨he came, did not come⟩ peculiar to $\mathscr{S}_0$ addressing $\mathscr{S}_1$. From here one moves from 0 to 1 then to 2, and then start once more since no $\mathscr{S}_0$ nor $\mathscr{S}_1$ in 1 or 2 is anticipated, pre-constructed.

Concerning *n'est-ce pas*, it is a biased negative question; in fact it is a request for confirmation. The problem of tags in English derives very smoothly from all this.

– *he is here, isn't he?*

We recontruct the interrogation as though it emanated from $\mathscr{S}_1$, and this brings us back to the place which $\mathscr{S}_1$ has not occupied

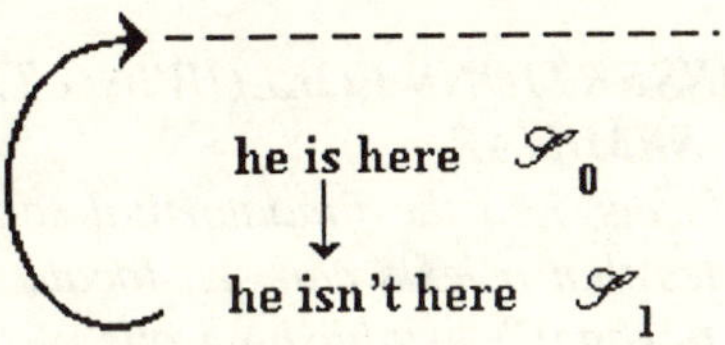

- he isn't here, is he?

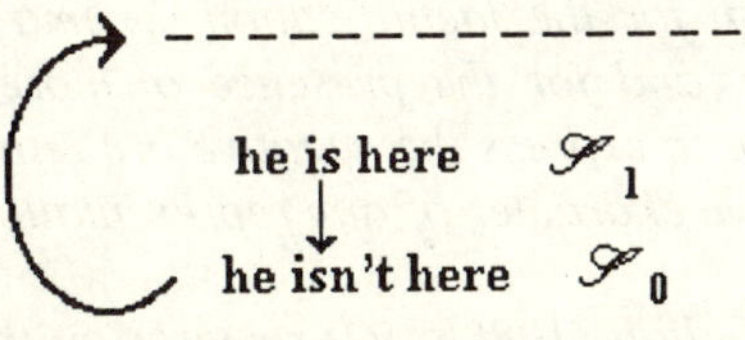

In French, *vraiment?*, *hein?* [*eh?*, *what?*, *huh?*]

Ah, tu es content, vraiment? [*So / Oh you're glad, are you?*]

Ah, tu es content, hein? [*So / Oh you're glad, eh? / what? / huh?*]

I'm glad.

– *Oh you are.*

or

– *Oh are you?*

One repeats, almost like an echo. $\mathscr{S}_1$ is asked to reconfirm that he did indeed say what he said:

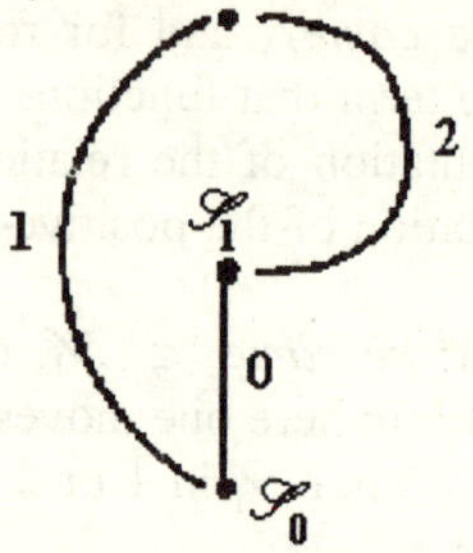

Oh you are glad is attributed to $\mathscr{S}_1$; $\mathscr{S}_0$ says "I think that you aren't glad", and so asks for confirmation.

In *Oh you're glad, perhaps?* the same analysis obtains, but the utterance signifies "would you go so far as to say that ... " or "how could go so far as to say that ... ". Furthermore, the expected value is more clearly in **(p')** than with *vraiment*.

ON CONSTRUCTING ASSERTIONS FOLLOWING THE D.E.A. SEMINAR

In his paper on schematic forms, i.e., the fundamental schemata of the SRμ (Culioli 1987a), Culioli notes that a lexis can self-locate or locate another lexis "(interpropositional linkage)", establishing one of three types of links: concomitance, consecution, or concomitance–consecution, from which one can derive " the diverse relationships said to be of subordination" (p.117)

Culioli sees an explanation for the identification schema's specialized markers, e.g., in Thai, Khmer, and for the presence of more than simply negative adjuncts to the positive to express the negative in Vietnamese, Japanese, etc. in the typically positive character of any representation of the lexis (Culioli 1988b: 97).

Concerning the negative, Culioli (1988b: 94) remarks on the impossibility of constructing an SRμ without a negative operator: "thus one can gloss ∉ Sit as 'not located with respect to the system of enunciative co-ordinates', 'is not valid', 'is not the case".

In order for an utterance to be well-formed, its terms must be situated: must have a site, i.e., "be stabilized in schema in relation to another term" (Culioli 1987a:119), and the stabilizing characteristics of each term (for ex-

ample: the quantitative and qualitative operations of determination in which it can enter) must be compatible" (120-121).

In Culioli (1989), he adds that the construction of an assertive utterance not only entails an assertive shape, but also requires that if a term contains a non-finite marker it must be related to another by means of interagentive or localizing relationships (p.209). In short, a predicative relation must contain "an overtly instantiated term" (p.211)

CHAPTER 5

MODALIZING

EDITOR'S INTRODUCTION

In his first statement on modalizing (Culioli, Fuchs & Pêcheux 1970:8), Culioli proposes a four-way description of modality:

1. positive, negative, injunctive, etc.

2. certainty, probability, necessity, etc.

3. judgmental [appréciative]: 'it is sad that ... ; happily'

4. intersubjective relationships.

His article on exclamatory utterances (Culioli 1974 passim) links the judgmental modality to quantitative and qualitative components of determination marked in the utterance, including operations such as scanning.

The sixth of the 1975-1976 D. E. A. Lectures includes more detail on the four modalities. Modality 1 is now composed of: assertive, interrogative and injunctive (p.69-71). Modality 2 comprises "the probable, the likely, the possible"; not ontological modalities (as in semiotics — p.72), but "a relationship between uttering and utterance, and enunciator and utterance" (p.71). The intersubjective relationships of Modality 4 consist of: "the deontic— 'one must honour one's parents', wishing, and permitting" (p.72). Culioli adds that the categories enumerated as contents of the various Modalities are not to be interpreted as mutually exclusive, and gives the example of the injunctive, which can be assertive (to form certain hypotheticals) or, in other instances ("pleas, suggestions"), part of Modality 4 (p.73).

His major work devoted to modality (Culioli 1978a) examines and analyses contexts including a modal **bien** *and the particular operation of scanning — leading to a boundary that will be crossed — of which* **bien** *is a marker. Starting with the translation for the title of the film "They shoot horses, don't they?": "On achève bien les chevaux", the linguist constructs a relationship such that the scanning and crossing entail deriving from the lexis of the first utterance, a paraphrastic family of second utterances, constrained by "context, situation, discursive pre-constructs, etc." (p.302).*

In the modality marked by the future tense, this type of scanning can be glossed by "will end up" (p.310). As for the conditional, it

> *marks the construction, on Sit_0, of a fictitious origin–locator Sit_0^1 from which one views [aims at, without intentionality (p.310)] a predicative relation [...] this signifies that by constructing Sit_o^1, $\mathscr{S}_0$ posits that the predicative relation is validatable, which does not imply that the relation will necessarily be validated nor invalidated [...]. (p. 312)*

The fictitious locator also enables the enunciator to be dissociated from the locutor, thus not to endorse nor guarantee what is uttered (ibid.).

EXCERPTS FROM THE D.E.A. SEMINAR

Our classification will revolve around two central points: on the one hand, intersubjective relationships, on the other the problem of quantification / qualification.

There are two possible configurations of intersubjective relationships:

a. first, an enunciator–co-enunciator relationship such that the utterance produced or recognized is fundamentally organized around the enunciator. An utterance is produced by means of which one evokes or refers to a situation in such a way that whoever produced the utterance guarantees what he has said, and is therefore ready to defend it against any one. This is what is traditionally referred to as an assertion. In this instance an intersubjective relationship necessarily exists [...] and within language. The relationship between subjects is a centred one, relating back to the enunciator–guarantor; it is therefore developed, structured, centred with respect to him, and fundamentally refers to him.

b. the second occurs when the relationship with the co-enunciator plays an essential part — whether it be problems of causation, coercion or of desiring applied to oneself or to others.

If I say, as I sometimes do: "modal component nil", it is not true: an assertion has a modal component. However, in the modal component of the intersubjective relationship appearing in an assertion, no direct action upon others is foreseen. For example: *Your brother left at 5 o'clock.* I am not saying: "You must leave at 5 o'clock" or "I want to leave at 5 o'clock, whether you like it or not", or "I am going to make your brother leave at 5 o'clock".

We have now singled out modalities 1 and 4; 1: assertion, 4: the causal component.

Modality 1

I also include the interrogative, which is, in fact, a hybrid of 1 and 4 and thus we have overlapping operations. We construct an intersubjective relationship that is an activator, exactly as in 4, since from this point of view it is indeed acting on others, activating an utterance. On the other hand, in the simplified instance by which we shall start, it is in fact asking an interlocutor to produce an assertion. For example:

Did your brother leave at 5 o'clock?
which prompts *yes my brother did indeed leave at 5 o'clock*
or *no my brother did not leave at 5 o'clock.*

I also add the injunctive, in the widest possible sense: from orders to pleas and even wishes, as well as requests and suggestions. It is something that appears to belong to domain 4, but which I place in 1 since it is the best example of an anti-assertion. In an assertion, one states that a certain situation is or is not; in the injunctive one says: "may a certain situation be or not be". Obviously this includes properties of the intersubjective modal form that I have just defined, yet it does belong to level 1, but only inasmuch as it is the opposite of an assertion. It is, in fact, a system which forms a loop, i.e., when one follows a certain course and classify elements, at some point one will be dealing with a term which is the reverse, so to speak.

Modality 4

Roughly speaking, an order is: A says to B: "whether you like it or not, do a certain thing". In the request, one is more polite, one says "one hopes that you like it"; in the suggestion "do you like what I like"; in the plea "I, myself, like [it]; I hope you like [it]", but the wish does not necessarily address itself to one person, as does the plea. It can be addressed to fate, to a divinity, or to all and sundry. I place causation, desiring / willing, coercion, deontics in modality 4.

With causation, one is pleased that something is done: it is a problem of valuation.

If we are dealing with self-referral, the problem will be one of desiring, willing, etc.

If it is a question of a relationship to another, including oneself seen as ancther, we shall be deaiing with a problem of coercion, of deontics. In coercion we are dealing with a relationship where there is necessarily valuation. If I say "he must finish his report by tonight", this signifies that, given that the validation is what is good, I am asking that the report be finished by tonight.

Hence there needs to be a [modal] distance with respect to the objective — even though this distance may possibly be eliminated — and a valuation.

[*Linguistics and the Problem of Reference*]

If we process *he must finish this report*, our starting point is the form *must*, a morpheme; from here we construct abstract forms, and we shall inquire as to the operations of which it can be a marker.

He must [*doit*] *finish the report by tonight* is ambiguous. The linguist's work in this instance is:

1. to state that it is ambiguous
2. to explain why it is ambiguous
3. to explain how, by prosodic or contextual additions, the ambiguity can be removed
4. to state why such and such an addition must be made to render it unambiguous.

He does not, however, give rules of interpretation; what is given is what is needed to construct the signification, and all we have on the referential values enables us to construct these referential values.

By signification I mean the global referential (cf. Frege's *Bedeutung*), but I have reduced it, in a much more traditional fashion, to the problem of reference and referential values. I rather quickly got rid of the reference, since I posited that there is no direct, unmediated relationship between an utterance and an event. It is always mediated. We are always dealing with a represented, constructed event. The problem of reference is one that is always caught between problems of truth values understood from a formal point of view: I give myself truth values and draw up tables, etc., and a problem of truth: does there exist a material counterpart, an object in the world? are we dealing with events in the world?

For the linguist this is catastrophic. The problem of referring to the world is not his concern. It is a consequence of our not working strictly extensionally. We [only] process properties, objects that we construct. From this point of view the problem of reference must be put aside.

Thus was I led to invent the term "referential values", and the ultimate problem of constructing a signification when people speak (cf. all the problems of presupposition, all the ideological layers vehiculated by discourse) is a socio-semiotic one. I also speak of referential values in lieu of aspectual values or modal values.

Modality 2

In this instance, there will be quantification on the gradient (Qnt), whereas in modality 3, we shall find Qlt (qualification). In effect we shall have a 1 – 4 relationship, and within it, a 2 – 3 relationship.

If we refer to what we have seen concerning the notional domain, we find a centred value, which will be what is true. For example: *X did that.* Then we shall be able to process the subjective certainty: in this instance, if in the centred Interior, this appears as:

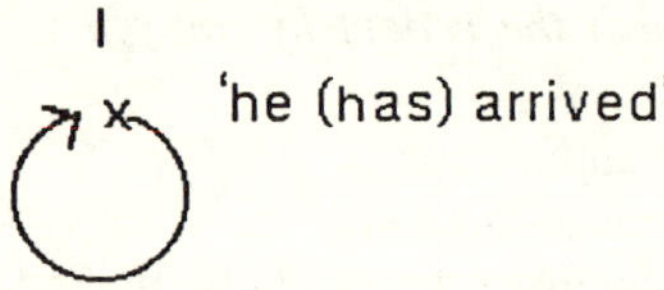

(I say nothing else, no more, no less.)

[*Weakened Certainty*]

As I widen the scope, I shall construct a domain of different values, such that, among other possibilities, I can find an instance including a different value that approaches the centred value:

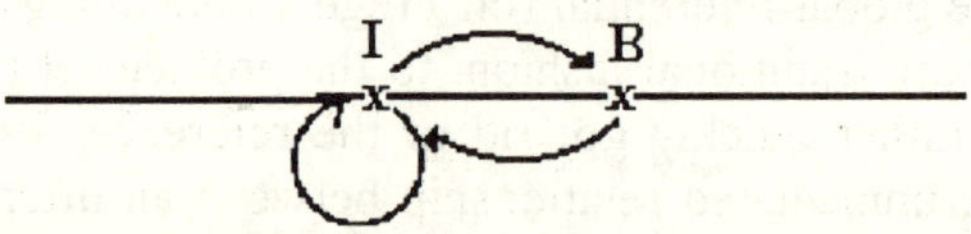

This yields **supposition**: *he must have returned; I believe he has returned — I think he has returned; There's every chance that — it is probable that ...* . Supposition must be understood in a slightly peculiar sense: I use it every time I construct a weakened certainty concerning something that is certain — when, for example, instead of saying: "he came", I say: "he must have come".

In other instances, probability, possibility, necessity will appear. Probability is a computation based on the chances that ... , i.e., a weakened certainty.

[*Possibility*]

The concept of possibility is extremely complex:

1. it means stating that it is a value among other positive ones; for example: there are many possible pathways.

2. *possible* refers to a distinction between *possible* and *impossible*: possible is what is not impossible.

3. it refers to a notion of eventuality: *it is possible that* ... ; this is somewhat of a hybrid of the first two. If we say "it is possible that ... " this signifies that it is possible that ... not ... ; it induces more than one value — and in so saying we process all the possibilities, and the negative is a part of this set. The notion of impossibility is a far different one. *Impossible* signifies: "one cannot even imagine saying that something might occur".

4. *possible* can also signify "it is *doable*".

We have here a whole cluster of values, but they are always characterized by one fundamental trait: there must be a modal distance, i.e., that with respect to what I refer to as the *enunciative locator* [*repère énonciatif*], there must be a viewpoint dissociated from the plane of assertion. For supposition, for example, there needs to be some distance to be able to provide an approximation; thus one must be in a position where one cannot produce anything but an approximation. As for possibility and probability, the same obtains: one must be able to envisage, but envisaging implies having lying before one something to do. One can always close the distance. For example, one can say: "I can erase the blackboard" and after having said this, one can add: "you see, I can erase the blackboard" and then one erases the board. In this instance, we almost always find a marker of realization, such as *there*, *you see*, *it's true that*, etc.

The possible activates at least two pathways.

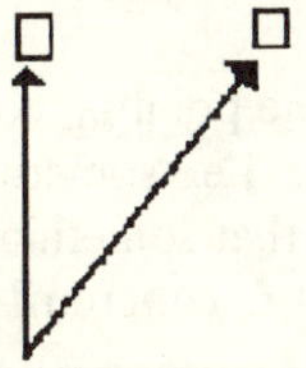

Both pathways can lead to possible values, equivalent values, i.e., positive ones. For example, I can say: "What can I have for dessert?" in reply to the question: "Would you like a dessert?", thus referring to possible desserts.

Now if I say: "it may rain, but then again it may not rain", in this instance the two values are *raining* and *not raining*, i.e., from the viewpoint of a domain, the positive value and the negative one.

If I say: "cats can be devastators", this signifies: it is possible, it is ima-ginable thus not impossible, it is not unimaginable that, hence "there are some that ... ". It also means : "there are some that ... not".

If one says that: "something is doable", it signifies that something may be done, or may not. It will not necessarily be done.

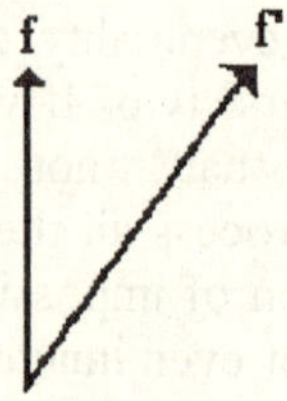

To say that it is doable signifies that one can take the pathway to f. It also means, however, that at some point this might not be the case: one could remain at the starting point, or perhaps try to start out, err then fail.

If one says that it is not doable, one cuts off the pathway to f, and one necessarily favours the other. One sees the fundamental difference that exists when the negative is activated:

something that can be done = 2 possibilities
something that cannot be done = only 1 = nothing
something that is not not-doable = some possibility exists.

Possibility is, therefore, Interior–Boundary — without the double arrow found in supposition; or Interior–Exterior.

[*Necessity and Supposition*]

In necessity, there exists one and only one value, and the detaching of which I have spoken: the distance with respect to the actual realization of something.

As for supposition, at some point t_0, concerning something which is either concomitant with or prior to it, i.e., something that has the properties of certitude, one says that one thinks that something took place, or is taking place:

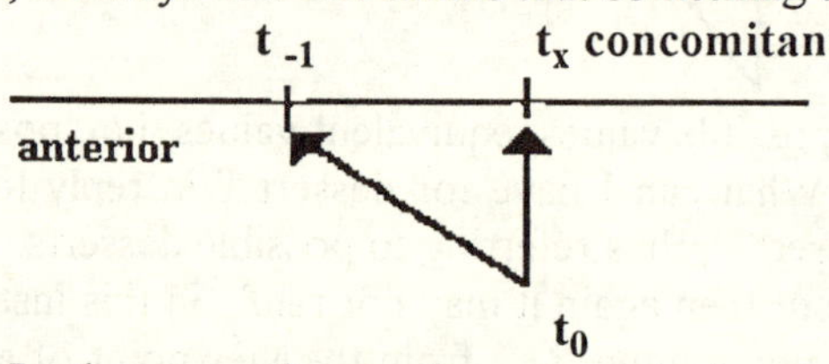

In the case of necessity, one *must* insert a distance in order to say that, given two points, there is only one path between these two points.

What we see here is a very old philosophical problem, namely the relationship between what is true and what is necessary. As soon as we process generic data for example, we are processing a relationship that, whatever the terms to which it applies, is always validated: we then have a necessary relationship.

In like fashion, we encounter the extremely ancient problem: "it must be since it is" and "it is because it must be". There is also the problem of seeing how the deontic, as a moral type of constraint, may be constructed upon it.

In assertions, there is, in part, one and only one path: in the instance of an assertion with a demontration, the latter consists in showing that there is only one path, thus what is false can be considered the equivalent of the absurd and the impossible. As for argumentation, or an assertion that simply states what has been noted, they fall under the heading of what I have called the "no more" [as in *no more, no less*]. When one deals with necessity, what one adds is that there is only one path.

There are thus two possibilities for what is necessary: one consists in having one pathway:

the other in having only one path:

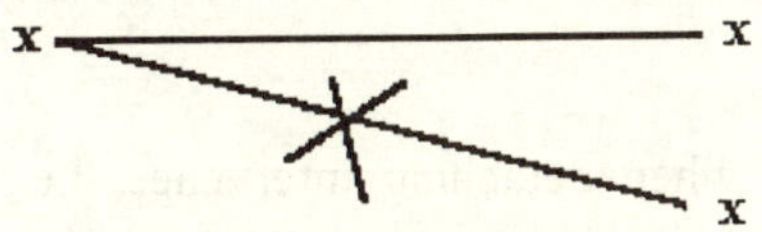

Modality 3

Here we are dealing with valuation of a qualitative nature: an evaluative modality. This includes: *it's natural, it's good, it's strange, it's shocking* ... Two instances can appear: one consists of an utterance of a near generic type often including anticipatory phenomena. For example: *what is good is that she should act this way* — an effectively ambiguous statement: one does not know whether she is acting thusly or is going to. In the other instance appears: *it is natural you should react in this manner*. The choice of *you* orients the interpretation: we surmise that the person has reacted. In any case, it is always an evaluation that one performs on the normality, naturalness, goodness, badness, happiness, sadness that ... . This evaluative modality can partly be associated with 2 or 1, partly with 4 also, but in fact it constitutes a domain of its own.

(Lecture of 13 March 1984)

Modality as a detached representation of reality

We are now going to examine in depth what we have touched upon superficially concerning modality. Modality, in the sense in which we use it here, supposes that there is representation.

If the act of touching or pointing is considered, one can see that one is dealing with present events: one cannot touch or point to something which is not present. Furthermore, in touching or pointing, my behaviour is not necessarily verbal: I can make a facial expression, a gesture, I can even bring about a transformation, for example, by throwing away or breaking an object I do not like. I can take something that I do like. One must, however, be careful not to call this modality. Non-verbal behaviour of desiring or rejecting cannot be considered modal behaviour even if it does represent an affect or certain relationships with objects or events.

In the area of pointing, there can be a tension in the direction of an object, i.e., this movement can transform the situation, one advances toward the object ... .We can see that from the perspective of the relationship which we can posit between verbal and non-verbal behaviour, there is a solution of continuity: a point resulting from ritualized behaviour, inasmuch as the gestures can be both founded in primordial activity and ritualized in a culture, for example, outstretched hands. All of this cannot, however, be called modality.

[*Detachability*]

The major transformation occurs when detaching intervenes, i.e., true language activity as activity by which we construct substitutes separable from reality. This is what we call **representation** in the framework of relationships between levels 1 and 2, i.e. construction of representations; and these representations will necessarily be designations [...] When does such a detaching occur?

– For example, in negation: through negation one creates constructs concerning what is not. We must not confuse it with negation by rejection: the act of breaking, of rejecting can be considered negative behaviour, of course, but this behaviour is not mediated by verbalization.

– When verbal behaviour applies to generics, obviously touching/pointing activities cannot apply; in generics, a part always transcends the individuality of an object or an event.

– An anaphora is necessarily detached, thus, a detachable substitute.

– When we process the class of instants, i.e., (to simplify) temporal or aspectual phenomena, we shall necessarily find "detachability": either phenomena referring to the already elapsed, or anticipatory phenomena. As soon as we say:

"The flower is no longer red"

we have processed the representation of a prior state. As soon as we say something like "so that's where you are, is it?", we have processed anticipation.

By extension, one can say that as soon as there is interlocutionary back-referencing, there is necessarily "detachability", inasmuch as, in a back-reference or in an exchange there necessarily exists a relationship, not with the vocal event that took place, but with the representation we derive from this vocal event. It is the representation that I construct of this phonetic event that triggers in me an exchange.

Pushing even further, one can say that assertions themselves contain a detached representation (cf., what we have indicated concerning the enunciator – co-enunciator relationship, and the notional domain as a constructed domain where, in uttering, one will mark that such and such a value is centred). An assertion, in the strictest sense of the term, i.e. when one says "here's what I think is true, I insist on saying it and on stating that it's what I believe", necessarily presumes a type of relationship that goes beyond simply stating what one has remarked. As soon as a language activity includes the construction of predicative relations that relate back to an enunciator–subject, there is necessarily detachability, and thus modality: modality is linked to this property of detachability.

Inasmuch as representation is necessarily verbalized, a problem of designation appears.

There is also a necessary cleavage between the singularity of the locution event, related to *locutors*, and the validation of that which refers us to the problem of the *enunciator*: there needs to be a subject to ensure permanence, a guarantee. Processing detached representations obliges me to insert both the locutor who says something, and a functor that will ensure that what is said is related back to a subject who is going to speak. Furthermore, what is said is not simply a verbal event, it is a way of referring to something, i.e., to the construction of a reference.

[*The Plane of Asserting*]

We can now take another look at each point. We construe a plane, that of asserting, and on this plane, is constituted the predicative relation (the orientation is already chosen) to which I have almost given an assertive form. It will be situated with respect to a complex system of enunciative locations: on the one hand λ will be an occurrence in a class of occurrences in a domain, and on the other, $\lambda \in$ Sit will be constructed. As an occurrence in a class of occurrences, it will be neither positive nor negative, nor between the two, nor any other value, but compatible with all of these.

If at some point λ becomes a positive assertion, λ is a part of the entire plane:

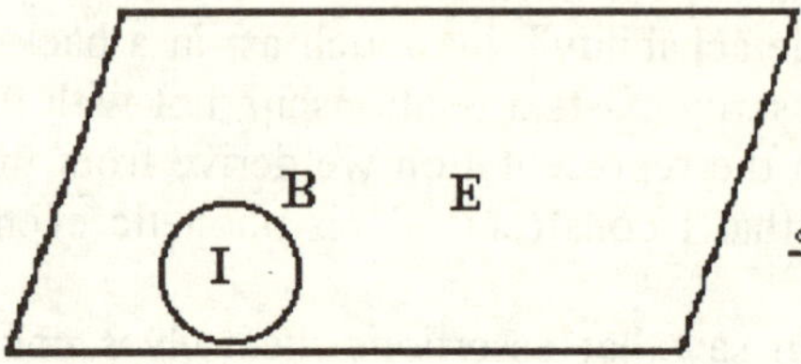

$\mathscr{D}$ = **domain**

For example: *The child is reading a book*
or *The child is not reading a book at all*
or *The child is indeed reading a book*

The child is not reading a book but only pretending, or *skimming through a book.*

If one considers that that is reading, the PR is placed in **I**; if one does not really call that reading, it is placed in **B**; if one judges that it is not reading a book at all, it is placed in **E**. One is therefore processing a set of possible values.

To say $\lambda \in$ Sit, is short for $Sit_2\ Sit_1\ \mathscr{S}it_0$. Saying that λ is an occurrence in a domain amounts to saying that to obtain a value, i.e. to be able to say whether λ is in I, B, or E, it must be located by the Situation.

Two instances may appear: one in which there is double centring, one where there is detaching and, from this viewpoint, a hiatus.

Double centring occurs when, putting to ourselves the problem of the distance 1 - 0, which applies to believing, considering: *I believe that*, *I think that*, *I consider that*, *according to me* ... , we say that it is we who commit ourselves to saying something.

For example, the difference between *The temperature is 12°* and *I'd say that the temperature is 12°*, or *I believe that the temperature is 12°*.

The temperature is 12° is a pure assertion; somewhere I have an objective standard that I have given myself. I have the assurance that it is trans-individual.

In the other instances, it is my experience that prompts me to say that ... .

Associated with this distinction, and represented here by **d**, is processing on the gradient to know whether it is truly centred or only approximately (i.e., whether some alternative value exists)

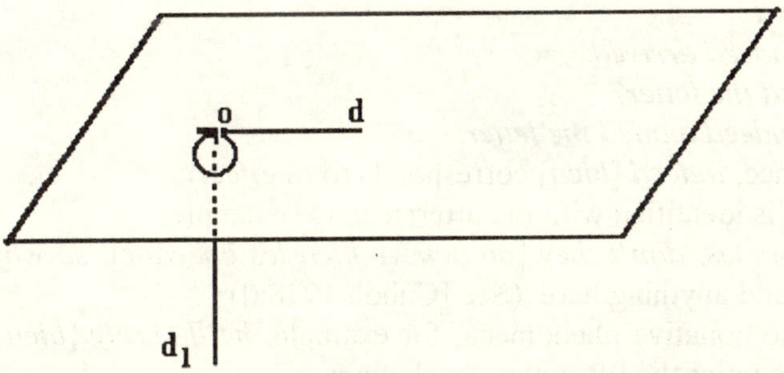

If one value is the correct one, every other value is either radically other, thus either outside the domain; or approximately the same — the difference being qualitative or quantitative. Each of us structures a whole notional domain of occurrences, i.e. of representations we construct, in such a way that, given the occasion, through our relationships with others, we compare our ways of designating.

Fictitious locating and examples of the same

Detaching produces another plane, such that between the second plane and the first we shall construct a relationship having the value of a break: ω. We cannot construct a solution of continuity enabling us to deal with a sort of uninterrupted neighbourhood, thus movement from one plane to the other. There is a hiatus. We construct a locator, which I have called fictitious locator $\mathscr{S}it_0{}^1$, detached from the time-based locating system.

We construct an image of the enunciator–subject $\mathscr{S}_0$ and of $\mathcal{T}_0$ that has the following properties: it is constructed with respect to $\mathscr{S}it_0$: $Sit_0{}^1$ is in fact $(\mathscr{S}_0^1, \mathcal{T}_0{}^1)$.

We shall sometimes process $\mathscr{S}_0$, $\mathscr{S}_0^1$, $\mathscr{S}_0^1\ \mathcal{T}_0{}^1$ with respect $\mathscr{S}_0\,\mathcal{T}_0$, etc., i.e., the parameters, so that we may find an *I* which, by means of successive identifications, refers to the person who says "I" when he says "I", etc.; and also construct a locator that will be off-centre. This will enable us to process the instances of which I have spoken: negation, modality 4 of the deontic type, generics, etc., with a higher degree of complexity.

[***Example: bien and croire bien***]

Now, let us look at a particular problem involving *croire* and *bien*.

When *bien* is used on the asserting plane, it may mark an operation of identification between occurrences, such that

– either there are two occurrences, and this is a pure and simple instance of identification, for example:

Has he arrived?
Yes, he has indeed arrived.
Has he mailed the letter?
Yes, he has indeed mailed the letter.
(In this instance, *indeed* [*bien*] corresponds to *in effect*)
– or the lexis is identified with the utterance, for example:
They shoot horses, don't they [*on achève bien les chevaux*], *so why not ... ?* and one can add anything here. (See [Culioli 1978a]).

There are also conative phenomena, for example: *he'll surely* [*bien*] *end up* ... and at some point the PR enters the domain.

As soon as *very* [*fort*] appears, we are processing a gradient. *Very* indicates the high degree: it marks that we are dealing with the attracting centre. *Very well* [*fort bien*] completely transforms the utterance.

They shoot horses, don't they? [*on achève bien les chevaux*] establishes a relationship between a non-verbalized — or possibly verbalized — pre-construct, and a second term. *They shoot horses very well* [*fort bien*] *don't they* is, ultimately, a kind of assertion concerning how to kill horses. If one says: "they shoot, don't they?", *bien* serves as the marker for setting up a relationship between two terms, and in all such instances, no gradient exists.

As for *they shoot very well* [*fort bien*] ... , it signifies that one can do this more or less *well*; hence, there is a gradient.

If we encounter *je crois bien* [*I think / I'm quite sure*], you are not dealing with a gradient, otherwise we would be able to process a homogeneous domain containing non-radical alterations: qualitative stability with alterations. We can immediately verify this by observing that * *je crois fort bien* [* *I very think*] is impossible.

[*Assertion / Interrogative / Hypothetical*]

Asserting, with its double centring and absence of detaching, induces one and only one value. Starting from the instance already examined:

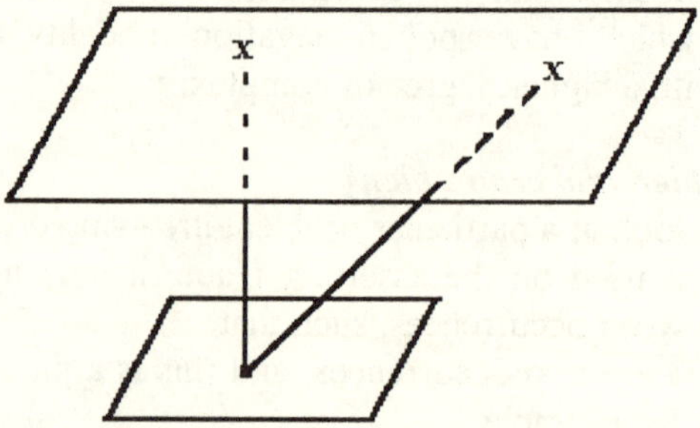

if one eliminates the distance, one cannot maintain both the right and the left, or perhaps one remains outside, below, not involved. If not, one must favour either a positive value or a negative one (the latter is always a value one has constructed on the positive one).

In the case of the interrogative, one places oneself outside the two values and deal once more with the problems we have examined [see previous chapter]. When one questions, one moves from one plane to the other:

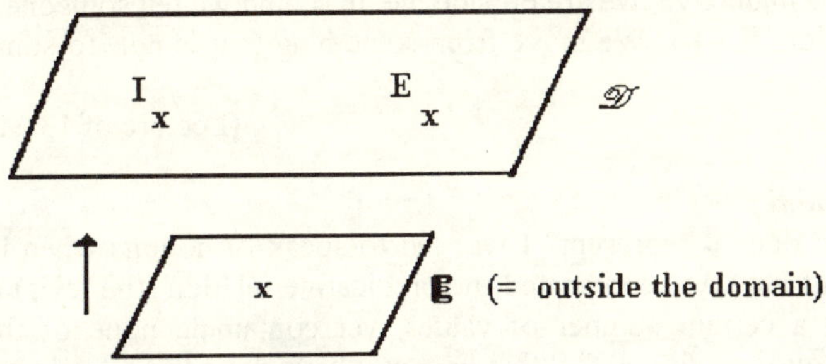

𝔼 signifies: outside of I – E, external to the plane. This is what occurs when one says: "but that's not what this is about".

If I move from 𝔼 to 𝒟 by means of a value I have chosen, I move from an external point to a positive–negative value and then to a positive one. However, I have noticed that some interrogative forms can, in fact, have the value of a hypothetical: *Were you to come* ... .

Were you to come is the equivalent of *if you were to come*. Now we can see that, with this type of processing, we shall be able to elucidate the construction of a hypothetical. A hypothetical is placing oneself outside, and positing that an event takes place. A hypothetical appears true, where , in fact, it is *false–true*, can be posited to be entirely imaginary and neither true nor false.

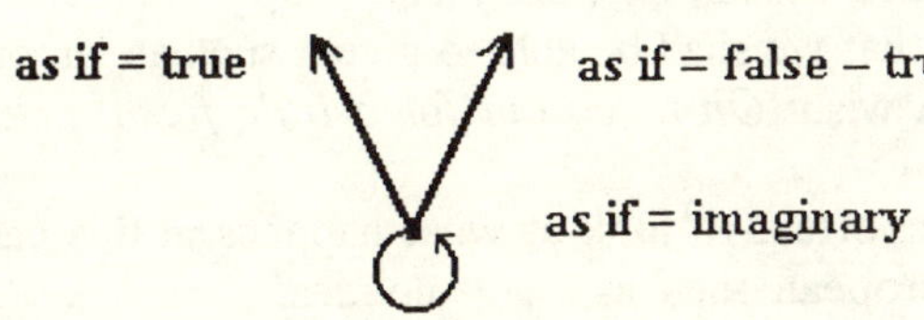

What enables the interrogative to also be a hypothetical? In the inter-rogative, all possible values are processed, and there is interaction between the two enunciators. In the hypothetical, we process neither relationships between two enunciators nor the two values. We proceed as though we knew one of the values, as though it were the right one, but in so doing, however, we do not blank out the other value, nor the fact that we are unable to state which is the correct value. In fact we process three values. Hypotheticals have the properties of assertions, but are not assertions.

For example: *If the weather is good tomorrow*, also signifies that the weather could very well not be good tomorrow, but we shall favour the possibility of it being good tomorrow.

In the injunctive, we are outside, i.e. in $\mathbb{E}$, and we tell someone to perform some action: $\mathbb{E} \rightarrow$ I. We move from something that is not, to something that is.

(Lecture of 13 March 1984)

[*The $\mathbb{E}$ plane*]

What does $\mathbb{E}$ represent? I was led to speak of notions when I attempted to find out how we represented the predicative relation (the lexis) as compatible with a certain number of values, yet containing none of these, cf. in French, "*qu'il ait fait ça*?" ["that he could have done this?"]. We must look at what happens when we designate and when we represent: representing is designating the representation. It is not an utterance in the perverted sense arising from the confusion of utterance and assertion. However, it has indeed been uttered inasmuch as it has a certain shape and has been recognized by another. This is why I constructed a space separate from that of assertion. (The assertive space being characterized by Sit_2 identified with Sit_1 identified with $\mathcal{S}t_0$, i.e., what occurs, occurs at the moment that I say it occurs: a privileged instance.) Space $\mathbb{E}$ is external to the very act of uttering by whose means I may give an assertive value ... At that point, $\mathbb{E}$ is indeed compatible with a structured domain I – E, but then again, one can remain outside. Thus it can be posited that $\mathbb{E}$ represents the mention of the notion — the minimal mention. From there, this detached minimal mention will always be plunged again into the enunciative space. It can be purely and simply the mention, compatible with all the values that we shall be able to give it such as: an order: *Knock before entering*; or a wish: *Oh to go out for a little fresh air!*; or a rejection: *Come?*.

It would be important to look at what happens in this case in languages other than Indo-European ones, as I have no idea.

We must distinguish two points:

1. As regards the conditional, for example *if I were to go to the cinema / movies*, we are not on the enunciative plane comprising I – E (the domain) applied to certainties or differed certainties. For there to be a hypothetical, a fictitious locator is needed. $\mathbb{E}$, which is neither true nor false, i.e. not validated,

also comes into play. These are the representations I construct. I shall activate a domain which consists of taking charge of validating, whether it be in the form of a promise, a loosely worded utterance, a deferred assertion. Activating the plane of I – E, forces me to favour either I or E. I must be outside and at a distance to be able to aim for one value but attain both. The closer I get, the more I must favour either I or E. Thus I need a pathway from **E** to this plane. That is the first point.

2. One value must necessarily be distinguished. If I have a target, a fictitious one in the instance of the conditional, I shall induce normally incompatible possibilities that I shall, however, be able to render compatible, since none is, in fact, validated. Moreover I move — even fictitiously — to the plane called $\mathscr{E}$; thus, from this viewpoint, I have constructed a distin-guished value. If there are two pathways, there will be valuating.

When dealing with an *assertive fiction*, E is always possible. We posit I without excluding E.

When we construct a hypothetical, we produce an anaphoric back-referencing equivalent to that constructed in a situation of *Pinpointing*, and *if* [*si*] (i.e., *thus* [*ainsi*]) will in fact provide us with that value: given the relation ⟨ I, going to the cinema ⟩, let it be so. Here we see the *trace* of this construct.

We shall also face a problem of modal strength. When we say: "be", or "let's give each other", we proceed as though we were constructing because we wished to construct, a particular fictitious value.

Let us examine the following example concerning hypotheticals:

And if he came?

It can induce two values:

1. what would happen?
2. this is a suggestion

Both instances, in fact, contain relationships between two terms. In the first instance, this is linked to problems of existential and aspectual connotations; and in the other, to problems of intersubjectivity: *what do you think about it? Are you for or against?*

The first instance signifies: "let's imagine that he does come; what would be the result?" This is an operation by means of which we predicate the existence of some event, in a fictitious manner inasmuch as we can say that we remain on the bottom plane. X could answer: "what a foolish idea!". We can, however, reply: "let us consider even the most improbable situations". X took *And if he came?* seriously, acting as if we favoured **I** on the plane we could call that of "reality", and we refer him back to the bottom plane by saying: it is an **I** derived from **E**.

(Lecture of 20 March 1984)

The Intersubjective Relationship (Modality 4)

Today we continue our work on modality 4, i.e., the intersubjective relationship. One very often hears that it consists of everything that constitutes *being able / can* [*pouvoir*] and *must* [*devoir*]. In fact, this encompasses a great deal, since it includes all modalities similar to *I need, I must have*. I shall therefore reduce it to a number of basic propositions so that we can see how to construct the problem. Above all, we must not use preconceived notions concerning the type of concept that might determine the different grammatical categories, such as possibility, necessity ... .

In fact we shall endeavour to explicate what these intersubjective re-lationships are. Given two points: **x**, **x**, we are going to examine the pos-sibilities; there are 3. The first is when two points are identified one with the other; this is the relationship of a subject with himself. Obviously the intersubjective relationship is always posited with respect to a predicative relation: there is always a hiatus. Here, however, it induces *I need, I want, it is my duty to, I wish, I am keen on / I insist on* ... . In some instances it signifies "it depends on you and you alone"; in others, that one is one's own interrogator. This relationship always entails *being in a position to, being able to* that indicates precisely what has been called an *intra*subjective value, i.e. one does not depend on someone else. For example: *I can give a hand* signifies: ''I am in a position to", i.e. "I am agreeable to, if you yourself wish". We will encounter, moreover, the relationship between enunciator and co-enunciator, that is to say either:

I wish – do you wish?

or *You wish – I accept* [*je veux bien*].

Bien with *vouloir* produces a new term and signifies "I accept". *Bien* indicates an identification, hence *if you wish, I accept* [*veux bien*]. We are therefore analysing an abstract relationship between two terms: I wish – you wish — cf. *will you* [*veux-tu*] *please shut up*. It is a relationship between two terms that are posited as being different. We can represent this instance by means of two loops and a relationship between them:

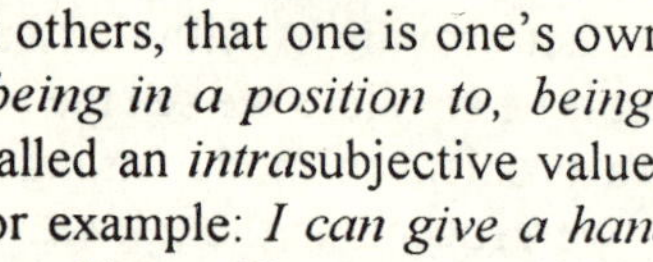

The third instance is an agent–patient relationship:

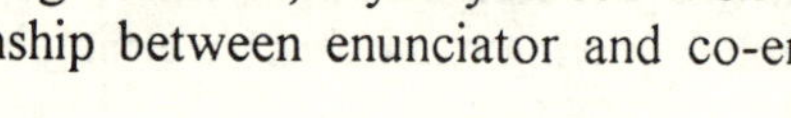

This does not necessarily involve one and only one predicate. Take for example *I wish to go out*; this signifies: "what interests me with respect to the predicative relation posited as possible, i.e., that can be validated or even invalidated (there is always this hiatus in the relationship with a predicative relation), is the positive value which I distinguish by means of valuing". Thus ⟨ I – going out ⟩, I wish that it will be realized."

All possible complications will immediately and massively appear, from *you say what you wish*, to *I want to go out!*, i.e., "don't stop me from going out". All we need to do is to fill in as many possibilities as we have combinations and we shall list all the values.

Another example: *I want to see you up in five minutes.*

One subjectivity dominates the other in the relationship called agentivity, and this relationship is not an effect of the verb *having to / must* [*devoir*] as such: we cannot at some particular point assign a value to a term. In order to discover the value, we must perform the entire analysis each time by means of a calculation procedure .

Being able to [pouvoir]: another look at the problem — a modal viewpoint

1. The first value corresponds to *being able to*: roughly what has been called "capacity".

Example: *I can run the 100 metres in 10 seconds.*

Here we have the interesting problem that I have called the problem of the **hiatus**. Someone may then say to us "do it" and we could succeed; we may, however, be capable of a great many things that we shall never do. We may also eliminate the hiatus by simultaneously doing what we say and saying it.

This first value corresponds to a looped relationship

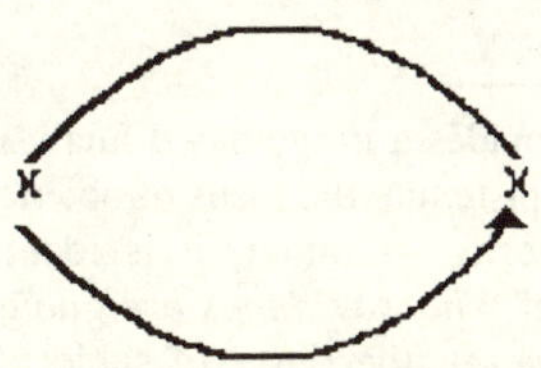

2. For the second value, I construct an enunciator – co-enunciator relationship, and the dialectic ensuing from *if you wish ...* . Usages are of the type: *may I help you?*, i.e., *I am able to help you if you wish.*

We can also encounter permission:

You may go out, i.e., *if you wish to go out, I shall not be an obstacle*, and that is permission.

This is the relationship I represented by an arrow:

X ⟶ X

which is roughly: making someone do something. *Letting* is not doing anything to prevent someone from doing something. *Preventing* is doing something so that someone cannot. *Not preventing* is not doing anything so that someone, as he pleases, does or does not do something. Hence *I do not prevent him* can differ from *I let him*. In *I do not prevent him*, I remain on the detached plane. I put myself on the sidelines. These, then, are root values.

3. The third value is epistemic, a handy term, but one that I do not very much like, as the values are sometimes superposed. If one says, for example, "He could not have opened the door", this signifies "it is unthinkable that he could have been able to". It must be fully understood that at some point we find both root and epistemic traits.[1] This third value occurs when one is outside, i.e., when one shifts back to modality 2: possibility. [...]

4. I shall add a fourth value: the *non-impossible*, i.e., *being able* as *that which is not impossible*.

The non-impossible re-enters the domain of possible values.

As regards the domain, if one says "I am able to", in relation to the domain, if circumstances required and/or if one wished it, one could produce this

[1] Langacker (1990) provides a usage-based analysis of the root/epistemic distinction: "In the senses we regard as epistemic, the locus of potency is the polar opposite of a focused well-delimited form of authority — rather, it is identified holistically as the nature of evolving reality itself. [...] (cf. *The way things are going, we should finish by noon*). Epistemic modals [... point] to yet another layer of subjectification [roughly corresponding to Culioli's *supposition* in Modality 2]. At issue are expressions like [...] *You must be tired. He may be finished by now*. [...] This usage reflects a shift in the domain where the notion of "momentum" is manifested: this conception is transferred from the evolution of REALITY ITSELF to the evolution of our KNOWLEDGE OF (PRESENT) REALITY. [...] . What remains a matter of future potentiality is the revelation of this state of affairs to the speaker (and secondarily, to the hearer) — the modals express the likelihood that, as the speaker's knowledge of current reality continues to expand, the profiled situation will prove to be a part of it" (336-337).

value, but obviously at the point where one says this, one is detached from this plane.

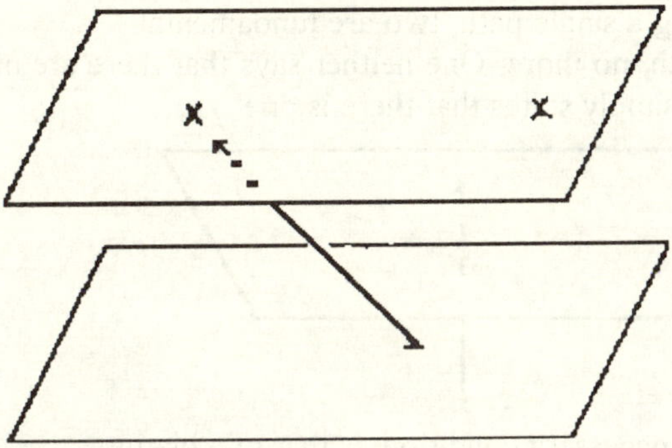

In the second instance, we find the same situation, except that here we have integrated inter-enunciator relationships, where previously the relationship was between an enunciator and himself. The possibility of two pathways still remains.

Contingency [*l'éventuel*] typically consists of two values both of which are possible: **I** and **E** are both possible values. When I say: "it might rain, it might not rain", I am completely external to the event *raining – not raining* that I am predicting for tomorrow. At the moment I say it, both are possible. I can be completely detached from the predictions.

With the non-impossible we find the traditional operation *there are instances where*. An aforeseen example is once again appropriate: *the French can be noisy* which signifies "it is not always possible to dissociate 'the French" and 'noisy', 'there are instances where' ... ". We recognize the operation for constructing the attracting centre. If we enter non-null values into the domain, we shall construct an organizer, i.e., typify.

The French can be noisy signifies: this is a national trait.

We cannot process *some Frenchmen are noisy* from a strictly quantitative viewpoint. Once more, we are processing intensionally. Furthermore, we need only add *how*, and *can* relates to the high degree:

How the French can be noisy!

(Lecture of 10 March 1984)

[*Linking the Detached Locator to the Plane of Assertion*]

When treating modalities, we are, of course, dealing with constructing the notional domain, and with the problem of constructing an enunciative locator such that there — possibly — appear both double centring, thus enabling the processing of a gradient, and the hiatus between a detached locator and the plane of assertion. We have also noted the problem of the path: we dealt with two instances — either only one path, or a bifurcation. There exist three ways of constructing a single path; two are fundamental:

– one path, no more. One neither says that there are more, nor that there are less. One simply states that there is one.

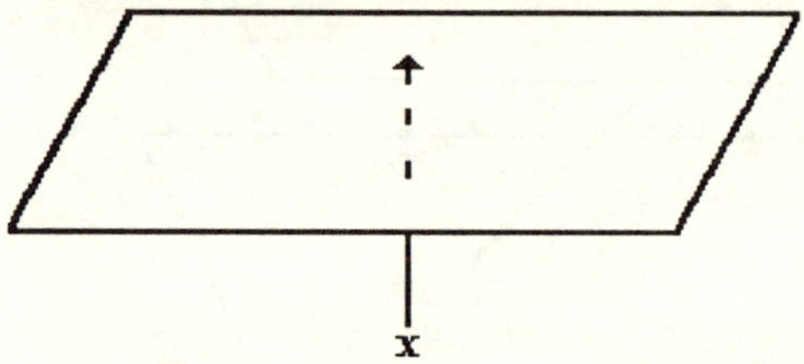

The only necessary condition, is that of a hiatus.

– The second way occurs when, processing a bifurcation, we eliminate all pathways save one, thus maintaining one and only one:

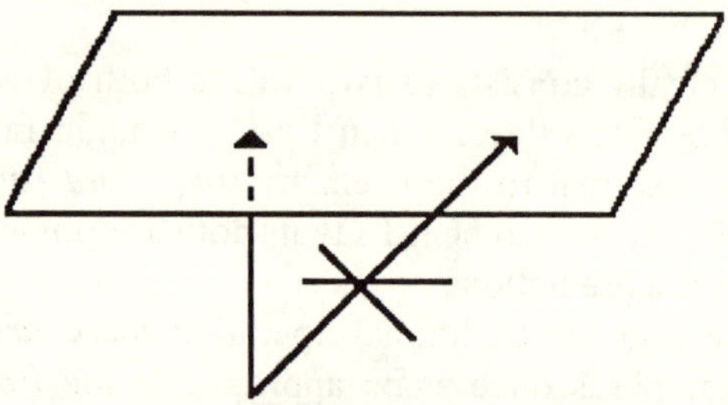

– The third corresponds to the instance where we have processed I and B. We construct the closed interval of possibilities that appears as a bifurcation, as well as *oscillations* such that, since we cannot specify the value of the centred point, we posit an approximate value and treat it as though it were the centred one. This is what is called *supposition or reckoning*, i.e. approximation, judgments concerning likelihood, such as:

He must have arrived.

At that pace, he should be there in 5 minutes.

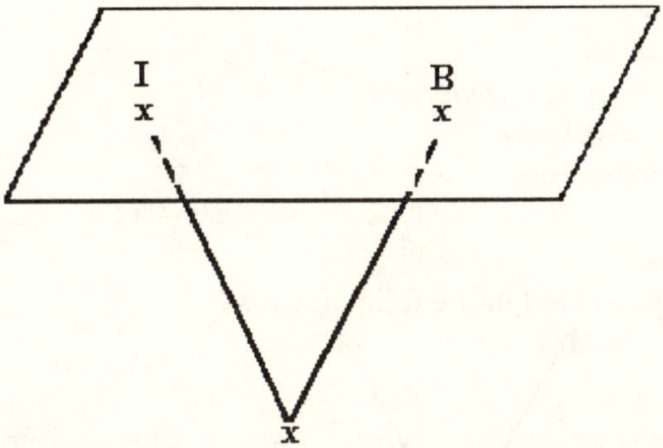

Starting from a very elementary distinction, by elaborating as we proceed, we shall integrate something much more complex: the number of operations that we perform will increase in a very complex fashion each time, and the work of the linguist will be to make explanatory statements when possible, i.e., in a high proportion of instances, and to say that in other instances he cannot explain ... .

For a given language, we shall be able to provide a description consisting of a coherent, homogeneous discourse on phenomena which, not being transposable from one language to another, are heterogeneous. Therein lies the problem of generalization.

[*Between Modality and Aspect*]

Now, we shall set out the problem that, in a sense, constitutes the tail-end of modalities and the beginning of aspects, using the following example as our starting point:

It can [*peut*] *rain tomorrow.*

We shall analyse it as having stable intonation patterns and an explicit context, i.e., that here there is none. We realize that it does not work very well and that we need an intonation so that the terms structure themselves with respect to one another, whereas *the dog is eating his mash*, can be said in a single tone.

Furthermore, * *it can (jolly, bloody, etc.) well* [*peut bien*] *rain tomorrow* is not well-formed, but:

– *it can (jolly, bloody, etc.) well rain tomorrow, I don't care* is acceptable.

– *it may* [*il se peut que*] *rain tomorrow* is better than: *it can rain tomorrow.*

– *it may well* [*il se peut bien que*] *rain tomorrow* is not very good [in French], whereas:

– *it could rain tomorrow*
– *it could well rain tomorrow*
– *it can very well [fort bien] rain tomorrow*
– *it could very well rain tomorrow*
– *it may very well rain tomorrow*
are all acceptable.

How can we account for this?

Being able to can be represented in the following way:

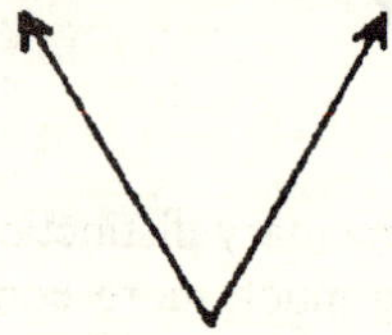

Bien can be a marker either of identification, or of a scanning operation (cf. *you'll finally end up [finiras bien par]* ...).

On the one hand, *being able to* induces a positive value; on the other, a scan on the occurrences. Let us examine *either* [*ou bien*] ... *or* [*ou bien*] ... . *Bien* here signifies: "either such and such a value ... or such and such a value", it is in fact the marker of an operation of assertion.

In *you'll finally end up* scanning takes place on conative occurrences.

In *even though* ... [*bien que* ...] the same analysis applies: *whatever the degree, the manner that* ... .

The problem is always the same: one constructs a notional domain, a class of occurrences, and one scans. Scanning between two terms corresponds to identification, pure and simple.

We realize that in * *it can well rain tomorrow*, we have constructed a string that is not centred, as *can* relates to a two-term bifurcation, and that *well* [*bien*], inasmuch as no relationship of identification is established, marks a scanning operation. Instances of this type necessarily include an *inter*lexis relationship; here it will be concessive in character.

If I integrate *very well* [*fort bien*], I am processing a gradient: in the set of what is thinkable, one can state that such and such an event is more likely than another. If I centre the domain, by using the marker *very* [*fort*], then the utterance is perfectly acceptable *it can very well rain tomorrow*.

With *it could*, one can construct *it could well rain tomorrow*. *Could* is a construct based on a fictitious locator of a distinguished value, even if this value is not the one that eliminates the others, for example:

[*if we were* or] *we (could)/would be*[*serait*] *on a desert island*. In saying this, we stay on the detached plane E.

In contradistinction to *can* which maintains equiponderance (even though a value may be distinguished, it is not distinguished to the point of eliminating the equiponderant character of the bifurcation), *could* marks explicitly the construction of a fictitious locator: it functions as if there were a locator enabling the location of the utterance. The conditional distinguishes a value (i.e., lets us posit that value **I** is realized) and favours positive occurrences, and thus the domain of non-null values. The instance is of the type I have called "scans with prospects", i.e., not a scan that then requires another's proposition to be located, but rather a proposition that includes its very conditions for centring and locating.

In the interrogative, as opposed to the affirmative, *bien* will appear quite normally, and not *fort bien*:

Where ***can*** [stress corresponding to *bien*] *he be?*

The response cannot be: * *he* ***can*** *be in the cellar*, but one may answer: "he can very well [fort bien] be in the cellar". Yet one cannot ask:

* *Where can he very well be?*

An interrogative is a scan, here of the class of occurrences of which *where* is the **image**. *Bien* is the marker of this scanning operation: it is compatible and is necessarily located, since in the interrogative the relationship is constructed with respect to the other enunciator. By inserting *very*, one would have centred the domain; however, scanning and centring cannot coincide.

ON MODALIZING FOLLOWING THE D.E.A. SEMINAR

Concerning the injunctive, Culioli (Culioli and Paillard 1987:528), and his collaborator, Denis Paillard, emphasize the intersubjective component of the modality and, in particular, the importance of constructing the relationship of $\mathscr{S}_1$ to ***p****. Whereas traditionally only that of $\mathscr{S}_0$ to* ***p*** *is taken into account, the former, not stabilized, gives the "silent" $\mathscr{S}_1$ the last word as he can choose to validate either* ***p*** *or* ***p'****.*

In a paper on bien *(Culioli 1988a), the linguist divides instances analysed in Culioli 1978a into two classes: "Operations in the Interior of the domain" (p.158); "Operations performed on the entire domain, and in particular, on the Boundary" (p.159). This last type provides us with an analysis of not entirely satisfactory, nor unsatisfactory solutions to problems posed by another locutor. Scanning the Interior, the domain of possible solutions, does not reveal a good solution; moving on to the Exterior (impossible solutions) proves fruitless. However, just before leaving the Interior the scan manifests a set of at least one conceivable solution; conversely, on entering the domain of possible solutions from the Exterior, "one encounters at least one conceivable solution. This double movement constructs the Boundary" (ibid.).*

CHAPTER 6

ASPECTS AND QUANTIFIABILIZATION

EDITOR'S INTRODUCTION

The first mention of aspect (Culioli, Fuchs, Pêcheux 1970: Note VIII, p.22) underlines the "relationship between the aspectual marks" of a verb, and "determinants applying to an argument", albeit in this general and allusive fashion.

In Culioli 1971, aspectual values are described in terms of open and closed intervals (p.10 et sq.); no specification is proposed concerning the quantitative or qualitative components of the states or processes, other than the links with diathesis (which we shall examine in the next chapter).

For the sake of classifiying and presenting an orderly vision of verbal activity, limited to samplings taken from a few Western Indo-European languages, modality, aspect and tense have traditionally been separated — to the detriment of their relationships (Culioli 1973:84). Culioli joins them in a "vector of properties" (ibid.)

He sets out (Culioli 1976:221) 4 types, "orders", of aspectual problems:

1. *Aktionsart (varying ways of expressing the same process in different languages).*
2. *involving modality*
3. *involving quantification*
4. *temporal topology:*

i.e., given a boundary between two domains, there will be elements, either just to the right or just to the left of the boundary, or in the 'interior' left or right. Every element bears an interval whose distance can be either infinite, canceled, or representable.

In Culioli 1978b, he examines 4 domains concerning aspect:

1. *the notional domain as described in Culioli 1978a (See above,Chapter 3).*
2. *"operations of quantitative/qualitative determination, such as evaluating the degree of intensity or extension (completeness)" (p.183)*

3. modality; and

4. "the category of instants" (p.185), a more detailed theorization of "temporal topology", which he opposes to those domains on which operations of quantification can apply (ibid.).

A paper devoted to an analysis of the quantifier quelque *(Culioli 1983b) includes a (brief) study of the iterative aspect and its relationship to scanning. The iterative comprises "no unique interval or point", and each repetition can be construed as "entering the domain, leaving it, re-entering it, etc." Each departure from the validatable into potentiality, as well as the general value of "unrealization", is produced by "scanning a set of points, without privileging any point (or closed interval) with respect to the situation of uttering, [i.e., $\mathcal{S}_0\mathcal{T}_0$]".*

EXCERPTS FROM THE D.E.A. SEMINAR

Quantification Linked to the Type of Scanning

[*Aspect, Modality, Quantification*]

Before tackling problems of aspect, I would like to examine the following utterances which will serve as our introduction to the aspectual domain, since they confront us with the problem of the relationships between aspect, modality, and quantification. Compare:

– * *Some money* [in the original *de l'argent*] *is useful.*
– *Some money; that's* [, *ça c'est*] *always useful.*
– *Some money would be useful.*
– *Money is useful.*

Analyzing these utterances brings us back to another problem, a classic:

– *A whale is a mammal.*
– *The whale is a mammal.*
– * *At this rate , a whale will have disappeared in 10 years.*
– *At this rate, the whale will have disappeared in 10 years.*

or:

– *A window lights up a room.*
– **A window was first introduced in the Middle Ages.*
– *The window was first introduced in the Middle Ages.*

[*Granular Scanning*]

The indefinite article *a* functions as a marker of the operation of scanning with Extraction. This is what I have called *granular scanning* (i.e., when we can preserve individuation), as opposed to *smooth scanning* (i.e., when individuation disappears and operations are performed globally [on the class]).

Each time we deal with an aspectual–temporal value that produces a fragmentation, i.e. an individuation, the individuation is preponderant, and the indefinite article can no longer function as an operator of scanning. For a scan to take place, there can be no heterogeneous zone: when the [French] present perfect [and the English past] appears, two zones are necessarily constructed: *not yet*, and *from now on*. If somewhere an operation of qualification activates an anaphoric relationship, then the utterance is once more well-formed. For example:

Such a window was first introduced in the Middle Ages.

We can say "until the Middle Ages, they had openings ... . Then oiled paper windows appear. Such windows were first fashioned in such and such a region during the Middle Ages ... ".

A is the marker for a number of operations. This is why we shall find well-formed and ill-formed utterances, and why we shall be able to check our operations. Terms in themselves are nothing: they are *traces* of operations that take place.

In *a whale is a mammal*, *a mammal* is considered to be a defining property. There is no temporal determination and *a whale* refers to *a, a, a* and not to *a, two, three*.

[*Smooth Scanning and Smoothing*]

Let us return to our first group of utterances.

1. *Money is useful*, marks the performance of a strictly *smooth* scanning operation on *money*: without any partition, fragmentation or sampling. We relate back to the notion. The utterance appears not to refer in any way to a break made between two zones that might correspond to a sampling, where a segment would be isolated. *Is useful* is a form of present indicative that does not refer to any interruption, partition, or heterogeneity: every occurrence has the same properties at all times.[1]

---

[1] Langacker 1990:87 proposes that "the perfective/imperfective and count/mass distinctions are precisely identical" *mutatis mutandis*: "The component states of a process (each profiling a relation) are analogous to the component entities constituting the region profiled by a noun". As for the mass noun (in Culioli's example: 'money') and the imperfective ('is'): " a. The region profiled by a mass noun is construed as being internally

In this instance there is *scanning–scanning*: indivisible, on the one hand, and on the other, unsegmented. It is a generic utterance in the strictest sense of the term. We have constructed a domain to which all the occurrences we can imagine belong.
2. As for **some money is useful*, we start with *some money*, i.e., a quantification Qt_1 on *money*. *Is–useful*, however, is always considered to have the property of being representable as not–closed, therefore open. There results a contradiction, and thus ill-formedness, since one term refers to a demarcation and the other refers neither to a demarcation nor a break.
3. In instance number 2:
Some money; that's always useful or
Some money; that's very useful
we reinforced the assertion with *that's* and *always*. Thanks to *always* we performed an operation of *smoothing*. This signifies that we act as though we "erased" the specific circumstances, and state that the description is a property (cf. "he's always complaining").

[*Quantification Nullified by Back-referencing*]

Concerning the instance *that's very useful*, we are dealing here with much more complexity. It is a peculiar case because we need either an enunciative operation of locating that will apply to the degree, given *very*, or a spatial-temporal parameter, given *always*. There remains the problem of back-referencing by *that* [*ce*]. In French, one can thematize by performing an anaphoric operation of global back-referencing with a deictic — *ce* or *ça*:

Some money; that [*c'*] ... .

This nullifies the operation of quantification activated by *some money*, as long as the global back-referencing itself voids the property of divisibility, of fragmentation. It is as though we were brought back to square one, our prototype: *money*.

Moreover, if what is back-referenced is generic, the human/non-human opposition is deleted:

– A father, ça se respecte [* *one respects that*, i.e., *must / should be respected*]

---

homogeneous. b. A mass is indefinitely expansible/contractible (any subpart is itself a valid instance of the category).[...] " a. The component states of an imperfective process are construed as all being effectively identical. b. An imperfective process is indefinitely expansible/contractible (any series of component states is itself a valid instance of the category)."

– *A city, ça se visite* [* *one visits that,* i.e., *must / should be visited*]

– *Some bread, ça se mange* [* *one eats that — no well-formed English equivalent can be constructed on this quantitative 'some'*]

– *Brothers, ça s'aide* [* *that helps one another,* i.e., *must / should help one another*]

It is, however, impossible to find a non-generic reference in such an instance, for example a human proper noun: * *Paul, that can be treated.*

With proper nouns referring to places, [however,] the utterance is well-formed, for example:

Marseille, ça se visite [*must / should / can be visited*] *in two days.*

[*Well-formedness: Homogeneity*]

4. In *Some money would be useful*, or *Some money would be useful to us*, we notice that *would*, like *will*, brings about a fragmentation. This signifies that for the moment we are in one state and will move on to another. Dealing with two states means that we can distinguish two zones, consequently no scanning is possible. Thus we realize that we can reduce the problem to one of well-formedness: we can only accept two parts if they are homogeneous.

ON ASPECTS AND QUANTIFIABILIZATION FOLLOWING THE D.E.A. SEMINAR

In Culioli & Denis Paillard (1987 passim), he and his collaborator demonstrate a correspondence, in Russian, between the perfective and utter-ances favouring $\mathcal{S}_0$'s privileged value: ***p****, and between the imperfective and $\mathcal{S}_1$'s position:* ***p, p'****. The only exception being the perfective in expressions of politeness or wishing, where the enunciator withdraws in favour of another "($\mathcal{S}_1$, whence politeness), or in the face of an uncontrollable force (fate, whence wishing)" (p.532).*

CHAPTER 7

ASPECT, DIATHESIS AND QUANTIFIABILIZATION

EDITOR'S INTRODUCTION

The second statement concerning aspect (Culioli, Fuchs & Pêcheux 1970: Note VIII, p.22) mentions the existence of a link between intransitivity, reflexivity and aspectual considerations. Note IX (p.23), specifies that the active voice is primitive; the passive, derived from the active. However, in Culioli (1976, Lecture 16:193), referring to studies on Zulu, as well as Uto-Aztecan languages (including Langacker & Munro 1975), the linguist specifies that "the passive schema is not simply the converse of the active one" but includes an operation of identification — "a real equative" in French as well. The passive of:

'Jean is driving the car' ['Jean conduit la voiture']

is not rendered by:

'The car is driven by Jean' ['La voiture est conduite par Jean']

but rather by:

'The car is driven' and 'It's Jean' ['La voiture est conduite' et 'C'est Jean']

"i.e., a relationship of identification is established between 'a driver of a car' and 'Jean as driver of the car'".[1]

As noted in Culioli, Fuchs & Pêcheux (1970:10) and further explicated in Culioli (1973:84), the category of Agent, hence agentivity, is part of a "vector of properties" comprising "Agent, Animate, Determined". The last underlines the intrinsic link with quantifiabilization.

In Culioli (1971), he states that the selection between the diathetic values of the relator, as evinced in the orientation of the surface text (when that relator is instantiated by a verb), can be calculated by applying the operation of location to its basic aspectual values: open and closed (10-13). He adds

[1] Langacker (1990: 127 sq.) also denounces the Chomskyan simplification. "Passive clauses do not derive from active clauses"; however, he insists on the semantic import of the three grammatical morphemes indicative of the passive (in Culioli's example: '*est*', the past participial inflection and '*par*').

that these aspectual values and problems depend on properties of the verbs themselves (Culioli (Lecture 10) 1976:122): "in the form of distribution needed to take this comparison into account, predicates like 'eating', 'breaking', or 'attacking' would be seen to induce the values O[pen] and C[losed] in ways that differ."

As first shown in Culioli (1973:84), quantifiabilization is a complex operation involving both quantity and quality since notions may comprise properties rendering them individuatable by quality as well as quantity ("Some foods make me ill"), and others not individuatable.[2] *Of the latter, Culioli distinguishes two types: "the* **dense** *(some butter)", the* **compact** *[...] (for example: the WHITENESS of the snow)".*

Culioli (1975:5) explicates quantity / quality operations, referring to the latter component as "comprehension (quality, property)" by setting out three types: (1) "relationships between comprehension and number [... e.g.,] in English, ***there isn't any butter*** *signifies 'there is't the slightest quantity of butter; whereas,* ***any butter is good*** *signifies 'any variety of butter is good [...]'; (2) "operations of totalization* ***(all ducks have webbed feet)*** *[...]; (3) "concatenated operations" [... e.g.,]* ***I like reading certain novels*** *signifies 'among novels, there are novels (possessing a particular property) that I like reading'".*

The linguist describes the notional domain as comprising occurrences and, therefore as quantifiable (Culioli 1983b:26). He then provides a more detailed description opposing **discrete**, *and, in particular,* **compact** *and* **dense**. *The former is "indivisible, a nominalized predicate [with or without the force of a subjective qualification — ibid., footnote 7], on which no operation of sampling can be performed".*[3] *The dense, however, is a hybrid category "possessing properties of the compact, but on which sampling can be performed by means of an enumerator [*dénombreur*]" (idem).*

EXCERPTS FROM THE D.E.A. SEMINAR

During this last lecture, we shall examine the relationship between a problem of diathesis and problems of aspect, based on the following example:

---

[2] Langacker specifically accounts for the coexistence of these two categories of quantifiabilization in certain mass nouns (wine, beer, glue) by positing a "multidimensional domain organized in terms of specific qualitative parameters (solidity, color, taste, discreteness / continuity, texture, and so on" (Langacker 1987:206)

[3] However, such "abstract nouns — like their more concrete counterparts — designate regions that can be either bounded or unbounded", if one accepts the conceptual validity of the "count / mass [noun] distinction". (Langacker 1987:207)

– *The curtain is torn*
– *The curtain has been torn*

This is a well-known problem, and we shall try to see how far we can advance with the conceptual tools we have constructed. Basically, there are two we can use: one thanks to our work here, the other, to the text on the role of metalinguistic representations [Culioli 1982]. We shall also benefit from the distinction drawn between *discrete*, *dense*, and *compact*. These are fundamental properties associated with a notion. This distinction is very often used specifically in analyzing noun formation, but can be proposed for general application.

[*Properties of Quantifiabilization, and Diathesis*]

[*The Discrete*]

We shall speak of the *discreteness* of what is individuatable, and all that derives from this trait; in particular when individuation exists, there are holes, gaps. Between one object and the next, however, there must necessarily be a solution of continuity. The second property is that we shall be able to order, i.e., that we shall construct an ordinal classification: 1st., 2nd., 3rd. occurrence. As for the designation, it can refer either to the notion, being individuatable, though not yet individuated; or to individuals. Verbs such as *tearing*, *breaking* are of this type.

The Dense

This applies to notions that refer to a reality with which we can perform operations, possibly of a discrete character, but then only by means of an *enumerator*. Without one, we cannot individuate. This is fundamental. Let us look at an example: *water*. Either we say: "a glass of water", in which case we have our enumerator and we are processing discreteness, or we say "some water", "a bit of water"; however, unless we have some yardstick, whatever it may be, we cannot say: "once some water, twice some water", "once a bit of water, twice a bit of water".

Let us examine *greeting*, an example analyzed by Catherine Fuchs and Anne Marie Léonard in *Vers une théorie des aspects.*[4] If you greet someone, you perform a ritual which, once finished, does not have to be repeated. Components include the likes of: *once* [*une fois que*], *when you've greeted*. However, it is obvious that you can greet, greet, greet and, in contradistinction to *tearing* or *breaking*, the reality remains intact. *Greeting* does not lead to a

[4] *Les systèmes du français et de l'anglais.* (=Connaissance et langage 6). Paris: Mouton / École des Hautes Études en Sciences Sociales. 1979.

point where you can say: *that's it; it's over / gone*, as would *crossing*, for example.

The Compact

This applies to what is indivisible in the strictest sense. The dense consisted of the indivisible and non-individuatable, and the discrete, of the individuatable. The compact includes, for example, an operation of localization — *being with respect to. Following* is an example of a verb corresponding to this operation. We can, however, be dealing with a localization with agentivity, or an abstract spatial one without agentivity:

– *5 is followed by 6.*

– *6 follows 5.*

but also

– *Pierre follows Marie.*

– *Marie is followed by Pierre.*

In the first instance, a complement is necessary: * *5 is followed.*

In the other, *Pierre is followed* is acceptable.

[*Links with Open and Closed Aspects*]

Open / Closed Intervals and the Adjacent

Once we have said this, we immediately see the difference between:

The curtain is torn and

The child is followed.

By projecting such an utterance onto the class of instants, we shall derive a whole set of interesting properties that I shall not review here. If, however, we wish to see how to construct a representation obliging us to move through a network of intervals, we shall construct two points inducing the following situation with *not yet*: we establish a relationship such that some point is a boundary marker indicating an alteration:

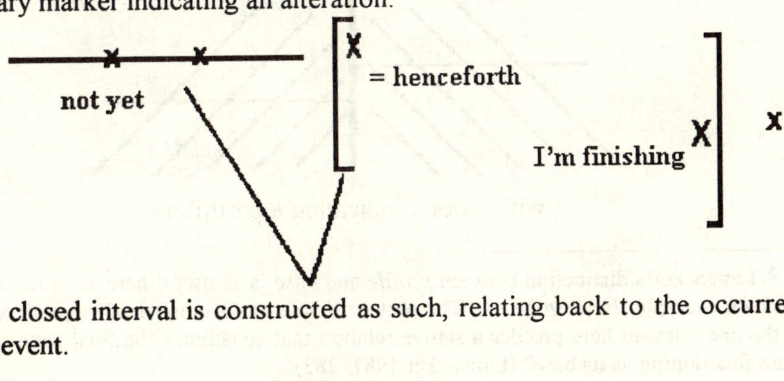

A closed interval is constructed as such, relating back to the occurrence of the event.

Now we can mark open or not-bounded intervals, by constructing the complement:

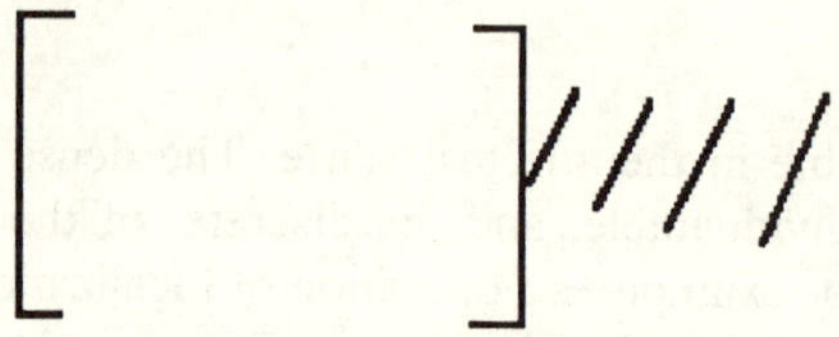

= every point can be identified with every other; it is an open interval: there is no partition.

The complement of the event is either open or unbounded: *open* signifies: "it's over now / it's alright now / that's done it now" [*ça y est maintenant*]; whereas if one hears: "Look, it's torn", one understands that at some point it was not torn, but that one's attention is not focused on *that's it, it's torn.*[5]

It is precisely what has been called the *adjacent* (*parakeimenos* in Greek) and the term is still used in modern Greek to refer to this form.

We can now return to our initial problem:

[#...# = the text string] #the curtain is torn#

We shall examine each of the markers: *is* and *torn*, in order to ascertain which operations they mark, and if we can determine their value here.

A verb such as *tearing* can be graphed as follows:

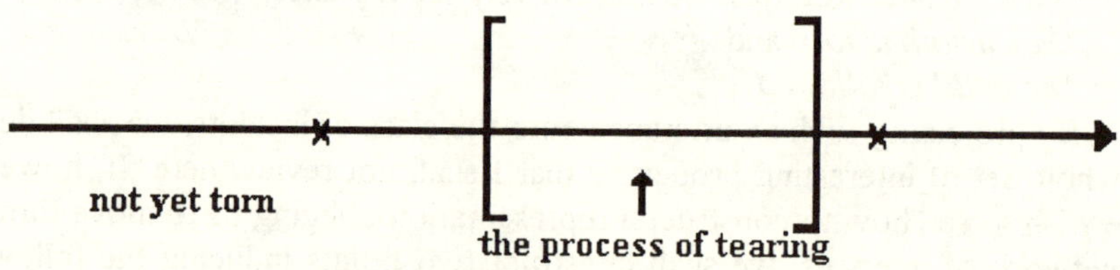

or:

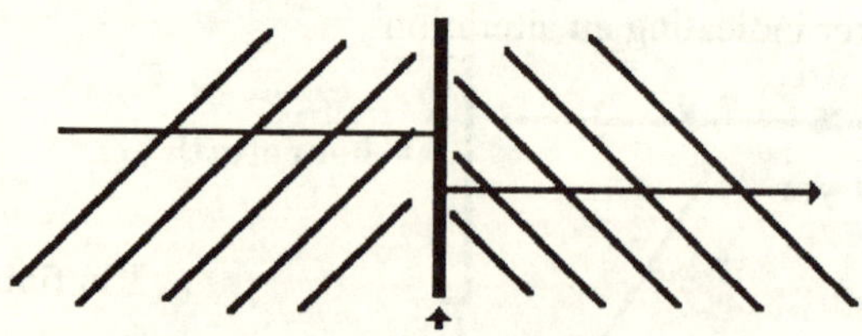

with a point indicating a partition.

[5] Langacker's distinction between *profile* and *base* is as useful here as in the analysis of his own example: *He is gone* — "The past participle has a number of semantic variants [...]; the one relevant here profiles a stative relation that constitutes the final state of a [...] process functioning as its base" (Langacker 1987: 283).

[*Agentivity*]

[*Teleonomy*]

A second problem, one of agentivity, inevitably appears: is there an agent or not? This is linked to one of the fundamental characteristics of agentivity as a cognitive property, which can itself be broken down, and comprises, in particular, a property concerning the teleonomy of the event, i.e., is the event intentional or non-intentional? In teleonomy, this is also related to: is it good or bad? is it done to x's detriment? in x's favour? is it indifferent? Teleonomy also includes: is it a success or is it a failure? Failing refers to conation, i.e., trying. From the notion of teleonomy, we derive a whole set of parameters of properties important for these problems.

[*Stative: No Agent; Changing States: Agent*]

Each time our predicate exhibits this type of schema, i.e., a two-place predicate:

$\langle (\ )_0\ r\ (\ )_1 \rangle$

we have two possibilities: first, an operation that will possibly clear place_0 and construct a place for an agent:

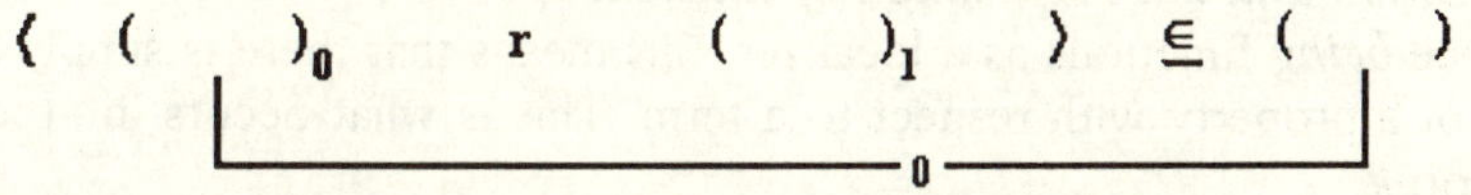

Then, once this place has been emptied, we fill the two places by means of a second operation. This results in a schema manifesting some very interesting properties, given the involvement of both operations — the typical feature of the French [or English] past participle: it can have an agentive value, and it can refer to a property external to any agentivity. We find this ambiguity in *torn*.

As we have represented it here, we intuitively relate the text string #the curtain is torn [*est déchiré*]# to *it is in the state of having a tear*.

The relationship marked by $_0$ (i.e., the one that consists in saying: *torn by*) having been eliminated, this one remains:

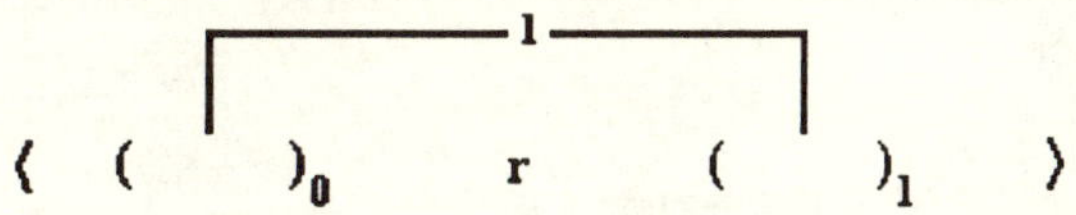

The two places form a loop and there is no longer any agent in the relationship.

Conversely, when there is movement from one state to another, there is agentivity, and no agentivity when there is none: when no transformation continues to occur, there is no longer any agent of transformation. Then we shall find markers that will differentiate this double value. Take the French verb *être*: as a present indicative [here, *est*], it is compatible with closed, open, and open–closed intervals. Because it is a present, it indicates a localization.

Then the form ending in *é* in French [*déchiré*, *torn*] induces the following values:

1. *this anyway*, which means that the value $_0$ is nct excluded, but will only appear in certain circumstances. Fundamentally, the relationship is reflexive:

$$\langle\ (\quad)_0 \quad r \quad (\quad)_1\ \rangle$$

2. from the point of view of an interval, or of diathesis, it is compatible with all values: open, closed. For example, *eaten* is compatible with both active and passive.

[*Localization and the Predication of Existence*]

Since *being* functions as a localizer, this means that there is simply localization of a property with respect to a term. This is what occurs in #the curtain is torn#.

In the absence of markers, it inevitably induces the *parakeimenos* value, i.e., the complement of the closed interval which, in fact, indicates the event. This is related to the fact that the verb *being* [*être*] is a completely neutral one. Given a first term, we find here the property of the fundamental primitive operation, that of being located by two identifications:

– the first indicates that an occurrence is located with respect to its predicate:

x is x = is what it is

– the second, that an ocurrence is located with respect to an abstract, spatial localization: *is in the spot where it is*, which enables the construction of the predication of existence:

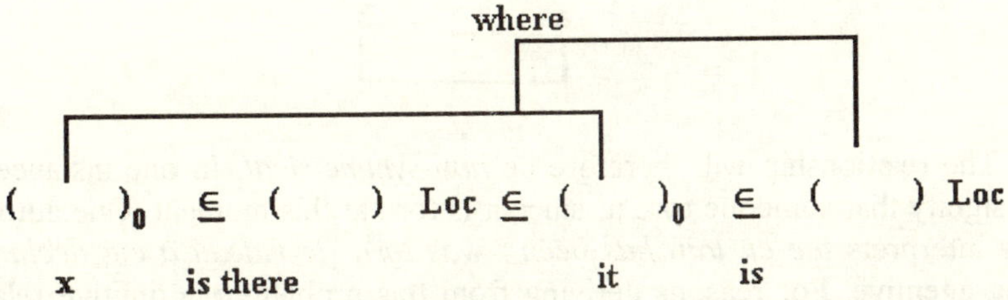

This provides us with a first operation external to the way of giving a response. The verb *being* will refer to an identification: in *being*, there is stability. *Being* is also used as an existential predication, for example: *God is*; *there are examples which* ... .

Then again, *being* comprises a property of stabilization, of a stabilized character, that renders it compatible with both the value of identification and that of localization, and at the same time it does not indicate a partition. Conversely, if we use *être* [*being*] with a form of the French *passé simple* or present perfect, this immediately induces a privileged value.

If we choose a verb such as *following*:

#the person is followed#

because of its indivisibility, the value that would eliminate pathway$_0$ cannot appear. *Following* necessarily indicates a relationship between two terms. The predicate disappears as possessor of properties of definition. It can never be rendered discrete, i.e., be interpreted as: *now* [*ça y est*] *he is followed*. We can never consider an occurrence finished. For example:

a été déchiré [*has been torn*]

It can refer to two possibilities:

on the one hand, *being torn* — unbounded open, stative [ ] —×→

Ex.: *Oh, the curtain is torn!*

and on the other: closed [ ] [ ] non-stative

Ex.: *In a wink, the curtain is torn, the furniture is* ... .

On the one hand, *being torn* with a form of the past participle activates two possibilities, one referring to *the curtain is torn*, and the other to *in a wink, the curtain is torn, the furniture smashed, etc.*

[*Non-symmetrical Relationships and Crossing*]

On the other, in *a été déchiré* [*has been / was torn*] *avoir* [*having*] is the marker whose fundamental property is *non-symmetry*: the relationship is necessarily between a locator and a locatum, such that:

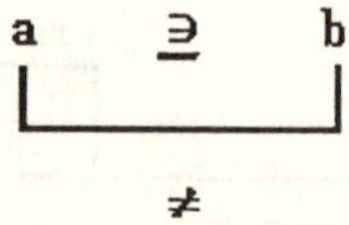

The relationship will therefore be *non-symmetrical*. In one instance, this can signify that someone tore it, since it is torn at this moment. One automatically interprets *the curtain has been / was torn* [*le rideau a été déchiré*] as being agentive. For reasons deriving from this problem of primitive relationships, in very many instances we introduce a relationship that refers to animates and even to human animates. The other instance can refer to two states: *a été déchiré* [*was torn*] can signify that it was torn, but is no longer. In this instance, the assymetry applies to t_2m and t_2n. This means that, as regards the property *being torn* as a stative, I indicate that the present state does not correspond to the prior state.

Let us examine the instance *is cleaned / cleans itself* [*se nettoie*]. The verb *cleaning*, is a prototypical teleonomic verb, including even a culturally intentional teleonomy. When one says *this motor is cleaned*, it means that someone must do the cleaning. If you say: "such operations are often carried out in the neighbourhood", everyone understands that people carry them out. Likewise, everyone understands that in *I am followed*, you are followed by an animate. The same prevails in *being beaten*.

In *a été déchiré* [*has been / was torn*], there will be a differentiation between a first and a second moment, which implies that you signify the existence of a prior moment when the curtain was not torn, and the present moment when it is. Between the two zones, an alteration is inevitable. When *avoir* appears, you will necessarily find agentivity, thus a necessary crossing of a boundary, movement from one zone to another:

1. if one says: "this curtain was torn" [*a été déchiré*] — first value : *it was, someone mended it*;

2. *the curtain has been torn* [*a été déchiré*] — second value: *it wasn't, somebody tore it*.

Simply by integrating the verb *avoir* [*having*], you imply that there are two states, thus solution of continuity from one state to another.

ON ASPECT, DIATHESIS AND QUANTIFIABILIZATION FOLLOWING THE D.E.A. SEMINAR

[no significant additions found before 1990; the opposition between ***discrete / dense / compact*** *is once more explored by Culioli & Jean-Jacques Franckel (1992), and by Culioli himself (1992), paper summarized below, in the Conclusion]*

CONCLUSION

After examining Antoine Culioli's works on cognition and representation during this twenty-two-year period, it behoves us to underline two types of coherence, aside from that of his representational model: diachronic and synchronic — continuity and harmony. Throughout the preceding chapters, by comparing the Seminar text with those prior and subsequent to it, a consistent pattern of development and consolidation emerged, including but one point of major transformation: the topological{XE "topological"} description of the notional domain based on prototypicality{XE "prototypicality"} from 1981 on. A cursory analysis of Culioli's latest paper (1992) at the time of this writing will show the same methodological constructs and interests. It was delivered as the keynote address, both retrospective and programmatic, to a round table discussion on his theory and its ramifications organized on the occasion of his retirement as head of the *Laboratoire de Linguistique formelle* (Paris 7 – CNRS URA 1028).

Among the seminal problems which evolutions in linguistics have caused him to set out, he stresses once more: the relationship between language and languages{XE "language and languages"} (p.4); metalanguage and formalization determining the construction of a metalinguistic system of representation "on which I have never ceased to work" (p.5); those created by naïve theories either of communication between an emitter and a receptor (the "black box"), or of autonomous syntax, and semantics, and the basis of the Cooperative Principle the "intention to signify" (*ibid.*).

The solutions that he chooses to emphasize are the **lexis{XE "lexis"}** (also defined here as "a sort of schema{XE "schema"} that provides possible pathways [to the construction of an utterance], some of which are activated by choice depending on circumstances — either determined or contingent —, others, in certain instances, are necessarily activated") (p.6); topological{XE "topological"} representation (7-8); constructing locator{XE "locator"}–locatum{XE "locatum"} relationships (including that of the "fictitious locator{XE "locator, fictitious"}"), the situation of uttering{XE "situation of uttering"} and localization{XE "localization"} (8-9); relationships of identification{XE "identification"} and differentiation{XE "differentiation"} on a gradient{XE "gradient"} in relation to the attractor{XE "attractor"} (9-10); and the necessary complexity of the model (10-11). He devotes an important segment to the relationships between *individuation*{XE "individuation"}, *quantifiabilization*{XE "quantifiabilization"}, the *discrete*{XE "discrete"}, the *dense*{XE "dense"} and the *compact*{XE "compact"}, leading to the schema of localization{XE "localization, schema of"}, thence to the predication of existence, and thus "to constructing a theory of assertion, the interrogative, etc. that will enable us to set out the problem of modality in relation to problems of aspect in what is, for me a more satisfactory way [...]" (11-13). He links certain relationships and distance, including the "primitive" distance: 0, 1 (∅ distance / some distance), that "suffices to set out [...] problems of modality, in particular those linked to the notion of bifurcation, pathway, etc.", then he poses a problem based, as in the works seen above, on a **paraphrastic family** (14). Finally, on the linguist's work he expresses the wish that his reasoning have verifiable coherence, and if coherence is stated to be local, that rules be drawn up to ensure truly coherent local activity (15).

On the synchronic side (Culioli 1989:203): "[...] some sceptic might then grumble and say: '*Constructive* all right! But who is the constructor?', [Culioli] would unwincingly reply: 'The linguist of course', since the linguist experiments and simulates language activity, namely utterances [...]"

By not only admitting, but actually proclaiming his subjectivity, the subjectiveness of his constructs, Culioli reminds us of a fundamental component constantly structuring his research: all representations of reality are subjective and require rigorous subjective processing[1]. The coherent and effective metalinguistic system of representation he has constructed based on a specific set of analyses performed on individual usage events (texts in context and situation), constitute his response to this need. This consistency between the character of the phenomena processed and that of its treatment underlines the contrast with analyses of "linguistic objects" without context or situation, and the "objectivity" of their apparatus and of the conclusions drawn.

Antoine Culioli's research in this sense exemplifies what he refers to in the 1983-1984 D.E.A. Seminar as his "heuristic approach". The metalinguistic system of representation is always "under construction", as it continues growth both (1) internally, formally constructing unforeseen, yet verifiable, utterances through complexification, and (2) through input from external sources and the necessary reaction to an utterance not previously inventoried in some family of natural languages (Culioli 1992:11). Thus, even if the relationships between levels II (utterances) and III (metalinguistic representa-

[1] Thus, Culioli's position is clear with respect to what Dirk Geraeerts (1993:123) sees as an example of ambiguity in Lakoff's characterization of semantic linguistics as not objective: does he refer to its subject matter or to its method?

tions{XE "representations, metalinguistic"}) become visibly tighter, Culioli (e.g., 1989:212-213) maintains the hypothetical status of the relationship between levels II and I (pre-utterance constructs: notions, schemata{XE "schemata"} and operations), i.e., of the fundamental analogy between the metalinguistic system's representation of verified utterances, and the representation of the cognitive{XE "cognitive"} components of uttering by utterances.

REFERENCES

A. Works by Antoine Culioli

1968a. "À propos du genre en anglais contemporain". *Les Langues modernes* 3.326-334.

1968b. "La formalisation en linguistique". *Cahiers pour l'analyse* 9.106-117 (Repr. as part 1 of Culioli, Fuchs, Pêcheux 1970).

1971a. "À propos d'opérations intervenant dans le traitement formel des langues naturelles". *Mathématiques et Sciences humaines* 34.7-15.

1971b. "Un linguiste devant la critique littéraire" *Cahiers de la Faculté des Lettres de l'Université de Clermont-Ferrand*. 61-79

1973. "Sur quelques contradictions en linguistique". *Communications* 20.83-91.

1974. "À propos des énoncés exclamatifs". *Langue française* 22.6-15.

1975a. "Notes sur détermination et quantification: définition des opérations d'extraction et de fléchage". [Pages 1-14 of a document printed and circulated within the framework of the *Projet interdisciplinaire de traitement formel et automatique de langues et du langage (PITFALL)*]. Département de Recherches Linguistiques (DRL), Université de Paris 7.

1976a. "Comment tenter de construire un modèle logique adéquat à la description des langues naturelles". *Modèles logiques et niveau d'analyse linguistique* ed. by Jean David & Robert Martin, 35-47. Paris: Klincksieck.

1976b. "Transcription du Séminaire de D. E. A. de M. A. Culioli : 'Recherche en Linguistique. Théorie des Opérations Énonciatives'". Paris: Département de Recherches Linguistiques, Univ. Paris 7.

1978a. "Valeurs modales et opérations énonciatives". *Le Français moderne* 46.4.300-317.

1978b. "Valeurs aspectuelles et opérations énonciatives: l'aoristique". *La Notion d'aspect. Actes du colloque organisé par le Centre d'Analyse syntaxique de l'Université de Metz (18-20 mai 1978)* ed. by Jean David & Robert Martin (= *Recherches linguistiques*, 5), 181-193. Paris: Klincksieck. (Repr. in *Linguistique, énonciation: Aspects et détermination* ed. by Sophie Fisher & Jean-Jacques Franckel (= *Connaissance et Langage*, 7), 99-114. Paris: École des Hautes Études en Sciences Sociales, 1983.)

1978c. “Linguistique du discours et discours sur la linguistique”. *Revue philosophique* 4.481-488.

1979a. “Conditions d'utilisation des données issues de plusieurs langues naturelles”. *Modèles linguistiques* I: 1.89-103.

1980. “Rapport sur un rapport”. *La Psychomécanique et les théories de l'énonciation. Actes de la Table Ronde tenue à Lille les 16 et 17 mars 1979*, 37-47. Lille: Presses Universitaires de Lille.

1981. “Sur le concept de notion”. *Bulletin de Linguistique appliquée et générale*. Besançon. 8.62-79 (Repr. in Culioli 1990.47-65.)

1982a. *Rôle des représentations métalinguistiques en syntaxe. Communication présentée à la session plénière du XIIIème Congrès International des Linguistes, Tokyo, 29 août-4 septembre 1982.* (= ERA 642, complément au 2).Paris: DRL., Paris 7.

1983. “The Concept of notional domain”. *Les universaux en linguistique. Actes du colloque international de Gummersbach.* (Repr. in Culioli 1990, 67-81.)

1983b. “A propos de *quelque*” in *Linguistique, énonciation. Aspects et détermination.* ed. by Sophie Fisher. & Jean-Jacques Franckel (= *Connaissance et langage*, 7). 21-29. Paris: EHESS.

1984. “Théories du langage et théories des langues”. *Benveniste aujourd'hui. Actes du colloque CNRS, Tours, 1983*, tome I, 77-85. Paris: Société pour l'Information grammaticale.

1986a. “La Frontière”. *Cahiers Charles V* 8. (Repr. in Culioli 1990, 83-90.)

1986b. “Stabilité et déformabilité en linguistique”. *Études de lettres.* special issue: *Langage et Connaissances*. 3-10. Lausanne: Université de Lausanne. (Repr. in 1990, 127-134.)

1987a. “Formes schématiques et domaine”. *Bulletin de Linguistique appliquée et générale* 13.7-15. (Repr. in Culioli 1990, 115-126.)

1987b. “La linguistique, de l'empirique au formel”. *Sens et place des connaissances dans la société : 3e confrontation*, 37-67. Paris: CNRS. (Repr. in Culioli 1990, 9-46.)

1988a. “Autres commentaires sur *bien*”. *Mélanges Stéfanini: Grammaire et histoire de la grammaire. Hommage à la mémoire de Jean Stéfanini*, 169-180. Aix-en-Provence: Université de Provence. (Repr. in 1990, 157-168).

1988b. “La négation: marqueurs et opérations”. *La Négation. La négation sous divers aspects. Actes du colloque, Neuchatel, 22-23 octobre 1987*, 17-38 (= Travaux du Centre de Recherches Sémiologiques, 56). (Repr. in 1990, 91-113.)

1989a. “Representation, referential processes and regulation. Language activity as form production and recognition”. *Language and Cognition* ed. by J. Montangero & A.Tryphon (= Jean Piaget Foundation Archives, Cahier 10). 97-124. (Repr. in Culioli 1990, 177-213.)
1989b. “Donc”. *Supostavitelno Ezikoznanie/Contrastive Linguistics*. Sofia. 14.5.16-20 (Repr. in Culioli 1990, 169-176.
)
1990. *Pour une linguistique de l'énonciation. Opérations et représentations*, tome I. Gap: Ophrys.
1992. “Ouverture”. *La Théorie d'Antoine Culioli. Ouvertures et incidences.* Gap: Ophrys. 3-15.

Culioli & Jean-Jacques Franckel 1992. “Structuration d'une notion et typologie lexicale. A propos de la distinction dense, discret, compact”. *Bulletin de Linguistique Appliquée et Génerale*. 17.7-12.
Culioli, Fuchs, Pêcheux 1970. *Considérations théoriques à propos du traitement formel du langage*. (Part 2: Notes, marked I to XI, with the collaboration of Catherine Fuchs and Michel Pêcheux, and “Lexis et méta-lexis — Applications au problème de déterminants” by Fuchs and Pêcheux). (= *Centre de linguistique quantitative de la faculté des sciences de l'Université de Paris*; *Documents de linguistique quantitative*, 7) Paris: Dunod.
Culioli & Denis Paillard 1987. “À propos de l'alternance imperfectif / perfectif dans les énoncés impératifs”. *Revue des Études slaves* 59:3.527-534.

B. Other Sources

Auroux, Sylvain. 1992. “La philosophie linguistique d’Antoine Culioli”. *La Théorie d’Antoine Culioli. Ouvertures et incidences*. Gap: Ophrys. 39-59.

Benveniste, Émile. 1966. *Problèmes de linguistique générale I*. Paris: Gallimard

1974. *Problèmes de linguistique générale II*. Paris: Gallimard

Chiss, Jean-Louis. 1986. “Charles Bailly: Qu’est-ce qu’une ‘théorie de l’énonciation’?”. *H.E.L.* 8:2.165-176.

Delesalle, Simone. 1986. “Introduction: Histoire du mot *énonciation*”. *H.E.L.* 8:2.7-22

Desclés, Jean-Pierre. 1992. “Au sujet des catégories grammaticales”. *La Théorie d’Antoine Culioli. Ouvertures et incidences*. Gap: Ophrys. 203-212.

Fuchs, Catherine. 1992. “De la grammaire anglaise à la paraphrase: un parcours énonciatif”. *La Théorie d’Antoine Culioli. Ouvertures et incidences.* Gap: Ophrys. 221-226.

Geraeerts, Dirk. 1993. “Des deux côtés de la sémantique structurale: sémantique historique et sémantique cognitive”. 15:1.111-129.

Guilhaumou, Jacques & Denise Maldidier. 1986. “De l’énonciation à l’événement discursif en analyse du discours”. *H.E.L.* 8:2.233-242

Joly, André & Daniel Rouland. 1980. “Pour une approche psychomécanique de l’énonciation”. *La Psychomécanique et les théories de l’énonciation*. ed. André Joly. Lille: Presses de l'université de Lille.

Langacker, Ronald W. 1987. *Foundations of Cognitive Grammar*. Vol. 1: *Theoretical Prerequisites*. Stanford: Stanford U. P.

1988a “An Overview of Cognitive Grammar”. *Topics in Cognitive Linguistics*. ed. by Brygida Rudzka-Ostyn (= *Current Issues in Linguistic Theory*, 50). 3-48. Amsterdam & Philadelphia: John Benjamins.

1988b “A View of Linguistic Semantics”. *ibid*. 49-90.

1990 *Concept, Image, and Symbol. The Cognitive Basis of Grammar*. (= Cognitive Linguistics Research,1). Berlin & New York: Mouton de Gruyter.

Milner, Jean-Claude. 1992. “De quelques aspects de la théorie d’Antoine Culioli projetés dans un espace non énonciatif”. *La Théorie d’Antoine Culioli. Ouvertures et incidences.* Gap: Ophrys. 19-38.

Normand, Claudine. 1986. “Les termes de l’énonciation chez Benveniste”. *H.E.L.* 8:2.191-206.

INDEX OF TERMS AND CONCEPTS

In the CURRENT ISSUES IN LINGUISTIC THEORY (CILT) series (edited by: E.F. Konrad Koerner, University of Ottawa) the following volumes have been published thus far or are scheduled to appear in the course of 1995:

1. KOERNER, Konrad (ed.): *The Transformational-Generative Paradigm and Modern Linguistic Theory.* 1975.
2. WEIDERT, Alfons: *Componential Analysis of Lushai Phonology.* 1975.
3. MAHER, J. Peter: *Papers on Language Theory and History I: Creation and Tradition in Language. Foreword by Raimo Anttila.* 1979.
4. HOPPER, Paul J. (ed.): *Studies in Descriptive and Historical Linguistics. Festschrift for Winfred P. Lehmann.* 1977.
5. ITKONEN, Esa: *Grammatical Theory and Metascience: A critical investigation into the methodological and philosophical foundations of 'autonomous' linguistics.* 1978.
6. ANTTILA, Raimo: *Historical and Comparative Linguistics.* 1989.
7. MEISEL, Jürgen M. & Martin D. PAM (eds): *Linear Order and Generative Theory.* 1979.
8. WILBUR, Terence H.: *Prolegomena to a Grammar of Basque.* 1979.
9. HOLLIEN, Harry & Patricia (eds): *Current Issues in the Phonetic Sciences. Proceedings of the IPS-77 Congress, Miami Beach, Florida, 17-19 December 1977.* 1979.
10. PRIDEAUX, Gary D. (ed.): *Perspectives in Experimental Linguistics. Papers from the University of Alberta Conference on Experimental Linguistics, Edmonton, 13-14 Oct. 1978.* 1979.
11. BROGYANYI, Bela (ed.): *Studies in Diachronic, Synchronic, and Typological Linguistics: Festschrift for Oswald Szemérenyi on the Occasion of his 65th Birthday.* 1979.
12. FISIAK, Jacek (ed.): *Theoretical Issues in Contrastive Linguistics.* 1981. Out of print
13. MAHER, J. Peter, Allan R. BOMHARD & Konrad KOERNER (eds): *Papers from the Third International Conference on Historical Linguistics, Hamburg, August 22-26 1977.* 1982.
14. TRAUGOTT, Elizabeth C., Rebecca LaBRUM & Susan SHEPHERD (eds): *Papers from the Fourth International Conference on Historical Linguistics, Stanford, March 26-30 1979.* 1980.
15. ANDERSON, John (ed.): *Language Form and Linguistic Variation. Papers dedicated to Angus McIntosh.* 1982.
16. ARBEITMAN, Yoël L. & Allan R. BOMHARD (eds): *Bono Homini Donum: Essays in Historical Linguistics, in Memory of J.Alexander Kerns.* 1981.
17. LIEB, Hans-Heinrich: *Integrational Linguistics. 6 volumes. Vol. II-VI n.y.p.* 1984/93.
18. IZZO, Herbert J. (ed.): *Italic and Romance. Linguistic Studies in Honor of Ernst Pulgram.* 1980.
19. RAMAT, Paolo et al. (eds): *Linguistic Reconstruction and Indo-European Syntax. Proceedings of the Colloquium of the 'Indogermanischhe Gesellschaft'. University of Pavia, 6-7 September 1979.* 1980.
20. NORRICK, Neal R.: *Semiotic Principles in Semantic Theory.* 1981.
21. AHLQVIST, Anders (ed.): *Papers from the Fifth International Conference on Historical Linguistics, Galway, April 6-10 1981.* 1982.
22. UNTERMANN, Jürgen & Bela BROGYANYI (eds): *Das Germanische und die Rekonstruktion der Indogermanischen Grundsprache. Akten des Freiburger Kolloquiums der Indogermanischen Gesellschaft, Freiburg, 26-27 Februar 1981.* 1984.
23. DANIELSEN, Niels: *Papers in Theoretical Linguistics. Edited by Per Baerentzen.* 1992.
24. LEHMANN, Winfred P. & Yakov MALKIEL (eds): *Perspectives on Historical Linguistics. Papers from a conference held at the meeting of the Language Theory Division, Modern Language Assn., San Francisco, 27-30 December 1979.* 1982.
25. ANDERSEN, Paul Kent: *Word Order Typology and Comparative Constructions.* 1983.

26. BALDI, Philip (ed.): *Papers from the XIIth Linguistic Symposium on Romance Languages, Univ. Park, April 1-3, 1982.* 1984.
27. BOMHARD, Alan R.: *Toward Proto-Nostratic. A New Approach to the Comparison of Proto-Indo-European and Proto-Afroasiatic. Foreword by Paul J. Hopper.* 1984.
28. BYNON, James (ed.): *Current Progress in Afro-Asiatic Linguistics: Papers of the Third International Hamito-Semitic Congress, London, 1978.* 1984.
29. PAPROTTÉ, Wolf & René DIRVEN (eds): *The Ubiquity of Metaphor: Metaphor in language and thought.* 1985 (publ. 1986).
30. HALL, Robert A. Jr.: *Proto-Romance Morphology. = Comparative Romance Grammar, vol. III.* 1984.
31. GUILLAUME, Gustave: *Foundations for a Science of Language.*
32. COPELAND, James E. (ed.): *New Directions in Linguistics and Semiotics.* Co-edition with Rice University Press who hold exclusive rights for US and Canada. 1984.
33. VERSTEEGH, Kees: *Pidginization and Creolization. The Case of Arabic.* 1984.
34. FISIAK, Jacek (ed.): *Papers from the VIth International Conference on Historical Linguistics, Poznan, 22-26 August. 1983.* 1985.
35. COLLINGE, N.E.: *The Laws of Indo-European.* 1985.
36. KING, Larry D. & Catherine A. MALEY (eds): *Selected papers from the XIIIth Linguistic Symposium on Romance Languages, Chapel Hill, N.C., 24-26 March 1983.* 1985.
37. GRIFFEN, T.D.: *Aspects of Dynamic Phonology.* 1985.
38. BROGYANYI, Bela & Thomas KRÖMMELBEIN (eds): *Germanic Dialects:Linguistic and Philological Investigations.* 1986.
39. BENSON, James D., Michael J. CUMMINGS, & William S. GREAVES (eds): *Linguistics in a Systemic Perspective.* 1988.
40. FRIES, Peter Howard (ed.) in collaboration with Nancy M. Fries: *Toward an Understanding of Language: Charles C. Fries in Perspective.* 1985.
41. EATON, Roger, et al. (eds): *Papers from the 4th International Conference on English Historical Linguistics, April 10-13, 1985.* 1985.
42. MAKKAI, Adam & Alan K. MELBY (eds): *Linguistics and Philosophy. Festschrift for Rulon S. Wells.* 1985 (publ. 1986).
43. AKAMATSU, Tsutomu: *The Theory of Neutralization and the Archiphoneme in Functional Phonology.* 1988.
44. JUNGRAITHMAYR, Herrmann & Walter W. MUELLER (eds): *Proceedings of the Fourth International Hamito-Semitic Congress.* 1987.
45. KOOPMAN, W.F., F.C. Van der LEEK , O. FISCHER & R. EATON (eds): *Explanation and Linguistic Change.* 1986
46. PRIDEAUX, Gary D. & William J. BAKER: *Strategies and Structures: The processing of relative clauses.* 1987.
47. LEHMANN, Winfred P. (ed.): *Language Typology 1985. Papers from the Linguistic Typology Symposium, Moscow, 9-13 Dec. 1985.* 1986.
48. RAMAT, Anna G., Onofrio CARRUBA and Giuliano BERNINI (eds): *Papers from the 7th International Conference on Historical Linguistics.* 1987.
49. WAUGH, Linda R. and Stephen RUDY (eds): *New Vistas in Grammar: Invariance and Variation. Proceedings of the Second International Roman Jakobson Conference, New York University, Nov.5-8, 1985.* 1991.
50. RUDZKA-OSTYN, Brygida (ed.): *Topics in Cognitive Linguistics.* 1988.
51. CHATTERJEE, Ranjit: *Aspect and Meaning in Slavic and Indic. With a foreword by Paul Friedrich.* 1989.
52. FASOLD, Ralph W. & Deborah SCHIFFRIN (eds): *Language Change and Variation.* 1989.
53. SANKOFF, David: *Diversity and Diachrony.* 1986.

54. WEIDERT, Alfons: *Tibeto-Burman Tonology. A comparative analysis.* 1987
55. HALL, Robert A. Jr.: *Linguistics and Pseudo-Linguistics.* 1987.
56. HOCKETT, Charles F.: *Refurbishing our Foundations. Elementary linguistics from an advanced point of view.* 1987.
57. BUBENIK, Vít: *Hellenistic and Roman Greece as a Sociolinguistic Area.* 1989.
58. ARBEITMAN, Yoël. L. (ed.): *Fucus: A Semitic/Afrasian Gathering in Remembrance of Albert Ehrman.* 1988.
59. VAN VOORST, Jan: *Event Structure.* 1988.
60. KIRSCHNER, Carl & Janet DECESARIS (eds): *Studies in Romance Linguistics. Selected Proceedings from the XVII Linguistic Symposium on Romance Languages.* 1989.
61. CORRIGAN, Roberta L., Fred ECKMAN & Michael NOONAN (eds): *Linguistic Categorization. Proceedings of an International Symposium in Milwaukee, Wisconsin, April 10-11, 1987.* 1989.
62. FRAJZYNGIER, Zygmunt (ed.): *Current Progress in Chadic Linguistics. Proceedings of the International Symposium on Chadic Linguistics, Boulder, Colorado, 1-2 May 1987.* 1989.
63. EID, Mushira (ed.): *Perspectives on Arabic Linguistics I. Papers from the First Annual Symposium on Arabic Linguistics.* 1990.
64. BROGYANYI, Bela (ed.): *Prehistory, History and Historiography of Language, Speech, and Linguistic Theory. Papers in honor of Oswald Szemérenyi I.* 1992.
65. ADAMSON, Sylvia, Vivien A. LAW, Nigel VINCENT and Susan WRIGHT (eds): *Papers from the 5th International Conference on English Historical Linguistics.* 1990.
66. ANDERSEN, Henning and Konrad KOERNER (eds): *Historical Linguistics 1987.Papers from the 8th International Conference on Historical Linguistics,Lille, August 30-Sept., 1987.* 1990.
67. LEHMANN, Winfred P. (ed.): *Language Typology 1987. Systematic Balance in Language. Papers from the Linguistic Typology Symposium, Berkeley, 1-3 Dec 1987.* 1990.
68. BALL, Martin, James FIFE, Erich POPPE &Jenny ROWLAND (eds): *Celtic Linguistics/ Ieithyddiaeth Geltaidd. Readings in the Brythonic Languages. Festschrift for T. Arwyn Watkins.* 1990.
69. WANNER, Dieter and Douglas A. KIBBEE (eds): *New Analyses in Romance Linguistics. Selected papers from the Linguistic Symposium on Romance Languages XVIIII, Urbana-Champaign, April 7-9, 1988.* 1991.
70. JENSEN, John T.: *Morphology. Word structure in generative grammar.* 1990.
71. O'GRADY, William: *Categories and Case. The sentence structure of Korean.* 1991.
72. EID, Mushira and John MCCARTHY (eds): *Perspectives on Arabic Linguistics II. Papers from the Second Annual Symposium on Arabic Linguistics.* 1990.
73. STAMENOV, Maxim (ed.): *Current Advances in Semantic Theory.* 1991.
74. LAEUFER, Christiane and Terrell A. MORGAN (eds): *Theoretical Analyses in Romance Linguistics.* 1991.
75. DROSTE, Flip G. and John E. JOSEPH (eds): *Linguistic Theory and Grammatical Description. Nine Current Approaches.* 1991.
76. WICKENS, Mark A.: *Grammatical Number in English Nouns. An empirical and theoretical account.* 1992.
77. BOLTZ, William G. and Michael C. SHAPIRO (eds): *Studies in the Historical Phonology of Asian Languages.* 1991.
78. KAC, Michael: *Grammars and Grammaticality.* 1992.
79. ANTONSEN, Elmer H. and Hans Henrich HOCK (eds): *STAEF-CRAEFT: Studies in Germanic Linguistics. Select papers from the First and Second Symposium on Germanic Linguistics, University of Chicago, 24 April 1985, and Univ. of Illinois at Urbana-Champaign, 3-4 Oct. 1986.* 1991.

80. COMRIE, Bernard and Mushira EID (eds): *Perspectives on Arabic Linguistics III. Papers from the Third Annual Symposium on Arabic Linguistics.* 1991.
81. LEHMANN, Winfred P. and H.J. HEWITT (eds): *Language Typology 1988. Typological Models in the Service of Reconstruction.* 1991.
82. VAN VALIN, Robert D. (ed.): *Advances in Role and Reference Grammar.* 1992.
83. FIFE, James and Erich POPPE (eds): *Studies in Brythonic Word Order.* 1991.
84. DAVIS, Garry W. and Gregory K. IVERSON (eds): *Explanation in Historical Linguistics.* 1992.
85. BROSELOW, Ellen, Mushira EID and John McCARTHY (eds): *Perspectives on Arabic Linguistics IV. Papers from the Annual Symposium on Arabic Linguistics.* 1992.
86. KESS, Joseph F.: *Psycholinguistics. Psychology, linguistics, and the study of natural language.* 1992.
87. BROGYANYI, Bela and Reiner LIPP (eds): *Historical Philology: Greek, Latin, and Romance. Papers in honor of Oswald Szemerényi II.* 1992.
88. SHIELDS, Kenneth: *A History of Indo-European Verb Morphology.* 1992.
89. BURRIDGE, Kate: *Syntactic Change in Germanic. A study of some aspects of language change in Germanic with particular reference to Middle Dutch.* 1992.
90. KING, Larry D.: *The Semantic Structure of Spanish. Meaning and grammatical form.* 1992.
91. HIRSCHBÜHLER, Paul and Konrad KOERNER (eds): *Romance Languages and Modern Linguistic Theory. Selected papers from the XX Linguistic Symposium on Romance Languages,University of Ottawa, April 10-14, 1990.* 1992.
92. POYATOS, Fernando: *Paralanguage: A linguistic and interdisciplinary approach to interactive speech and sounds.* 1992.
93. LIPPI-GREEN, Rosina (ed.): *Recent Developments in Germanic Linguistics.* 1992.
94. HAGÈGE, Claude: *The Language Builder. An essay on the human signature in linguistic morphogenesis.* 1992.
95. MILLER, D. Gary: *Complex Verb Formation.* 1992.
96. LIEB, Hans-Heinrich (ed.): *Prospects for a New Structuralism.* 1992.
97. BROGYANYI, Bela & Reiner LIPP (eds): *Comparative-Historical Linguistics: Indo-European and Finno-Ugric. Papers in honor of Oswald Szemerényi III.* 1992.
98. EID, Mushira & Gregory K. IVERSON: *Principles and Prediction: The analysis of natural language.* 1993.
99. JENSEN, John T.: *English Phonology.* 1993.
100. MUFWENE, Salikoko S. and Lioba MOSHI (eds): *Topics in African Linguistics. Papers from the XXI Annual Conference on African Linguistics, University of Georgia, April 1990.* 1993.
101. EID, Mushira & Clive HOLES (eds): *Perspectives on Arabic Linguistics V. Papers from the Fifth Annual Symposium on Arabic Linguistics.* 1993.
102. GARGOV, Georg and Petko STAYNOV (eds) : *Explorations in Language and Cognition. Selcted Papers from the workshop : The notion of cognitive in linguistics, September 1989.* n.y.p.
103. ASHBY, William J., Marianne MITHUN, Giorgio PERISSINOTTO and Eduardo RAPOSO: *Linguistic Perspectives on Romance Languages. Selected papers from the XXI Linguistic Symposium on Romance Languages, Santa Barbara, February 21-24, 1991.* 1993.
104. KURZOVÁ, Helena: *From Indo-European to Latin. The evolution of a morphosyntactic type.* 1993.
105. HUALDE, José Ignacio and Jon ORTIZ DE URBANA (eds): *Generative Studies in Basque Linguistics.* 1993.
106. AERTSEN, Henk and Robert J. JEFFERS (eds): *Historical Linguistics 1989. Papers from the 9th International Conference on Historical Linguistics, New Brunswick, 14-18 August 1989.* 1993.

107. MARLE, Jaap van (ed.): *Historical Linguistics 1991. Papers from the 10th International Conference on Historical Linguistics, Amsterdam, August 12-16, 1991.* 1993.
108. LIEB, Hans-Heinrich: *Linguistic Variables. Towards a unified theory of linguistic variation.* 1993.
109. PAGLIUCA, William (ed.): *Perspectives on Grammaticalization.* 1994.
110. SIMONE, Raffaele (ed.): *Iconicity in Language.* 1995.
111. TOBIN, Yishai: *Invariance, Markedness and Distinctive Feature Analysis. A contrastive study of sign systems in English and Hebrew.* 1994.
112. CULIOLI, Antoine: *Cognition and Representation in Linguistic Theory. Translated, edited and introduced by Michel Liddle.* 1995.
113. FERNÁNDEZ, Francisco, Miguel FUSTER and Juan Jose CALVO (eds): *English Historical Linguistics 1992. Papers from the 7th International Conference on English Historical Linguistics, Valencia, 22-26 September 1992.*1994.
114. EGLI, U., P. PAUSE, Chr. SCHWARZE, A. von STECHOW, G. WIENOLD (eds): *Lexical Knowledge in the Organisation of Language.* 1995.
115. EID, Mushira, Vincente CANTARINO and Keith WALTERS (eds): *Perspectives on Arabic Linguistics. Vol. VI. Papers from the Sixth Annual Symposium on Arabic Linguistics.* 1994.
116. MILLER, D. Gary: *Ancient Scripts and Phonological Knowledge.* 1994.
117. PHILIPPAKI-WARBURTON, I., K. NICOLAIDIS and M. SIFIANOU (eds): *Themes in Greek Linguistics. Papers from the first International Conference on Greek Linguistics, Reading, September 1993.* 1994.
118. HASAN, Ruqaiya and Peter H. FRIES (eds): *On Subject and Theme. A discourse functional perspective.* 1995.
119. LIPPI-GREEN, Rosina: *Language Ideology and Language Change in Early Modern German. A sociolinguistic study of the consonantal system of Nuremberg.* 1994.
120. STONHAM, John T. : *Combinatorial Morphology.* 1994.
121. HASAN, Ruqaiya, Carmel CLORAN and David BUTT (eds): *Functional Descriptions. Transitivity and the construction of experience.* 1995.
122. SMITH, John Charles and Martin MAIDEN (eds): *Linguistic Theory and the Romance Languages.* 1995.
123. AMASTAE, Jon, Grant GOODALL, Mario MONTALBETTI and Marianne PHINNEY: *Contemporary Research in Romance Linguistics. Papers from the XXII Linguistic Symposium on Romance Languages, El Paso//Juárez, February 22-24, 1994.* 1995.
124. ANDERSEN, Henning: *Historical Linguistics 1993. Selected papers from the 11th International Conference on Historical Linguistics, Los Angeles, 16-20 August 1993.* 1995.
125. SINGH, Rajendra (ed.): *Towards a Critical Sociolinguistics.* n.y.p.
126. MATRAS, Yaron (ed.): *Romani in Contact. The history, structure and sociology of a language.* 1995.
127. GUY, Gregory R., John BAUGH, Deborah SCHIFFRIN and Crawford FEAGIN (eds): *Towards a Social Science of Language. Papers in honor of William Labov. Volume 1: Variation and change in language and society.* n.y.p.
128. GUY, Gregory R., John BAUGH, Deborah SCHIFFRIN and Crawford FEAGIN (eds): *Towards a Social Science of Language. Papers in honor of William Labov. Volume 2: Social interaction and discourse structures.* n.y.p.
129. LEVIN, Saul: *Semitic and Indo-European: The Principal Etymologies. With observations on Afro-Asiatic.* 1995.
130. EID, Mushira (ed.) *Perspectives on Arabic Linguistics. Vol. VII. Papers from the Seventh Annual Symposium on Arabic Linguistics.* 1995.